D1187515

AMERICAN HISTORY BY ERA

The Colonial Period: 1607–1750

VOLUME 2

Brenda Stalcup, *Book Editor*

Daniel Leone, *President*
Bonnie Szumski, *Publisher*
Scott Barbour, *Managing Editor*

GREENHAVEN
PRESS®

THOMSON

™

GALE

San Diego • Detroit • New York • San Francisco • Cleveland
New Haven, Conn. • Waterville, Maine • London • Munich

Cover credit: © Hulton/Archive by Getty Images

Dover Publications, 89, 137
Library of Congress, 38, 156, 223
North Wind Picture Archives, 122
Prints Old and Rare, 70

Cover inset photo credits (from left): Planet Art; Corel; Digital Stock; Corel; Library of Congress; Library of Congress; Digital Stock; Painet/Garry Rissman

LIBRARY OF CONGRESS CATALOGING-IN-PUBLICATION DATA

The colonial period: 1607–1750 / Brenda Stalcup, book editor.
    p. cm. — (American history by era; v. 2)
Includes bibliographical references and index.
ISBN 0-7377-1039-X (pbk. : alk. paper) — ISBN 0-7377-1040-3 (lib. : alk. paper)
    1. United States—History—Colonial period, ca. 1600–1775. I. Stalcup, Brenda.
II. Series.
E188 .C725 2003
973.2—dc21
                                    2002032216

Printed in the United States of America

CONTENTS

sent expeditions up from Florida to spy on the English colonists, but they never made an all-out attempt at eradicating Jamestown.

5. The Dutch Colony of New Netherland

A few years after the first English settlers arrived at Jamestown, the Dutch established the colony of New Netherland in the region that is now called New York. New Netherland was particularly notable for its religious tolerance and the diverse ethnic and national origins of its inhabitants.

Chapter 2: The Pilgrims and the Puritans

1. The Origins of the Puritans

The Puritan movement initially sought to purify the Church of England and to reform English society. Their efforts earned them the hostility of the royal family and the high church officials. Confronted by a rising tide of persecution, some Puritans decided to leave England and establish colonies in the New World, where they hoped to be free to practice their religion as they saw fit.

2. The Arrival of the Pilgrims

The Pilgrims were the first group of settlers who came to America searching for religious freedom. They drafted a set of laws called the Mayflower Compact, which circumvented the authority of the English king and placed power squarely in the hands of the colonists.

3. Squanto's Relationship with the Pilgrims

Squanto's aid to the Pilgrims during their first year in Plymouth was crucial to their survival. However, the full story of Squanto's dealings with the Pilgrims is far more complex. As an emissary to the fledgling colony, he walked a difficult tightrope between the English settlers and the various Indian tribes of the region.

colony of Rhode Island as a bastion of religious
freedom and tolerance.

3. Migrations from Massachusetts

Dissatisfied with various aspects of life in the
Massachusetts settlements, some Puritans ven-
tured to new territories in Connecticut.

4. The Constitution of the United Colonies of New England

In 1643, four Puritan colonies in Massachusetts
and Connecticut agreed to join together as the
New England Confederation, the first federalist
union formed in America.

5. The Conquest of New Sweden and New Netherland

The Swedish and Dutch settlements in North
America fell under British control in 1664 and
were transformed into the colony of New York.

6. The Founding of the Carolinas

The region originally called Carolina was established as one colony. However, it soon became evident that the northern and southern provinces
were quite different in their geography, agriculture, social life, commercial endeavors, and attitudes toward slavery.

7. French Expansion in the Interior of the Continent

During the 1670s and 1680s, the colonists of New
France sent a number of expeditions down the
Mississippi River in order to explore and lay claim
to the rich lands of the interior continent.

Chapter 4: Religious Persecutions and Enthusiasms

Chapter 5: Relations Between the Colonists and the Native Peoples

Ireland, Scotland, Germany, and other European countries.

D uring the sixteenth century, events occurred in North America that would change the course of American history. In 1512, Spanish explorer Juan Ponce de León led the first European expedition to Florida. French navigator Jean Ribault established the first French colony in America at Fort Caroline in 1564. Over a decade later, in 1579, English pirate Francis Drake landed near San Francisco and claimed the country for England.

These three seemingly random events happened in different decades, occurred in various regions of America, and involved three different European nations. However, each discrete occurrence was part of a larger movement for European dominance over the New World. During the sixteenth century, Spain, France, and England vied for control of what was later to become the United States. Each nation was to leave behind a legacy that would shape the political structure, language, culture, and customs of the American people.

Examining such seemingly disparate events in tandem can help to emphasize the connections between them and generate an appreciation for the larger global forces of which they were a part. Greenhaven Press's American History by Era series provides students with a unique tool for examining American history in a way that allows them to see such connections. This series divides American history—from the time that the first people arrived in the New World from Asia to the September 11, 2001, terrorist attacks—into nine discrete periods. Each volume then presents a collection of both primary and secondary documents that describe the major events of the period in chronological order. This structure provides students with a snapshot of events occurring simultaneously in all parts of America. The reader can then gain an appreciation for the political, social, and cultural movements and trends that shaped the nation. Students reading about the adventures of individual European explorers, for instance, are invited to consider how such expeditions compared in purpose and consequence to earlier and later expeditions. Rather than simply learning that Ponce de León was the first Spaniard to try to colonize Florida, for example, students can begin to understand his expedition in a larger context. Indeed, Ponce's voyage was an extension of Spain's desire to conquer the Caribbean and Mexico, and his expedition was to inspire other Spanish explorers to head north from Hispaniola and New Spain in search of rich empires to conquer.

Another benefit of studying eras is that students can view a "snapshot" of America at any given moment of time and see the various social, cultural, and political events that occurred simultaneously. For example, during the period between 1920 and 1945, Charles Lindbergh became the first to make a solo transatlantic flight, Babe Ruth broke the record for the most home runs in one season, and the United States dropped the atomic bomb on Hiroshima. Random events occurring in post–Cold War America included the torching of the Branch Davidian compound in Waco, Texas, the emergence of the World Wide Web, and the 2000 presidential election debacle in which ballot miscounts in Florida held up election results for weeks.

Each volume in this series offers features to enhance students' understanding of the era of American history under discussion. An introductory essay provides an overview of the period, supplying essential context for the readings that follow. An annotated table of contents highlights the main point of each selection. A more in-depth introduction precedes each document, placing it in its particular historical context and offering biographical information about the author. A thorough chronology and index allow students to quickly reference specific events and dates. Finally, a bibliography opens up additional avenues of research. These features help to make the American History by Era series an extremely valuable tool for students researching the political upheavals, wars, cultural movements, scientific and technological advancements, and other events that mark the unfolding of American history.

INTRODUCTION

The colonial era of the United States lasted for over a century and a half, a time period nearly as long as the history of the nation following independence in 1776. From the very beginning of the colonial era, the settlers who came to the New World were distinguished by an uncommonly strong sense of self-determination. They tended to be independent thinkers—in religion, in politics, in societal issues. They placed a high premium on liberty and personal autonomy. The colonial period was marked by an almost constant undercurrent of unrest, of dissatisfaction with the status quo that led to radical attempts to rework society. In many respects, the seeds of the American Revolution were present from the very first days of the colonies.

To some extent, the unique character of the American colonists was due to the process of self-selection. It took a certain type of person to decide to break all ties with the past and set out on a hazardous ocean crossing for an unknown land. Those who were meek and cautious, who valued security and order, did not willingly volunteer for such an uncertain endeavor. Most early settlers, therefore, were risk takers, with all that trait implies: a strong sense of self-confidence, a thirst for adventure and excitement, an unwillingness to be boxed in. They sought opportunities for land and riches that could not be found in Europe, beset as it was by overpopulation and rigid rules governing one's place in society. Other early colonists were impelled by the less worldly motive of religious freedom, but they were no less risk takers for that. In fact, the colonies that formed for religious reasons were usually the ones that were most willing to defy royal edicts, to rebel against their imperial overlords, and to insist on their right for liberty.

This tendency to strive for freedom was most pronounced in the thirteen English colonies. Although the Spanish and the

French founded colonies in sections of what later became the United States, these regions never evidenced the same drive toward independence. There were certainly many adventurers and opportunists among the Spanish and French colonists, but the colonies themselves stayed firmly under the control of their respective monarchies. Several factors explain this difference. First, Spanish and French settlements were typically established by military expeditions; the settlements were governed by the head officers, who imposed strict military discipline. The regiments were accompanied by missionaries from the various Catholic monastic orders, who ensured that the colonists remained faithful to the official religion of their homeland. In both cases, the primary interest in colonization was to exploit the resources of the New World for the benefit of the mother country. Few women or established families migrated to the Spanish and French colonies; the settlements were peopled by young men, mostly soldiers and traders, who had little incentive to remain for long.

On the other hand, by the end of the colonial period, the thirteen English colonies included a considerable number of settlers from other parts of Europe. Many of these colonists were religious dissenters—Huguenots from France, for example, or Pietists from Germany—who desired the freedom to worship and live as they saw fit. In this sense they resembled their English neighbors, and they played an important part in forming the independent nature of the original thirteen colonies.

ENGLISH COLONIZATION BEGINS

Prior to 1607, a handful of English settlements had been planted on the North American continent, but none of these ventures had endured for long. By the time that the first permanent English colony took root, Spain already possessed outposts in the territory that is now Florida and New Mexico. The French had long ago laid claim to New France, encompassing present-day Canada. Although France's first permanent settlement, Quebec, would not be established until 1608, its initial attempts at colonization had been longer-lived and more successful than those of England. The English were actually latecomers to North America, and in 1607 there was no hint that by the eighteenth century they would dominate the continent.

The first English colony to survive was Jamestown, located in the Chesapeake Bay region of Virginia. Initially, Jamestown

had much in common with the typical Spanish or French settlement: The colony consisted only of men, most of whom
dreamed of getting rich quick through the discovery of gold or
the fabled Northwest Passage, which would provide Europeans
with an expeditious trade route to Asia through the American
continent. Jamestown was designed to be a money-making enterprise: The colonists had been sent out under the auspices of
the Virginia Company of London, a joint-stock company that
held a royal charter authorizing it to make settlements in North
America. The company's stockholders expected to receive a
considerable profit for their investment in the colony.

The reality of life in the fledgling settlement was much
harsher than anyone expected. From the moment they arrived,
the colonists, who were low on food supplies after the long
ocean crossing, had to start trying to raise crops in an unfamiliar environment. However, they could not devote enough time
to agricultural work because of the company's insistence that
they search for gold and other valuable resources to be shipped
to England, as well as explore the local waterways in an attempt
to find the Northwest Passage. "As a result of all of these outside activities," writes historian Oliver Perry Chitwood, "only
four acres of corn were planted in the spring of 1608."[1] To make
matters worse, a large percentage of the initial settlers were
townsmen who were unfamiliar with farming or upper-class
gentlemen who scorned manual labor.

The colonists paid an appalling price for the lack of emphasis on self-sustainable agriculture. Throughout the first few
years of the settlement, hundreds of people died. As Chitwood
explains,

> The main reasons were disease and famine. The immi-
> grants underwent a costly experience in becoming ac-
> climated, or in passing through the "seasoning"
> process, as the early writers termed it. The swamps and
> lowlands near Jamestown were favorable breeding-
> places for malaria, and this disease was especially
> prevalent. . . . Much of the illness that proved fatal
> would not have been so had not the power of the
> colonists to combat disease been weakened by the mal-
> nutrition of their bodies through a lack of proper food.[2]

Jamestown reached its lowest point during the dreadful winter
of 1609–1610, or the "starving time" as it came to be called. The

colonists resorted to grubbing for roots and berries, to eating rats, snakes, and horsehides. When even these provisions ran low, they turned in desperation to cannibalism, devouring the corpses of those who had already succumbed to hunger or disease. By the spring of 1610, their numbers had been reduced from five hundred to sixty, and the survivors almost abandoned Jamestown as a failed experiment.

Eventually, the stockholders of the Virginia Company realized that the best way to ensure the success of the colony was to attract people who wanted to stay in America permanently. Rather than young men seeking to make a fast fortune, they needed dedicated individuals willing to work industriously toward long-term goals. To this end, the company sought out a different sort of colonist, one who had personal responsibilities to meet. In the words of historian Charles M. Andrews, "The appearance of families—wives, children, and servants—show[ed] that the company at last was beginning to understand what a colony ought to be."[3]

The Virginia Company also altered its policy concerning land ownership, granting fifty-acre tracts to new migrants. With land in England in short supply and rarely available to any but the rich, the prospect of land ownership proved to be a tremendous draw for potential colonists. Additionally, the company expanded the settlers' civil rights and increased their level of participation in the governing of the colony. These two elements would be crucial in England's colonization of North America, according to historical authors Bruce Catton and William B. Catton:

> Land and self-government: the colonial impulse derived from these, and the entire colonial edifice would be built upon them—not because rulers, founders, or organizers especially wanted it that way, but because ordinary Englishmen were not prepared to come forward in sufficient numbers if these items were not included in the package.[4]

In this way, the English approach toward colonization would markedly differ from that of the Spanish and the French. At the same time, however, the English settlers' sense of entitlement to self-government would fuel a growing desire for colonial independence.

The second colony founded by the English was, like Jamestown, sponsored by a joint-stock company with the intent of profiting from the resources of the New World. But there was a key difference in the makeup of these settlers: Forty-one of the passengers on the first voyage to this new colony were religious dissidents fleeing oppression. With the arrival of these dissidents—the Pilgrims—at Plymouth Bay in the winter of 1620, the tenor of the English colonies would experience a fundamental change.

Throughout the American colonial period, the religious situation in the motherland was extremely volatile. England had been a predominately Protestant nation since the 1500s, when King Henry VIII renounced Catholicism and established the Anglican Church as the official religion of the country. Because the English monarch served as the head of the Anglican Church, any religious dissent could be viewed not just as heresy but as treason against the Crown. English Catholics and non-Anglican Protestants alike depended on the goodwill of the reigning monarch, which might be withdrawn at any moment due to seemingly unrelated political considerations. Moreover, all of England's rulers during this era based their policies on their own religious beliefs and their personal attitudes toward religious freedom. Each time a new monarch was installed, the level of religious tolerance in the country changed; religious groups that had previously enjoyed royal favor would suddenly find themselves subjected to the most severe persecution.

The Puritans actually originated in the 1560s as a reformist party within the Anglican Church. They believed that "the Anglican Church had not sufficiently altered or reformed the ritual and organization of the Catholic Church,"[5] explains author Faith Jaycox. Most Puritans wanted to stay within the Anglican Church; they simply wished to "purify" it by removing the remaining vestiges of Catholicism. "By 1600," historian Esmond Wright notes, "the Puritans were divided into two groups: Congregationalists, who were organized as small independent churches made up only of true believers, and Presbyterians, who wanted a central authority and accepted all comers into the faith."[6] The members of a small radical faction of the Congregationalist branch of Puritanism were known as the Separatists because they had given up on the idea of reforming the Anglican Church from within and sought to separate themselves completely from its control.

The Pilgrims who landed at Plymouth were Separatists who

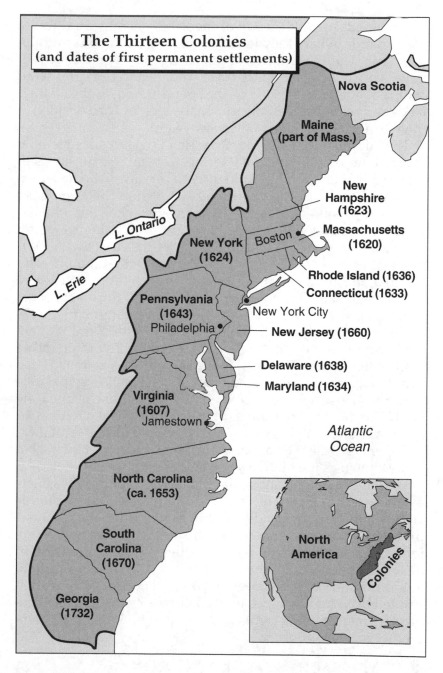

The Thirteen Colonies
(and dates of first permanent settlements)

Nova Scotia

Maine
(part of Mass.)

New
Hampshire
(1623)

L. Ontario

New York
(1624)

Boston

Massachusetts
(1620)

Rhode Island (1636)

Connecticut (1633)

L. Erie

Pennsylvania
(1643)

New York City

Philadelphia

New Jersey (1660)

Delaware (1638)

Maryland (1634)

Virginia
(1607)

Jamestown

Atlantic
Ocean

North Carolina
(ca. 1653)

South
Carolina
(1670)

North
America

Colonies

Georgia
(1732)

had withdrawn from the Anglican Church in 1606. According to English law, their congregation thereby became illegal; the group suffered constant harassment, and some members were imprisoned. In 1608, many of the Pilgrims relocated to the Netherlands, where they found more acceptance. But by 1619, it became clear that Spain was preparing to invade the Netherlands, which it had formerly ruled, and the Pilgrims grew concerned about their fate should the Spanish conquer the Netherlands and reimpose Catholicism on the region. They decided to migrate again, this time to the New World.

The Pilgrims' ship, the *Mayflower*, left England on September 16, 1620. Accompanying the Pilgrims were more than sixty soldiers, skilled laborers, and indentured servants who had been recruited for the colonization effort. When the *Mayflower* reached the banks of Massachusetts in November, the colonists realized that they had traveled too far north, but with winter setting in, there was no time to beat down the coast toward Virginia. They had landed outside the territory that their charter covered, meaning that they had no lawful right to settle there and no legal basis for a government. The Pilgrims were especially concerned about the loyalty of the non-Pilgrim members of the group. "Some of these latter," Bruce Catton and William B. Catton relate, "when the decision to land at Plymouth rather than go to Virginia was being made aboard *Mayflower*, had been heard to remark that this freed them from all authority, that they could now proceed to do exactly as they chose in the new land."[7] So the Pilgrim leaders drew up a document allowing for self-government of the colony and convinced all the adult men, whether Separatists or not, to affix their signatures to what became known as the Mayflower Compact.

Under the circumstances, the Mayflower Compact was necessary to ensure Plymouth's survival. But it also was a unique and even revolutionary document, as it granted the colonists prerogatives of government usually reserved for the Crown. John Quincy Adams, the sixth president of the United States, described the Mayflower Compact as "the first example in modern times of a social compact or system of government instituted by voluntary agreement conformably to the laws of nature, by men of equal rights and about to establish their community in a new country."[8]

THE MASSACHUSETTS BAY COLONY

While the Mayflower Compact was almost certainly a spontaneous measure, resorted to only when need unexpectedly arose, the next group of Puritans to migrate to Massachusetts took premeditated steps to guarantee self-government. The charter granted to the Massachusetts Bay Company failed to include the usual provision that the company keep its home office in England. Taking advantage of this oversight, the Puritan settlers decided to bring the charter with them, thereby transferring the whole government of the colony to the New World. In a secret meeting shortly before their departure from England, John Winthrop and eleven other Puritan leaders signed an agreement that in effect bought out the non-Puritan investors of the Massachusetts Bay Company, transforming it from a commercial enterprise into a community of religious dissenters.

Carrying the charter to the North American continent was a stroke of genius. As historian Sally Smith Booth explains,

> Physical possession of legal documents was considered essential during the seventeenth century. Although a primitive system of record keeping had been developed, original charter documents were vastly more credible than copies. . . . Without being able to examine the instrument, English courts would be unable to legally justify revocation of the document.[9]

With the charter safely in Massachusetts, the likelihood of direct oversight or interference from England became extremely low. "Investors, or for that matter king's ministers, who wanted to interfere with the internal affairs of the Massachusetts Bay Colony would have to cross the Atlantic to do so,"[10] writes historian Arthur Quinn. By taking the charter across three thousand miles of ocean, the Puritans had freed themselves to direct their government howsoever they pleased.

The Massachusetts colonists promptly established what history professor Alan Taylor calls "the most radical government in the European world: a republic, where the Puritan men elected their governor, deputy governor, and legislature."[11] Instead of being governed by men appointed by company stockholders or the Crown, citizens voted for their elected officials, who were colonists like themselves and answerable to no higher authority in England. But though Massachusetts organized itself as a republic, it was not in any way a democracy. The Puritans had come to America to create a model society, a biblical commonwealth firmly grounded in the tenets of their faith and dedicated to the glory of God. They specified that only male colonists who had been accepted as members of a Puritan church would be considered citizens and given the right to vote. Thus, they sharply curtailed the possibility that non-Puritan settlers would gain political power in the colony. Full church membership was carefully controlled; in 1640, for example, only one-fifth of the adult male population had voting privileges.

By 1634 at the latest, the British government discovered that the charter for the Massachusetts Bay Colony was missing. English officials had received allegations of disorder and misrule in Massachusetts, and when they investigated the situation, they realized that the Puritans had taken the charter with them. The colonial leaders were ordered to return the charter; they refused point-blank and instead began to strengthen New England's defenses in case England attempted to seize the charter by force. British and colonial officials hotly contested the issue in legal documents and courtrooms until 1638, when the king, beset by troubles at home, abandoned the effort to retrieve the charter. Massachusetts had won the first round in the battle for colonial autonomy.

BACON'S REBELLION

A generation later, the first major armed rebellion against British colonial rule erupted in Virginia in 1676. The revolt was primarily directed at the royal governor, William Berkeley. During his first tenure as Virginia's governor in the 1640s, Berkeley had gained popularity among the colonists by leading a victorious campaign against the Indians. However, after he was reappointed as governor by King Charles II in 1660, Berkeley alienated many Virginians by showing favoritism toward his cronies when granting land or political offices. He stacked the House of Burgesses, Virginia's representative assembly, with men he had personally appointed and then refused to hold new elections for the House for more than a decade. In 1670, the right to vote was taken away from all colonists who were not landowners.

The settlers were also angry about economic problems in the colony. The British had recently passed laws that gave them a monopoly in the trade of tobacco, Virginia's main crop. Virginian planters and farmers were no longer allowed to sell their tobacco to anyone but British merchants, and soon the price of tobacco plummeted. At the same time, British merchants raised the prices on the finished goods that they sold to the colonists. Heavy taxes and a scarcity of good agricultural acreage contributed to the economic squeeze felt by many colonists. While

Virginian planters went into debt, Berkeley flaunted his wealth and lived in ostentatious luxury, which only deepened resentment against him.

Nathaniel Bacon was himself a young English aristocrat who had only just arrived in Virginia in 1674, where he served on the governor's council. Nevertheless, as Bacon labored to carve out a tobacco plantation on the western frontier of the colony, he found himself sympathizing with the grievances of his less fortunate neighbors. "The poverty of the Country," he declared in 1675, "is such that all the power and sway is got into the hands of the rich, who by extortious advantages, having the common people in their debt, have always curbed and oppressed them in all manners of ways."[12] Bacon soon emerged as the leader of the rebellion that bears his name, an uprising that crossed class lines by encompassing in its ranks planters and indentured servants, farmers and slaves.

VIOLENCE ON THE WESTERN FRONTIER

The immediate cause of Bacon's Rebellion was discontent concerning Berkeley's Indian policy. As the number of settlers on the western frontier grew, they competed more and more with the Indians of the region over ownership of the land and its resources. Raids and skirmishes became increasingly common in Virginia's backcountry during the early 1670s. Then, in July 1675, a white overseer was murdered; seeking revenge, a local militia killed a band of innocent Indians. The Indians retaliated, which led to more reprisals from the colonists, and before long the western territory was in a state of war. Berkeley, however, refused to authorize an offensive campaign against the Native Americans. Instead, he promoted a purely defensive strategy that centered on the construction of an extensive system of frontier forts, which would be funded through yet another hike in the colonists' taxes.

The frontier settlers were outraged by Berkeley's plan. They believed that the forts would be, in Taylor's words, "ineffective and wasteful follies that added to their tax burden while further enriching the governor and his cronies, who reaped the construction contracts."[13] Defying Berkeley's orders against offensive action, Bacon assumed command of a force of three hundred volunteers and launched an expedition against the Indians in the spring of 1676. When news of the vigilante campaign reached Berkeley, he declared Bacon and his followers traitors.

At this juncture, Bacon and his volunteer force left off fighting Indians and marched on the capital at Jamestown. He demanded a military commission authorizing him to lead troops against the Indians. It was granted by the House of Burgesses, which also proceeded to pass a series of reform measures called Bacon's Laws. One law restored the franchise to free men who were not property holders; others placed protections on the rights of ordinary citizens, addressed the economic plight of Virginia's farmers, and limited the power of the governor and other appointed officials.

Meanwhile, Bacon raised a small army of over a thousand men from all walks of life and led them into the wilderness to fight the Indians. In his absence, Berkeley regained control of Jamestown and once again declared Bacon a rebel and a traitor. Bacon responded by attacking the capital, forcing Berkeley to flee across Chesapeake Bay for safety. His troops looted the estates of the wealthy—including Berkeley's own property—and torched the town. Bacon appeared to be on the verge of gaining control over the entire colony. Then fate struck him down: He suddenly fell ill and died of a fever in October. Bereft of his leadership, the rebellion rapidly fell apart. Berkeley rounded up the insurgents and executed twenty-three of the most prominent rebels.

Historians have varying opinions about the significance of Bacon's Rebellion. Many believe that it was a foreshadowing of the American Revolution that would follow exactly one hundred years hence. They point out that the grievances expressed by the Virginians in 1676 were similar to those that sparked the Revolution in 1776: issues of taxation, exploitive trade laws, lack of political representation, dissatisfaction with English governors who did not have the colonists' best interests at heart. Conversely, other historians argue that Bacon's Rebellion was merely a power struggle between Berkeley and Bacon. These scholars contend that the rebels had no real intent to break away from England and form an independent state; rather, their main objective was to kill Indians indiscriminately in order to steal their land.

But while it may never be possible to ascertain the exact goals that Bacon and his followers had in mind, it does seem clear that ideas of liberty motivated at least some of those involved in the insurrection. Anthony Arnold, one of the ringleaders who was captured after Bacon's death, expressed such sentiments shortly before his execution. "Kings have no rights," he told the royal judges,

> but what they got by conquest and the sword, and he who can by force of the sword deprive them thereof has as good and just a title to them as the King himself. If the King should deny to do me right I would think no more of it to sheath my sword in his heart or bowels than of my mortal enemies.[14]

In an age when kings were still thought to have a divine right to rule, these words were more than treasonous—they were revolutionary.

UNREST IN NEW ENGLAND

Bacon's Rebellion was the most important popular uprising before the Revolution, but clashes between the colonies and the British authorities persisted throughout the colonial period. Massachusetts remained a particularly obstinate colony, ignoring the Crown's frequent requests to see its charter while conducting internal affairs to suit itself. In 1664, as historians Oscar Theodore Barck Jr. and Hugh Talmage Lefler explain,

> The defiant Bay Colony . . . declared that Parliament had no right to legislate for it, or the king to supervise its laws and courts—that Massachusetts was "not obliged to the king but by civility.". . .
>
> For more than a decade . . . , Massachusetts continued to evade the trade laws, to enact measures—or "resolves"—contrary to those of England without sending them to London for approval, and to disfranchise the majority of her inhabitants, including about two thirds of her wealthiest merchants. The colony also forcibly extended its jurisdiction over New Hampshire and Maine. This semi-independent and belligerent attitude was discussed by various governmental agencies in England.[15]

In 1676, the British government dispatched an investigator, Edward Randolph, to the colony. He uncovered evidence of widespread smuggling, noncompliance with royal orders, and—ironically enough—persecution of religious dissenters. When Randolph returned to England the following year, he maintained that Massachusetts had usurped royal authority through twenty-four "assumed powers" that it exercised without justification. He recommended that the colony's independence be curbed by placing it under the direct control of the Crown.

The English government immediately took steps to rein Massachusetts in, initiating legal proceedings that eventually resulted in the revocation of the colony's charter in 1684. Before Massachusetts officially became a royal colony, however, its legislature repealed all the tax laws in a final show of defiance. The royal government of the colony got off to a shaky start without the ability to collect any taxes, and the Massachusetts colonists continued to circumvent unpopular laws whenever they could. Finally, in 1686, King James II created the Dominion of New England, which encompassed Massachusetts, Plymouth, Connecticut, Rhode Island, New Hampshire, and Maine. Two years later, New York and New Jersey were also incorporated into the Dominion. A single royal governor, Edmund Andros, was appointed to oversee the Dominion. The popularly elected legislatures of the individual colonies were abolished, leaving the residents without benefit of representation.

The Dominion of New England constituted a kind of supercolony intended to streamline the administration of the region. But as historian Lawrence H. Leder notes,

> The advantages of this consolidation—better quality officials, uniform laws and taxes, simplified administration, and coherent defense policies—did not outweigh its inherent difficulties. Poor communications throughout a widespread territory, obstacles presented by strong local loyalties, and hostilities created by abolition of representative government would prove serious stumbling blocks for the new government.[16]

Both the Dominion and Governor Andros proved to be intensely unpopular among the New Englanders. Andros exacerbated the situation by eliminating many civil liberties, intentionally hampering the activities of municipal governments, and invalidating all land titles issued under the original Massachusetts charter. He offended the Puritans by mocking their beliefs and by appropriating a Congregational meetinghouse for Anglican church services.

Andros was not the only unpopular ruler at the time, however. In England, James II had aroused resentment over his heavy-handed policies and arbitrary decrees. Furthermore, James was the first Catholic monarch to rule England for more than one hundred years, and some of his policies concerning religion alarmed the Protestant majority of the nation. They were reassured, though, by the fact that he would be succeeded by his Protestant daughter, Mary, from his first marriage. But when the king's second wife gave birth to a son and heir who was sure to be raised Catholic, parliamentary leaders decided to take action. They invited Mary and her husband, William of Orange, governor of the Netherlands, to rule England in tandem. His support dwindling, James fled the country in 1688, and William and Mary were proclaimed the lawful monarchs of England.

When word of the Glorious Revolution reached Boston in April 1689, the colonists staged a bloodless coup of their own. Working on the assumption that Andros did not represent the new regime in England, the residents of Boston deposed Andros and several other appointed officials. The colonists regained control of Massachusetts, voted to resume their former mode of government, and dismantled the Dominion of New England. A few weeks later, Plymouth, Connecticut, and Rhode Island also reverted to their old forms of government. In New York, the colonial militia under the command of Jacob Leisler seized control of the government in May, installing Leisler as governor. A third uprising occurred in July when Protestants in Maryland, led by John Coode, wrested power away from the proprietary government.

The colonists who instigated these revolts did so without any indication that their actions would be approved of in the mother country. And in fact, William and Mary were not inclined to allow the colonies this much freedom. It took several years for England to reestablish firm control over the settlers, and in the process the British government struck several compromises with the colonies that extended their liberties. While the monarchs never attempted to reinstitute the Dominion of New England, they refused to restore the original charter of the Massachusetts Bay Colony and instead retained it as a royal colony, albeit with more rights than it had enjoyed under the Dominion. In New York, when Leisler hesitated to accept the appointment of a royal governor, he was arrested for treason and executed. Four years after his death, Parliament exonerated him of all charges, but the measure was too little, too late: The bitterness in New York over the aftermath of Leisler's Rebellion would persist for years.

A LEGACY OF FREEDOM

As demonstrated in the accounts above, the American colonists had already developed a strong tradition of striving for freedom well before the beginning of the 1700s. The events described here are just some of the challenges that the colonists presented to the British government. "For more than one hundred and fifty years," Booth writes, "English and plantation governments were bombarded with a never ending series of petitions, grievances, and remonstrances from quarrelsome and dissatisfied colonists."[17] And although they preferred to protest peacefully, if these measures failed, the colonists were not averse to resorting to violent means. The American Revolution did not arise from a vacuum; rather, it was the culmination of tensions that steadily built up throughout the colonial period of American history. From the earliest settlers in Jamestown and Plymouth to the native-born provincials of the mid-1700s, the colonists insisted on their rights to life, liberty, and the pursuit of happiness.

NOTES

1. Oliver Perry Chitwood, *A History of Colonial America*. New York: Harper & Row, 1961, p. 59.
2. Chitwood, *A History of Colonial America*, p. 58.
3. Charles M. Andrews, *Our Earliest Colonial Settlements: Their Diversities of Origin and Later Characteristics*. Ithaca, NY: Cornell University Press, 1959, p. 38.
4. Bruce Catton and William B. Catton, *The Bold and Magnificent Dream: America's Founding Years, 1492–1815*. Garden City, NY: Doubleday, 1978, p. 76.
5. Faith Jaycox, *The Colonial Era: An Eyewitness History*. New York: Facts On File, 2002, p. 82.
6. Esmond Wright, *The Search for Liberty: From Origins to Independence*. Cambridge, MA: Blackwell, 1995, p. 507.
7. Catton and Catton, *The Bold and Magnificent Dream*, p. 86.
8. Quoted in Francis Dillon, *The Pilgrims*. Garden City, NY: Doubleday, 1975, p. 137.
9. Sally Smith Booth, *Seeds of Anger: Revolts in America, 1607–1771*. New York: Hastings House, 1977, p. 36.
10. Arthur Quinn, *A New World: An Epic of Colonial America from the Founding of Jamestown to the Fall of Quebec*. Boston: Faber and Faber, 1994, pp. 122–23.

11. Alan Taylor, *American Colonies*. New York: Viking Penguin, 2001, p. 165.

12. Quoted in Herbert Aptheker, *The Colonial Era*. New York: International Publishers, 1959, p. 65.

13. Taylor, *American Colonies*, p. 149.

14. Quoted in Aptheker, *The Colonial Era*, p. 67.

15. Oscar Theodore Barck Jr. and Hugh Talmage Lefler, *Colonial America*. New York: Macmillan, 1968, pp. 202–203.

16. Lawrence H. Leder, *America—1603–1789: Prelude to a Nation*. Minneapolis, MN: Burgess, 1972, p. 92.

17. Booth, *Seeds of Anger*, p. xiii.

Early Settlements

CHAPTER 1

THE FOUNDING OF JAMESTOWN

THE VIRGINIA COMPANY OF LONDON

Established in Virginia in 1607, Jamestown was not England's first attempt at colonizing North America, but it was the first English settlement that survived. The following document was written in 1606 by the council members of the Virginia Company of London, which sponsored the Jamestown settlers. The Virginia Company intended this document to serve as a guide for the colonists upon their arrival in the New World. Much emphasis is placed on the selection of a site that would be easy to defend—an important concern for the settlers, who anticipated attacks from the local Native Americans and the Spanish (who held prior claims to the land in Virginia). In addition, the council members give advice on the proper construction of Jamestown and the cultivation of crops.

But as the instructions make clear, the company also expected the colonists to immediately begin searching for precious metals and a route to Asia, even before they had finished building their shelters and planting the crops they would need to survive. Due in part to these expectations, the Jamestown colony got off to a rough start, with many settlers succumbing to starvation, exposure, or disease. The settlement eventually became prosperous not through the discovery of gold, as the Virginia Company anticipated, but through the cultivation of tobacco, which became its staple commodity.

Edward D. Neill, *History of the Virginia Company of London*, Albany, NY: Joel Munsell, 1869.

Instructions given by way of advice by us whom it hath pleased the King's Majesty to appoint of the Counsel for the intended voyage to Virginia, to be observed by those Captains and company which are sent at this present to plant there.

As we doubt not but you will have especial care to observe the ordinances set down by the King's Majesty and delivered unto you under the privy seal; so for your better directions upon your first landing we have thought good to recommend unto your care these instructions and articles following.

CHOOSING A SITE

When it shall please God to send you on the coast of Virginia, you shall do your best endeavour to find out a safe port in the entrance of some navigable river making choice of such a one as runneth farthest into the land, and if you happen to discover divers portable rivers, and amongst them any one that hath two main branches if the difference be not great make choice of that which bendeth most toward the North-west for that way you shall soonest find the other sea.

When you have made choice of the river on which you mean to settle be not hasty in landing your victuals and munitions, but first let Captain [Christopher] Newport discover how far that river may be found navigable that you make election of the strongest, most wholesome and fertile place for if you make many removes besides the loss of time, you shall greatly spoil your victuals and your casks, and with great pain transport it in small boats.

But if you choose your place so far up as a bark of fifty tuns will float then you may lay all your provisions ashore with ease, and the better receive the trade of all the countries about you in the land, and such a place you may perchance find a hundred miles from the river's mouth, and the further up the better for if you sit down near the entrance, except it be in some island that is strong by nature, an enemy that may approach you on even ground may easily pull you out, and if he be driven to seek you a hundred miles [in] the land in boats you shall from both sides of the river where it is narrowest, so beat them with your muskets as they shall never be able to prevail against you.

And to the end that you be not surprized as the French were in Florida by Melindus [i.e., Pedro Menéndez de Avilés] and the Spaniard in the same place by the French [in 1564, the French attempted to surreptitiously establish a colony in territory claimed by Spain; the following year, a Spanish fleet led by Menéndez crushed the French colony in a surprise attack], you shall do well to make this double provision, first erect a little stoure at the mouth of the river that may lodge some ten men, with whom you shall leave a light boat, that when any fleet shall be in sight they may come with speed to give you warning. Secondly you must in no case suffer any of the native people of the country to inhabit between you and the sea coast for you cannot carry yourselves so towards them but they will grow discontented with your habitation, and be ready to guide and assist any nation that shall come to invade you, and if you neglect this you neglect your safety.

When you have discovered as far up the river as you mean to plant yourselves and landed your victuals and munitions to the end that every man may know his charge you shall do well to divide your six score men into three parts, whereof one party of them you may appoint to fortifie and build of which your first work must be your storehouse for victual; the other you may imploy in preparing your ground and sowing your corn and roots; the other ten of these forty you must leave as centinel at the haven's mouth. The other forty you may imploy for two months in discovery of the river above you, and on the country about you which charge Captain Newport and Captain [Bartholomew] Gosnold may undertake of these forty discoverers; when they do espie any high lands or hills Capt. Gosnold may take twenty of the company to cross over the lands, and carrying a halfdozen pickaxes to try if they can find any minerals. The other twenty may go on by river, and pitch up boughs upon the banks' side by which the other boats shall follow them by the same turnings. You may also take with them a wherry such as is used here in the Thames, by which you may send back to the President for supply of munition or any other want that you may not be driven to return for every small defect.

You must observe if you can whether the river on which you plant doth spring out of mountains or out of lakes, if it be out of any lake, the passage to the other sea will be the more easy, and is like enough that out of the same lake you shall find some spring which run the contrary way toward the East India Sea, for the great and famous rivers of Volga, Tauis and Dwina have three heads near joynd, and yet the one falleth into the Caspian Sea, the other into the Euxine Sea, and the third into the Polonian Sea.

In all your passages you must have great care not to offend

the naturals, if you can eschew it, and imploy some few of your company to trade with them for corn and all other lasting victuals if you have any and this you must do before that they perceive you mean to plant among them, for not being sure how your own seed corn will prosper the first year, to avoid the danger of famine, use and endeavour to store yourselves of the country corn. . . .

And how weary soever your soldiers be, let them never trust the country people with the carriage of their weapons, for if they run from you with your shott which they only fear, they will easily kill them all with their arrows. And whensoever any of yours shoots before them, be sure that they be chosen out of your best markesmen, for if they see your learners miss what they aim at, they will think the weapon not so terrible and thereby will be bould to assault you.

Above all things do not advertize the killing of any of your men, that the country people may know it; if they perceive that they are but common men, and that with the loss of many of theirs, they may deminish any part of yours, they will make many adventures upon you. If the country be populous, you shall do well also not to let them see or know of your sick men, if you have any, which may also encourage them to many enterprises. . . .

BUILDING THE TOWN

It were necessary that all your carpenters and other such like workmen about building do first build your storehouse and those other rooms of publick and necessary use before any house be set up for any private person, and though the workman may belong to any private persons yet let them all work together first for the company and then for private men.

And seeing order is at the same price with confusion it shall be adviseably done to set your houses even and by a line, that your streets may have a good breadth, and be carried square about your market place, and every street's end opening into it, that from thence with a few field pieces you may command every street throughout, which market place you may also fortify if you think it needfull.

You shall do well to send a perfect relation by Capt. Newport of all that is done, what height you are seated, how far into the land, what comodities you find, what soil, woods and their several kinds, and so of all other things else to advertise p'ticularly;

and to suffer no man to return but by pasport from the President and Counsel, nor to write any letter of any thing that may discourage others.

Lastly and chiefly the way to prosper and achieve good success is to make yourselves all of one mind for the good of your country and your own, and to serve and fear God the Giver of all Goodness, for every plantation which our Heavenly Father hath not planted shall be rooted out.

A Meeting of Cultures: The Indians and the Jamestown Colonists

Gary B. Nash

In the following excerpt from his book *Red, White, and Black: The Peoples of Early North America*, Gary B. Nash examines the interactions between the English colonists in Jamestown and the Indians who lived in the Chesapeake Bay region. In particular, he describes the relationship of Captain John Smith and Powhatan, the leader of a powerful confederation of several local tribes. According to the author, the actions of Powhatan and his daughter, Pocahontas, were often misinterpreted by Smith and the other colonists. Powhatan initially attempted to build an alliance with the colonists, Nash explains, but he soon grew to perceive Jamestown as a dangerous threat to his own people.

Nash is a professor emeritus of history and the director of the National Center for History in the Schools at the University of California in Los Angeles. His books include *Class and Society in Early America* and *Race, Class, and Politics: Essays on American Colonial and Revolutionary Society*.

Gary B. Nash, *Red, White, and Black: The Peoples of Early North America*, Englewood Cliffs, NJ: Prentice-Hall, Inc., 1992. Copyright © 1974 by Prentice-Hall, Inc. Reproduced by permission.

From the time that the first Jamestown expeditions touched shore, Indians and Englishmen were in continuous contact in North America. Moreover, permanent settlement required acquisition of land by white settlers—land that was in the possession of native people. That single fact initiated a chain of events that governed the entire sociology of red-white relations.

FIRST ENCOUNTERS

It is not possible to know exactly what Englishmen expected of the Indians as they approached the Chesapeake Bay in the spring of 1607. Nor is it possible to be certain whether the Indian destruction of a Spanish Jesuit mission on the York river in 1570 bespoke a generalized hostility toward Europeans. But it is likely, given the English belief that the Roanoke colony had been reduced to a pile of bones by the Indians a generation earlier, and given the Indians' sporadic experience with Europeans as a militaristic people—and a people who wished to interfere with their religious beliefs and practices—that neither side was very optimistic about the receptiveness of the other. The pessimistic view of the English must have been greatly intensified when the Jamestown expedition was attacked near Cape Henry, the most seaward point of land in the Chesapeake Bay region, where the first landfall was made. From this point on, the English proceeded with extreme caution, expecting violence and treachery from the Indians, even when they approached in outwardly friendly ways. When the one-armed Captain Christopher Newport led the first exploratory trip up the newly named James River, just weeks after a tiny settlement had been planted at Jamestown, he was confused by what he encountered. The Indians, a member of his group wrote, "are naturally given to trechery, howbeit we could not find it in our travell up the river, but rather a most kind and loving people." This account describes how the English were wined and dined by the Indians, who explained that they were "at oddes" with other tribes, including the Chesapeake tribe that had attacked the English at Cape Henry, and were willing to ally with the English against their enemies.

It is now known that the Indians of the region were accurately describing their situation when they said they were "at oddes" with other tribes. Some forty small tribes lived in the Chesapeake Bay region. Powhatan was the paramount chief of several dozen of these, and for years before the English arrived he had been consolidating his hold on the lesser tribes of the area, while warding off the inland tribes of the Piedmont. In this situation Powhatan may have seen an alliance with the English as a means of extending his power in the tidewater area while simultaneously neutralizing the power of his western enemies. At the same time, his unpleasant experience with Europeans, including a clash just three years before with a passing English ship whose crew had been hospitably entertained but then had killed a local chief and kidnapped several Indians, probably made Powhatan extremely wary of these newcomers.

John Smith and others were quick to comprehend the inter-tribal tensions as well as the linguistic differences among the Indians. But apparently they could not convince themselves that some tribal leaders could find their arrival potentially to their advantage. Perhaps because their position was so precarious, with dysentery, hunger, and internal strife debilitating their tiny settlement, they could only afford to regard all Indians as threatening. Hence, hostile and friendly Indians were seen as different only in their outward behavior. Inwardly they were identical— "savage," treacherous men who only waited for a chance to drive the English back into the sea from which they had emerged.

During the first months of contact, the confusion in the English mind surfaced again and again. In the autumn of 1607, for example, when food supplies were running perilously low and all but a handful of the Jamestown settlers had fallen too ill to work, the colony was saved by Powhatan, whose men brought food to keep the struggling settlement alive until the sick recovered and the relief ship arrived. Many saw this as an example of Powhatan's covert hostility rather than as an attempt of the chief to serve his own interests through an alliance with the English. "It pleased God (in our extremity)," wrote John Smith, "To move the Indians to bring us Corne, ere it was halfe ripe, to refresh us, when we rather expected . . . they would destroy us." As a man of military experience among "barbarian" people in other parts of the world, Smith was not willing to believe that the Indians, in aiding the colony, might have found the survival of the English in their own interest. Another leader of the colony could only attribute the Indians' generous behavior to the intervention of the white man's God. "If it had not pleased God to have put a terrour in the Savages heart," he wrote, "we had all perished by those wild and cruell Pagans, being in that weake estate as we were."

JOHN SMITH AND POCAHONTAS

In December 1607 Smith was captured during one of his exploratory incursions into Powhatan's country and marched to Werowocomoco, the seat of Powhatan's confederacy. Powhatan seems to have wanted to employ this opportunity to impress the English with his power and arranged a mock execution ceremony for Smith. At the critical moment, as the executioners prepared to deliver the death blows, the chief's favorite daughter, Pocahontas, threw herself on Smith to save him. About twelve years old, Pocahontas had been a frequent visitor to Jamestown, undoubtedly as an emissary of her father, and was well known to Smith. But rather than understanding the rescue in symbolic terms, as Powhatan's way of indicating his strength but also his desire to forge a bond with the newcomers, Smith and other Virginians took Pocahontas's gesture as a spontaneous outburst of love for the English—an un-Indian-like act attributable to English superiority or perhaps to God's intervening hand. Hostility was on the English mind, sporadic hostility had already occurred, and Powhatan's deliverance of the English leader, at a time when the colony was almost defenseless, was thus not conceived as a conciliatory act.

In the aftermath of the incident, Pocahontas became a kind of ambassador from Powhatan to the struggling Jamestown colony, an agent who became fluent in the English language and kept her father informed on the state of the internally divided Englishmen. By late 1608, more colonists had arrived in Jamestown, and Smith, as the new president of council, adopted an aggressive stance, burning Indian canoes, fields, and villages in order to extort food supplies and to cow Powhatan and his lesser chiefs into submission. Fully aware that Virginia could not be resupplied from England every few months and that the colonists were unable to sustain themselves in their new environment, Smith sought a forced trade with Powhatan. But by now, Powhatan had determined to let the Englishmen starve, a policy made manifestly clear not only by his refusal to trade corn but by his withdrawal of Pocahontas. On penalty of death, the young Indian daughter of the chief was forbidden to enter the English settlement. "Captain Smith," warned Powhatan at a confrontation of the two leaders in January 1609, "some doubt I have of your coming hither, that makes me not so kindly seek to receive you as I would [like]. For many do inform me your coming is not for trade, but to invade my people and possess my country."

Smith's response, as the leader of a colony where some men were deserting to the Indians while others starved, was to raid Indian villages for provisions and slaughter native people of both sexes and all ages. Powhatan responded by attacking the English wherever he could. Even the arrival of fresh supplies and several hundred new colonists in the summer of 1609 did not help, for the provisions were quickly exhausted, the men ravenously consuming more than they produced. When the relief ships departed in October 1609, with John Smith aboard one of them, Virginia embarked upon a winter of despair. Under the surveillance of Powhatan, who ambushed foraging colonists whenever he could, the death toll mounted. George Percy, Smith's successor, wrote that after the horses had been eaten, the dysentery-racked Virginians "were glad to make shift with [such] vermin as dogs, cats, rats, and mice." When these were exhausted, men resorted to "things which seem incredible, as to dig up corpses out of graves and to eat them—and some have licked up the blood which hath fallen from their weak fellows. And amongst the rest, this was most lamentable, that one of our colony murdered his wife, ripped the child out of her

John Smith

womb and threw it into the river, and after chopped the mother in pieces and salted her for his food, the same not being discovered before he had eaten part thereof."

Powhatan's policy of withdrawing from trade with the encroachers had succeeded. By the spring of 1610 the Spanish ambassador to England, Alonso de Velasco, reported accurately that "the Indians hold the English surrounded in the strong place which they had erected there, having killed the larger part of them, and the others were left, so entirely without provisions that they thought it impossible to escape." Virginia could be easily erased from the map, Velasco counseled his government, "by sending out a few ships to finish what might be left in that place." What the Spanish ambassador did not know was that two relief ships had reached Jamestown in May 1610 but found the situation so dismal that Sir Thomas Gates, arriving to assume the governorship of the colony, decided to embark the remaining sixty survivors, set sail for England, and admit that Englishmen could not permanently inhabit the shores of the Chesapeake. On June 7, 1610, Gates ordered the forlorn settlement stripped of its meager possessions, loaded the handful of survivors aboard, and set sail down the James River for the open sea. The ships dropped anchor for the night after reaching the Chesapeake Capes and planned to start the return ocean voyage on the following day.

On the next morning three ships hove into sight. They carried 150 new recruits sent out by the Virginia Company and a new governor, Sir Thomas West, Lord De la Warr. Jamestown, at its moment of extinction, was reborn.

INTERMITTENT FIGHTING

Newly armed and provisioned, the revitalized Jamestown colonists revived and extended their militaristic Indian policy in what amounted to an on-again, off-again war between 1609 and 1614. The new attitude toward the Powhatan Confederacy was apparent in the orders issued in 1609 for governing the colony. Three years before, the Virginia Company had instructed, "In all your passages you must have great care not to offend the naturals, if you can eschew it." Now the governor was ordered to effect a military occupation of the region between the James and York rivers, to make all tribes tributary to him rather than to Powhatan, to extract corn, furs, dyes, and labor from each tribe, and, if possible, to mold the natives into an agricultural labor force as the Spanish had done in their colonies. As the English settlement gained in strength, Smith's successors continued his policy of military foraging and intimidation. From 1610 to 1612 Powhatan attacked the colonists whenever opportunities presented themselves and the English mounted fierce attacks that decimated three small tribes and destroyed two Indian villages. Most of the corn that sustained the colony in these years seems to have been extracted by force from Powhatan's villages.

In 1613 the English kidnapped Pocahontas in a move designed to obtain a return of English prisoners and a quantity of weapons that the Indians had acquired over the years and to force payment of "a great quantitie of Corne," as Pocahontas's abductor, Captain Samuel Argall put it. Understanding that his daughter was not in harm's way, Powhatan made limited concessions to the English but refused to satisfy all the ransom conditions. In the following year, when the widower John Rolfe vowed to marry Pocahontas, Powhatan reluctantly assented to the first Anglo-Indian marriage in Virginia's history and signed a humiliating peace treaty. Pocahontas became the instrument of an uneasy truce between the two societies and returned to England with Rolfe and other members of Powhatan's Confederacy in 1616 in order to promote further colonization of the Chesapeake, She died on the eve of her departure for Virginia in 1617 after helping to raise the money that pumped new lifeblood into the Virginia Company and consequently sent hundreds of new fortune-seekers to the Chesapeake as part of the population buildup that would lead to a renewal of hostilities five years after her death.

CULTURAL INTERCHANGE

Notwithstanding misconceptions, suspicion, and violence on both sides, the English and the Powhatans lived in close contact during the first decade of English settlement and cultural interchange occurred on a broad scale. Although it has been a commonplace in the popular mind since the moment when Europeans and Native Americans first met that the Europeans were "advanced" and the Indians were "primitive," the technological differences between the two cultures, as anthropologist Nancy Lurie has reminded us, were equaled or outweighed by the similarities between these two agricultural societies. The main technological advantages of the English were their ability to traverse large bodies of water in wooden ships and their superiority in the use of iron to fashion implements and weapons. But the Indians quickly incorporated such iron-age items as kettles, fishhooks, traps, needles, knives, and guns into their material culture. In return they provided Englishmen with an understanding of how to use nets and weirs to catch the abundant fish and shellfish of the Chesapeake waters and introduced Europeans to a wide range of agricultural products that were unknown in Europe before the New World was reached. Englishmen in Virginia learned from the natives how to cultivate tobacco, corn, beans, squash, pumpkins, and other food products. Indians also introduced the English to a wide range of medicinal herbs, dyes, and such important devices as the canoe.

Such cultural interaction proceeded even while hostility and sporadic violence was occurring in the early years. It was facilitated by the fact that some Indians lived among the English as day laborers, while a number of settlers fled to Indian villages rather than endure the rigors of life among the autocratic English rulers and oppressive tobacco planters. This kind of interchange brought a knowledge and understanding of the other culture. Thus, even while the English pursued a policy of intimidation in the early years, they recognized the resilience and strength of the Indians' culture. Smith marveled at the strength and agility of the Chesapeake tribesmen, at their talent for hunting and fishing, and admired their music and entertainment. He noted that they practiced civil government, that they adhered to religious traditions, and that many of their customs and institutions were not unlike those of the Europeans. "Although the countrie people be very barbarous," he wrote, "yet have they amongst them such government, as that their Magistrats for good commanding, and their people for due subjections, and obeying, excell many places that would be counted very civill." Other Englishmen, such as the Anglican minister Alexander Whitaker, who proselytized among the Indians, wrote that it was a mistake to suppose that the Indians were merely savage people, "for they are of body lustie, strong, and very nimble: they are a very understanding generation, quicke of apprehension, suddaine in their dispatches, subtile in their dealings, exquisite in their inventions, and industrious in their labour." So, while both sides adjusted uneasily to the presence of the other, both were involved in cultural borrowing. It was a process between two peoples separated by a cultural gap that was not nearly so large as the Europeans found it convenient to imply by labeling one culture "savage" and the other "civilized."

THE WAR OF 1622

After the increase of population that accompanied the rapid growth of tobacco production, relations between the two peoples underwent a fundamental alteration. While giving Virginia an important money crop, the cultivation of tobacco created an enormous new demand for land. As more and more men pushed up the rivers that flowed into the Chesapeake Bay to carve out tobacco plantations, the Indians of the region perceived that what had previously been an abrasive and sometimes violent relationship might now become a disastrous one. Powhatan had retired in 1617, just as the cultivation of tobacco was beginning to expand rapidly. His kinsman, Opechancanough, who assumed leadership of the tidewater tribes, con-

cluded that he must embark upon a program of military renaissance and spiritual revitalization.

Opechancanough was battling not only against land-
encroaching Englishmen but against the diseases they were
spreading among the Indian population. The deadliest of all European weapons were the microorganisms brought ashore in
nearly every immigrant. In Europe these bacteriological infec-
tions—smallpox, diphtheria, scarlet fever, yellow fever, and others—had wrought demographic disaster in the fifteenth and sixteenth centuries. But infected populations had gradually built
up immunities against them. The Indians of the New World,
however, had no such immunity when the Europeans arrived
as human carriers of these pathogens. The effects were therefore swift and deadly. Whole tribes could be wiped out in a few
years, leaving vast areas depopulated. The greater the density
of Indian population, the swifter the spread of the disease. In
Mexico and other parts of the densely populated Spanish empire, the Indian population losses were far more catastrophic
than in more sparsely settled coastal North America. But in the
Chesapeake region minor epidemics had taken their toll in the
1580s and again in 1608. Between 1617 and 1619 another epi-
demic decimated the Powhatan tribes.

In leading a reorganization of his people, Opechancanough
relied heavily on Nemattanew, a war captain and religious
prophet whom the English called "Jack of the Feathers" for the
"fantastick Manner" in which "he wou'd often dress himself up
with Feathers . . . as though he meant to flye." A shadowy figure who came often to the English settlements, Nemattanew
had convinced his tribesmen that he was immortal and that
they would be immune to musket fire if they rubbed their bodies with a special ointment. In March 1622, as Opechancanough
was piecing together plans for a unified attack on the Virginia
settlements, Nemattanew was murdered by the English. His
death triggered the famous Indian assault two weeks later that
dealt the colony a staggering blow; but the highly combustible
atmosphere generated by a half-dozen years of white expansion
and pressure on Indian hunting lands was the fundamental
cause of the attack.

THE COLONISTS' RESPONSE

Although it did not achieve its goal of ending English presence
in the Chesapeake area, the Indian attack of 1622 wiped out al-

most one-third of the white population. Included among the victims was Opechancanough's nephew by marriage, John Rolfe. It was the final straw for the Virginia Company of London. Shortly thereafter it declared bankruptcy, leaving the colony to the governance of the Crown. The more important result was that those who survived the attack were left free to pursue a ruthless new Indian policy. Even though several leaders in the colony confided to men in England that the real cause of the Indian attack was "our owne perfidious dealing with them," it was generally agreed that henceforward the colonists would be free to hunt down the Indians wherever they could be found. No longer would it be necessary to acknowledge an obligation to "civilize" and Christianize the native. A no-holds-barred approach to "the Indian problem" would now be taken, once the Virginians' strength was sufficient. One Virginian, Edward Waterhouse, wrote revealingly after the attack:

> Our hands which before were tied with gentleness and faire usage, are now set at liberty by the treacherous violence of the Sauvages. . . . So that we, who hitherto have had possession of no more ground than their waste and our purchase at a valuable consideration to theire owne contentment gained; may now by right of Warre, and law of Nations, invade the Country, and destroy them who sought to destroy us; whereby wee shall enjoy their cultivated places, turning the laborious Mattacke [mattock; a tool for digging] into the victorious Sword . . . and possessing the fruits of others labours. Now their cleared grounds in all their villages (which are situate in the fruitfullest places of the land) shall be inhabited by us, whereas heretofore the grubbing of woods was the greatest labour.

A note of grim satisfaction that the Indians had succeeded in wiping out one-third of the English population can be detected. Now the colonizers were entitled to devastate Indian villages and take rather than buy the best land. John Smith, writing from England two years after the attack, noted that some men held that the attack "will be good for the Plantation, because now we have just cause to destroy them by all meanes possible." Edward Waterhouse expressed the genocidal urge that was prevalent when he reasoned that the Indians had done the colonists a favor by sweeping away the previous English reluctance to annihilate the Indians. He enumerated with relish the ways that the "savages" could be exterminated. "Victorie," he wrote, "may be gained many waies; by force, by surprize, by famine in burning their Corne, by destroying and burning their Boats, Canoes, and Houses, by breaking their fishing Weares [weirs], by assailing them in their huntings, whereby they get the greatest part of their sustenance in Winter, by pursuing and chasing them with our horses, and blood-Hounds to draw after them, and Mastives to teare them."

Once the thirst for revenge was slaked, the only debatable point was whether the extermination of the tidewater Indian tribes would work to the benefit or disadvantage of the colony. One prominent planter offered "reasons why it is not fitting utterlye to make an exterpation of the Savages yett" and then assured his neighbors that it was not genocide he was against but the destruction of a people who, if properly subjugated, could enrich all Virginians through their labor. But both subjugation and assimilation required more time and trouble than the Virginians were willing to spend. The simpler course, consistent with instructions from London to "root out [the Indians] from being any longer a people," was to follow a scorched earth policy, sending military expeditions each summer to destroy villages and crops. In 1629 a peace treaty was negotiated but then rejected because it was decided by the council that a state of "perpetual enmity" would serve the colony better. It was a policy predicated on the belief that acculturation of the two people, even if possible, was not desirable.

BLACK SLAVERY IN VIRGINIA

OSCAR REISS

The first recorded presence of Africans in the British colonies of North America occurred in 1619, when twenty blacks arrived in Jamestown. As author Oscar Reiss relates, these new arrivals were treated as indentured servants rather than slaves. They had the same rights as white indentured servants, Reiss explains, and as soon as they completed their indenture, they were free to buy land and keep their own indentured servants. Over time, however, the white colonists began to make a sharp distinction between the status of white and black servants. Reiss enumerates the various factors that contributed to the establishment of lifelong slavery for blacks in Virginia in the following excerpt from his book *Blacks in Colonial America*.

V irginia, the first permanent English colony on the shores of continental North America (1607), was the template for the development of black-white relations in the rest of the South. Most English colonies in seventeenth-century America were founded by religious dissenters who came to practice their religion as they thought proper (although to the exclusion of all others). By contrast, Virginians were Anglicans who came to make money for themselves and their sponsors. This meant physical work, which was foreign to the leaders of the group. Later in the century, it became apparent that the best way to make money for the few was a plantation economy built on the backs of stolen Africans.

Oscar Reiss, *Blacks in Colonial America*, Jefferson, NC: McFarland & Company, Inc., 1997. Copyright © 1997 by Oscar Reiss. Reproduced by permission of McFarland & Company, Inc., PO Box 611, Jefferson, NC 28640. www.mcfarlandpub.com.

BLACK "CARGO"

Twelve years after the colony's founding, in 1619, 20 blacks, including 3 women, disembarked in Jamestown. In 1618 Governor Samuel Argall of Virginia sent the *Treasurer* to the West Indies, supposedly to obtain and deliver a load of salt and goats. At sea, the *Treasurer* met a Dutch man-of-war, and the two attacked a Spanish frigate carrying over 100 blacks. The attackers took the "cargo" and sailed for Virginia, though they were separated by a storm. Several weeks later, the Dutch ship sailed into Hampton Roads, where the black cargo was traded for goods and supplies.

These new immigrants were treated as indentured servants, not as slaves. Most of these early blacks had been baptized on the African coast or in the Spanish colonies, and in 1619 it was still illegal for an Englishman to enslave Christians. The sale of indentured servants by captains of ships was a common practice in early colonial history. The Africans were traded for public provisions, and therefore they became "servants of the state" (similar to their position in early New Netherlands). They were assigned to officers of the colony and to planters associated with the administration of the colony. Also in 1619 100 young men and boys arrived from London to start their indenture contract. Both groups were treated in a similar fashion, and both would become freeholders in the colony if they survived the "seasoning" period and the depredations of the Native Americans. The blacks survived this early period better than their white coworkers. In the decade of the 1620s, black arrival was slow. The *Treasurer* brought one woman; the *James* brought Antonio in 1621; the *Margaret and John* brought Mary; in 1623 the *Swan* brought John Pedro. In 1623 Anthony and Isabel married and produced William, baptized in the Church of England. A head count in 1623 showed 1,275 whites and 22 blacks. Two years later there were 23 blacks and 1,095 whites and Indians. In 1629 a cargo of blacks captured from a Portuguese ship was exchanged for 85 hogsheads (a cask, often referring to a certain amount of liquor or occasionally other stored material) plus five butts of tobacco (also a term for casks equal to two hogsheads).

ATTEMPTS AT SEPARATION

The black and white indentured servants had more in common with each other than the whites had with the owners of their indenture contracts. The servants worked, lived, and ate with each other; they also socialized and bred. Their masters saw a danger in this intimate relationship and tried to drive a wedge between the two races. At first, this was done through different work assignments. African women worked with the men in the fields, while white women worked around the house. Then, whites were listed with a given and a family name, blacks with only a given name. For example: "A muster of Mr. Edward Bennett's servants included Wassell Wibling and Antonio, a negro, in the *James* 1621. . . . Mary, a negro woman in the *Margaret and John* 1622." A court record for Essex County: "September ye 10th, Ano Dom 1694. Certificate according to Act of Assembly is granted to Captain Richard Haile for two hundred & fifty Acres of Land for the Importation of five persons into this Colony by names Patrick Bradley, Elinor Corkeley, Andrew, Guy, Anne, Negroes." In the first true Virginia census in 1629, blacks were listed separately from Englishmen. In 1630 Hugh Davis was whipped in public for defiling himself (sleeping) with a black woman. Laws against miscegenation were passed in 1662, 1691, 1696, 1705, 1753, and 1765. By the end of the seventeenth century, intermarriage was illegal. In 1640 all inhabitants, "negroes excepted," were expected to bear arms for the security of the colony. The Anglican church, allied to the rich planters, helped to create this schism. Anglican priests preached that the blacks were not Christian and that they were different. When blacks began to undergo baptism in the church, a new reason for separation was needed so the church preached that there was a defect in the black's character solely related to being black. Eventually, the black was deprived of civil rights, his position in the community was lowered, and he fell outside the protection of the law. Finally, the site of origin of slaves had its effect. Early in the century, blacks came from the West Indies where they may have worked for two or three years. They were accustomed to the white man's ways, wore the same clothes, and had picked up enough English to communicate with whites. Later in the century, slaves were imported directly from Africa. They spoke no English and could not communicate with white workers. It should be noted that since they came from different tribes they could not communicate with each other either.

These attempts at separation were not uniformly successful. In 1676 Nathaniel Bacon led an insurrection of freedmen, servants, and slaves against the authorities. White free men joined because they had no hope for a future while the authorities, supported by the wealthy planters, were in control. They felt closer to the servants and blacks than they did to the rich. After Bacon's sudden death in 1676, the authorities offered amnesty to those who would put down their arms, and the rebellion collapsed. After the insurrection, fewer indentured whites were imported. They were replaced by blacks who were severely restricted in their activities.

THE INTRODUCTION OF SERVICE FOR LIFE

Early in the century, blacks who completed their indenture were free to obtain land; several took advantage of the head-rights law to obtain large grants of land. Anyone who imported servants, white or black, received 50 acres of land per individual. In one case, Richard Johnson, a black, purchased an indenture contract and kept a white man in servitude. However, by 1670 a black was forbidden to keep a white servant. Black landowners treated their black servants as their white neighbors did. For instance, Anthony Johnson, a Negro, was accused of holding a black as an indentured servant "longer than he should or ought." Johnson told the court that he had a claim on the servant for life, and he won his case (1640). From this decision one may assume that the concept of lifetime servitude already existed before the court's decision.

The acceptance by society of service for life predated its acceptance by law. Most authorities cite the case of John Punch as a landmark decision by the courts. In 1640 Hugh Gwyn brought back to Virginia three servants who had escaped to Maryland. Two were white, and John Punch was black. The court ordered that all three were to receive 30 lashes. The whites were to serve out their terms of indenture plus a penalty of one year to the owner and three years to the colony. The black could not be punished by increasing his term of servitude, because it was for life. The next step in the descent of the black into slavery was to make his progeny servants for life. In 1646, Francis Potts sold a Negro woman and boy to Stephen Charlton "to the use of him forever." In 1652 William Wittington sold to John Pott "a negro girl and her issue for their lifetime." What was accepted practice was written into law in 1661. According to this legislation, blacks could not be punished by adding time to their period of servitude, because they served for life. The decree further stated that if an English servant ran off with a black, he would serve his penalty time plus that of the black, because time could not be added to the black's lifetime of servitude. The following year a statute was added to the laws of Virginia stating that the child took the status of the mother. This decree was diametrically opposed to common law, which conferred the father's status on the child. If the usual condition applied, slavery would slowly have reached a point of extinction: while many white masters produced offspring with their slaves, many fewer white women engaged in miscegenation. The old common law against Englishmen enslaving Christians was next to be struck down. By a law in 1667, baptism did not change the status of the convert. Three years later, it was decided that all non-Christian servants who came to Virginia by ship were slaves for life. Those blacks who came by land (that is, from another colony) had to serve 12 years, and children had to serve until the age of 30. Finally, this loophole was closed in 1682 when all servants, except Turks and Moors, brought to this country whose native religion was not Christian were slaves.

Within a period of 50 years of their arrival in Virginia, the position of blacks was written in stone. They were slaves upon whose labor the plantation economy existed.

SPAIN'S REACTION TO THE COLONY AT JAMESTOWN

J. LEITCH WRIGHT JR.

The English colony of Jamestown was established on land that Spain claimed as its own. Although the Spaniards had no colonies in Virginia, they clearly saw Jamestown as a foreign threat to their dominance in the New World. In the following essay from *Anglo-Spanish Rivalry in North America*, J. Leitch Wright Jr. describes several Spanish attempts at undermining the colony at Jamestown, including the use of spies and the deployment of military expeditions from the Spanish fort in St. Augustine, Florida. However, he asserts, Spain never made a concentrated effort at expelling the Jamestown colonists, and thus the English gained a foothold in North America. A retired professor of history from Florida State University in Tallahassee, Wright is the author of *Florida in the American Revolution* and *The Only Land They Knew: American Indians in the Old South*.

D uring the latter part of the sixteenth century France, the Netherlands, and England had contested by force of arms the imperious policies of Philip II, the King of Spain. By their successes it was obvious in the early 1600s that Spanish hegemony in Europe was a thing of the past. And these same three nations were responsible for the destruction of Spanish hegemony in the Indies. Their inroads on Spanish colonies in the sixteenth century usually had been confined to raiding

J. Leitch Wright Jr., *Anglo-Spanish Rivalry in North America*, Athens: University of Georgia Press, 1971. Copyright © 1971 by the University of Georgia Press. All rights reserved. Reproduced by permission.

and privateering; in the seventeenth century they shifted emphasis to colonization and exploitation.

ENGLISH PLANS

Before or shortly after the turn of the century Spain grudgingly signed peace treaties with her opponents one by one, including an ambiguous 1604 treaty with England. Immediately after the proclamation of this treaty, if not earlier, Englishmen, vigorously searching for new sources of raw materials and markets, were busy formulating a multitude of New World enterprises in North and South America and the West Indies. . . .

The fact that there was peace, the terms of which—at least by the English interpretation—sanctioned such settlements, and the fact that English commercial and manufacturing interests were concerned with America not only as a source of bullion, or as a foothold to continue search for the Northwest Passage, or as an anti-Spanish privateering base, but also as the site of future populous colonies which would be an end in themselves by producing valuable naval stores, wines, and iron, stimulated interest in relatively uninhabited and otherwise unattractive Virginia. Two groups of backers, one in London, the other in Plymouth, organized a typical joint-stock company, the Virginia Company. The royal charter provided that the boundaries would be between thirty-four degrees (Cape Fear in present-day North Carolina) on the south and forty-five degrees (central Maine) on the north. Two settlements would be made within these bounds provided they were not in territory "actually possessed by a Christian prince." Prior English voyages, the writings of the Richard Hakluyts [two cousins of the same name who promoted English colonization of North America], and translations of classic Spanish works about the New World all made it plain that Spain had no settlements north of Cape Fear. The Spanish ambassador to England, Pedro de Zúñiga, ironically observed that though the charter specified that the two settlements would not be within one hundred miles of each other, it made no mention "of the distance at which they are bound to be from your majesty's subjects.". . .

In 1607 the London Company sent out three small vessels and one hundred forty-four settlers to found a colony. Because of the unfavorable experience at Roanoke Island they by-passed Albemarle and Pamlico Sounds and instead established themselves on the more navigable Chesapeake Bay. Keeping Menéndez's surprise of the French in mind [in 1565, Spanish captain Pedro Menéndez de Avilés destroyed a French colony in Florida], they spent some time looking for a suitable site. The Jamestown peninsula finally selected offered many advantages: a good harbor, ease of defense from the Indians by land, and time for ample warning of an attack by sea. At once they fortified Point Comfort at the mouth of the James to give warning to settlements up river. . . .

The privations, internal quarrels, governmental reorganizations, Indian hostility, and ultimate success of the colony are well known. At first, under the dictatorial leadership of John Smith the colony enjoyed a moderate degree of success. Then after his departure the colony's fortunes dipped to their lowest ebb during the "starving time." The few surviving colonists hung on, and with continual reinforcements from England, the tide began to turn. John Rolfe, through his marriage to Pocahontas, established friendly relations with the Indians and, through his importation of tobacco seeds from the Spanish Indies and his improved method of curing tobacco, gave the colony a substitute for gold or silver. In time the settlers erected new fortifications at Cape Henry and Cape Charles and concluded defensive alliances with the Indians to prevent "that all devouring Spaniard from laying his ravenous hands upon these gold shewing mountains," as stated in the Virginia Council's report of 1607.

THE THREAT TO SPAIN

Spain's attitude toward this new English plantation was the same shown toward the French in Florida. . . . The plans and progress of the Virginia Company were well-publicized: at once the Spanish people had their "hearts and their eyes fixed much upon" Virginia, as Charles Cornwallis reported to the Privy Council in 1608. Zúñiga vainly protested to James I, the English king, that this company was usurping provinces of *la Florida*, and at the same time he kept Madrid informed of Jamestown's fortunes.

For over a decade after 1607 the Spanish Council of War, denying England's right to settle here and doggedly insisting that this colony violated the recent treaty, considered sending a one-thousand, two-thousand, or even five-thousand-man expedition, organized in either New or Old Spain, to expel the Jamestown intruders. The danger, direct and indirect, to the Spanish Indies was painfully obvious. Not only was the Chesapeake athwart the return route of the treasure fleet, but given time this "gran cancer" might flourish, expand, and even threaten the heart of New Spain. For a variety of reasons— though not because the council felt exterminating the Virginia settlement would violate the peace treaty—none of its proposals were put into effect. There was a perennial lack of funds, and during the "starving time" when the settlers were reduced to eating vermin and, at least in one case, a fellow colonist, it appeared that Jamestown would succumb by itself. Also it was quickly obvious that the metal which the Englishmen brought from Virginia was "not as rich as had been thought." In fact, it was worthless. By the time Spain realized this colony was permanent, rival and more immediately dangerous ones were appearing in various parts of the New World. . . .

Prior to the colonizing activities of the Virginia Company, Spain had considered abandoning her Florida base at St. Augustine, removing the Christian Indians to Hispaniola in the West Indies, and erecting a new, smaller fort along the Florida peninsula to rescue shipwrecked mariners. After Jamestown she quickly abandoned these ideas. Fortunately her position in Florida was stronger now than it had been for two decades. Zealous Franciscan efforts had paid rich dividends in harmonious Indian relations, and the presidio at St. Augustine had been repaired so that the triangular wooden structure could truly be called a fort rather than a beehive. In addition, the Florida governor ordered Indians living along the coast to capture any Europeans who came ashore for wood and water. It was problematical whether or not the Indians would obey this order because of their numerous prior contacts with English and French ship captains. But it was an unfortunate corsair or colonist who, by whatever means, fell into Spanish hands. A sentence to the galleys was the best fate to be hoped for. At almost the same time that Virginia colonists were stepping ashore at Cape Henry, Spanish soldiers captured a band of French and English "pirates" and took them to St. Augustine, [where they] all were hanged.

SPANISH AGENTS IN JAMESTOWN

The Spanish position in Florida was steadily improving, but there was little the three-hundred-man garrison could do about Jamestown. There was even less that the distant frontier outposts in northeastern Mexico could do, although officials at both places advanced projects to expel the English. The first threat to Virginia came not from St. Augustine, or from Mexico, or from Spain, but rather from Spanish agents within the Jamestown colony itself—at least indications strongly suggest this. In the past half century Spanish confidants had accompanied most of the English colonization voyages to North America, and it would be illogical to think that none were passengers to Virginia in 1607. The Jamestown colonists were not a carefully screened group, and it would have been easy for the Spanish ambassador to include one or more sympathetic Catholics—this is precisely what he did with subsequent voyages. In any case, during the early critical years there were sputterings, grumblings, plots, and intrigues. Many were directed toward Smith and the autocratic manner in which he governed. In turn, he usually charged his antagonists with being Spanish agents. Doubtless most of them committed no offense except to oppose Smith; even so, there is probably at least some foundation for his allegations.

Scarcity of provisions in 1609 forced some of the colonists to split up into groups and to live with and off neighboring Indians. According to Smith there was a Spanish-inspired design, headed by "the Dutchman and one Bently" to incite the Indians to massacre the Englishmen while they were in such a precarious position. Smith sent William Volda to apprehend these two conspirators, but instead of taking them prisoner he joined in their insidious plot. Smith apparently defeated this scheme by executing the major participants. . . .

A MILITARY MISSION TO VIRGINIA

The first Spaniards definitely known to have visited Virginia came not surreptitiously as spies but openly on a Spanish vessel whose mission was to determine the exact state of the English plantation. The Spanish Council of War, which was considering the best method of dealing with this threat to the Indies, dispatched them. The Council ordered Governor Pedro de Ibarra at St. Augustine to make a reconnaissance to discover the precise location of the English settlements and the best route to attack them.

Accordingly, Ibarra outfitted Captain Francisco Fernández de Ecija with a pinnace, twenty-five men, and the Indian wife of a Spanish soldier as interpreter. Ecija, a long-time resident of St. Augustine, and commander of an infantry company, was well qualified for this mission. In 1605 he had commanded an expedition which captured French corsairs on the Savannah River [in present-day Georgia] and later that same year had made a reconnaissance as far north as Cape Romain [in present-day South Carolina]. Now his superiors ordered him to sail to Chesapeake Bay. . . . His first stop was at the Jordan River (Cape Fear) where Indians gave eye-witness accounts of how the whites had built a fort on the Jamestown peninsula, how they had secured it with heavy armaments, how numerous vessels traded there, and how others guarded the harbor. At the Jordan he rescued a Frenchman from the Indians. Though he had lived among them for many years and had almost forgotten his native tongue, in a short time he was able to confirm and elaborate their reports.

Ecija sailed for Jacán, as the Spaniards called Virginia, to see for himself. After passing through the capes at the entrance of the Chesapeake, he saw that the Indians had told the truth. A ship, a large one with two topsails and a great banner at its masthead, was on guard in the bay. It sailed in the opposite direction, and Ecija became suspicious. Was it purposely enticing him further into the bay? Not to be outdone, Ecija too sailed in the opposite direction—back through the capes and down to the North Carolina coast. . . . But foul weather off the treacherous Carolina coast forced him to seek refuge in the Jordan where he requestioned the Indians before finally returning to St. Augustine. His detailed report about the English in Jacán added little to information obtained long ago by the Spanish ambassador in London.

CONFLICT AT POINT COMFORT

To get a more accurate picture of conditions and specific settlements Spain increased her efforts to smuggle spies into Virginia. At the same time Philip III ordered another vessel to visit Jacán. In April 1611 the *Nuestra Señora del Rosario* cleared Lisbon. Aboard were Captain Diego de Molina, Ensign Antonio Pérez, and the pilot, Francis Lymbry. Molina and Pérez were native Spaniards, while Lymbry was an Englishman who lived in Madrid with his Spanish wife. Their official commission authorized them to search along the coast of *la Florida* for a wrecked Spanish man-of-war and to salvage its artillery. But this was merely an excuse to spy out the Virginia colony.

Molina and his confederates touched at Havana, Cuba, and St. Augustine before sailing boldly into the Chesapeake.

Quickly they detected signs of English activity at Point Comfort, and squads of Englishmen emerged from the forest to greet Molina as he stepped ashore from his longboat. The Spanish Captain patiently explained that he desired only to continue searching for the shipwrecked vessel. His English hosts warily replied that they would have to report this to their governor thirty miles up river at Jamestown. Meanwhile why not place the Spanish vessel in safety behind Point Comfort? Molina, Pérez, and Lymbry remained ashore, while John Clark returned with the other Spaniards to the *Nuestra Señora* to pilot her in the strange waters. Smouldering suspicion now broke into open flame. The Englishmen refused to let Molina and his two companions return to their ship. At the same time, the remaining Spaniards, becoming alarmed, refused to take shelter behind Point Comfort or to release the pilot Clark. The *Nuestra Señora* beat up and down before Point Comfort but, because Molina failed to give the prearranged signal, did not land. Fearing for their safety, the Spaniards fled the Chesapeake with the unwilling English pilot aboard. . . .

From Jamestown Clark was taken to Havana where Spanish officials recorded voluminous pages of his testimony concerning particulars of the colony, the outpost at Point Comfort, the main fort at Jamestown, the number of able-bodied men, the "pirates" that used Jamestown as a base, and a myriad of other details. From Havana Clark went to Madrid and, either because of expediency or religious conviction, became a Catholic en route. Once in Spain he was imprisoned, questioned, and finally released in exchange for Molina. Clark returned to London and piloted other ships to Virginia, including the *Mayflower* which landed at Plymouth in 1620. . . .

SPAIN'S FAILURE TO CARRY THROUGH

Jamestown's location was partly responsible for its protection. It was adjacent to the return sailing route to Europe which for Spanish naval commanders presented difficulties. A logical force to use against Virginia were the Spanish galleons which were in the West Indies awaiting to convoy the merchant ships to Europe. Supposedly while these merchantmen were protected at Portobello, Veracruz, and other ports and the trade fairs were in progress, the galleons could pay Jamestown a visit. Because of the prevailing winds and currents it was easy to sail from the West Indies to Jamestown, but it was difficult to return.

Should the galleons not get back to the West Indies in time to convoy the treasure fleet it would be disastrous. Theoretically the galleons could detour and stop at Jamestown while escorting the treasure fleet to Europe, but this was risky and never seriously considered. Had Jamestown been in the West Indies within easy reach of the galleons or been founded a half century earlier when the Spanish navy was stronger and the mother country not so exhausted from wars, then the English would have suffered the fate of the earlier French colonists.

Nevertheless rumors circulated throughout Europe that a powerful Spanish armada had departed for Virginia, that the galleons of the treasure fleet had paid Jamestown a visit before returning to Spain, or that Spain had actually destroyed the infant colony. These reports were still prevalent two decades after Jamestown's founding. In 1620 John Rolfe received supposedly reliable word of a forthcoming attack in the spring. With no place of strength to retreat to, few experienced soldiers, and poor ordnance, this news was disheartening. Five years later England and Spain were at war. The colonists, almost prostrate after the recent Indian massacre, braced themselves and hoarded their powder for the expected Spanish descent. Fortunately Spain was deeply committed in Germany, in defending Cádiz from a mismanaged English expedition, and in warding off the Dutch elsewhere in America; and this threat to Virginia, like every other, failed to materialize.

THE DUTCH COLONY
OF NEW NETHERLAND

MAX SAVELLE AND ROBERT MIDDLEKAUFF

Shortly after the English founded Jamestown, the Dutch began
to explore and settle in the area that is now New York, as Max
Savelle and Robert Middlekauff relate in the following selection
from their book *A History of Colonial America*. Savelle and Middlekauff describe the various towns, forts, and trading posts established by the Dutch in the region that they called New
Netherland. In addition, the authors examine the economic
growth of the colony, its cultural and social life, and the settlers'
desire for self-government.

Savelle was a professor of history at the University of Wash-
ington at Seattle for twenty years; his books include *The Colo-
nial Origins of American Thought* and *Seeds of Liberty: The Genesis
of the American Mind*. Middlekauff is the emeritus Preston
Hotchkiss Professor of American History at the University of
California in Berkeley. He is the author of *The Mathers: Three
Generations of Puritan Intellectuals, 1596–1728* and *Ancients and
Axioms: Secondary Education in Eighteenth-Century New England*.

T he colonization of America by Dutchmen was a manifes-
tation of the continuing expansion of the commercial life
of Holland, which paralleled in many ways the expansion of England. The growth of Dutch commerce is a part of the
story of the development of Holland as a nation and its challenge to the Hispano-Portuguese monopoly of the commerce of
the colonial world.

THE BIRTH OF AN INDEPENDENT HOLLAND

The Spanish Low Countries began their war of independence against Spain in 1565. This war had its origin in resistance to King Philip II's arbitrary regulation of commerce and his attempt to inflict upon the Protestant people of the Low Countries a restoration of the Catholic religion. During the course of the war, in 1579, the seven northern provinces (Holland) separated from the southern provinces, and in 1581 declared themselves independent of Spain. The southern provinces (Belgium) compromised their quarrel with Spain and remained under Spanish control. The war of Holland alone with Spain then continued until 1609, when a truce was arranged, at the expiration of which period the war was resumed and became a part of the Thirty Years War. Dutch independence was finally recognized by the Treaty of Münster in 1648.

As dependencies of Spain, the Low Countries had enjoyed rich profits from the Spanish and Portuguese colonial trade, for Cadiz and Lisbon were the terminal points for the overseas trade routes, and Dutch vessels went to these ports with cargoes of manufactured goods and other products of the north to take in exchange the spices of the Far East and the tobacco or hides or gold and silver from America. With their separation from Spain, however, and with the annexation of Portugal by Spain in 1580, the Dutch merchants found their vessels excluded from Portuguese and Spanish ports. Partly for this reason and partly because of the high profits to be derived from direct trade, Dutchmen began to sail directly to the Indies, east and west, where they traded in the markets of the colonies and preyed upon Spanish and Portuguese ships. These activities on both sides of the world were very profitable, and in 1602 the Dutch East India Company was formed for trade and warfare against Spain and Portugal.

HENRY HUDSON'S DISCOVERY

It was this company that engaged Henry Hudson, an Englishman, to go out in 1609 to search for a passage round America toward the Far East. He eventually came to a river that he called the Mauritius after Prince Maurice, but which later came to be known as the Hudson River in honor of himself, and sailed up that river to the head of navigation. In the course of his journey he traded up and down the river with the Indians, and the skins that he took back to Holland paid good profits. This was the beginning of the Dutch fur trade on the Hudson.

Following the expedition of Henry Hudson, other ships went to the river of Mauritius almost every year; and in 1614 Adriaen Block went on a voyage in which he not only engaged in trade but in exploration as well. On this voyage he sailed along the shores of Long Island Sound, probably as far as Block Island, and he probably entered the Connecticut River. As a result of his voyage, which was a profitable one, there was organized a group of merchants in Amsterdam called the New Netherland Company, who petitioned the Dutch Estates General [the parliament] for a patent which, when granted, gave them the right to send out four trading voyages in a period not exceeding three years. They built a fort on the river somewhat above the site of the present city of Albany, New York, but their monopoly ran out in 1618 and was not renewed; whereupon the trade along the river was opened to anyone who cared to engage in it.

It was at this time that the twelve-year truce made in 1609 was approaching its end and the English Pilgrims in Leyden were beginning to think of emigrating from Holland to America. The merchants interested in trade, led by William Usselinx, looking forward to the renewal of the war which was a foregone conclusion, proposed to organize a great trading company which would have the threefold objective of carrying on a profitable privateering warfare against the Spaniards in America, the establishment of colonies in the New World, and trade with the North American Indians. Their greatest interest was in war and commerce rather than in colonies; but it was expected that colonies would be useful bases of operations in the carrying on of their other activities. In 1621 the Estates General issued a charter to the Dutch West India Company. The company was composed of merchants in the various parts of the Netherlands, and each regional group had its own board of directors. These regional boards sent representatives to Amsterdam to form a council of nineteen men, eighteen of whom were representatives of the regional directorates and one of whom was appointed by the Estates General. This council of nineteen became the governing agency of the Dutch West India Company and worked out most of the policies that were carried out in the company's colony of New Netherland. The company was given a monopoly of all the commerce along the shores of America and in the Atlantic generally south of the tropic of Cancer. It was also given the right to maintain armies, make laws, punish offenders, make war and treaties with native princes or foreign powers. It was practically a state within a state. . . .

NEW NETHERLAND

The Dutch West India Company's first colonizing expedition, under the command of Cornelius Jacobsen May, was composed chiefly of French-speaking Protestants from the southern provinces of the Low Countries that had compromised their differences with Philip II. The settlers went first to Manhattan Island, on which the heart of New York City now stands. But since the company's intent in founding a colony revolved chiefly about the anticipated profits from the fur trade, they were divided into small groups, one of which went up the Hudson and established the trading post of Fort Orange, while another went over into the Delaware valley and built Fort Nassau. A third small party went to the mouth of the Connecticut, and a few stayed at the mouth of the Mauritius (Hudson) River. This place, because of its location, became the economic and political center of the colony. Of the other settlements, Fort Orange became the most important by reason of its strategic position relative to the fur trade.

The first settlement of the Dutch at the mouth of the Hudson was on what is now known as Governors Island. But as other ships followed the *New Netherland*, with more colonists and livestock, this island was found to be too small, and a permanent fort was built in 1625 at the lower end of Manhattan Island, with the town, called New Amsterdam, stretching eastward along the shore of the East River. Within the fort was the office of the Dutch West India Company, a market place, the residence of the governor, barracks, and the church. Outside, the land was laid out in "bouweries," or farms, where the settlers built their first permanent houses of bark. By the time Peter Minuit took charge as "director general" in 1626, the colony already had taken on a certain air of bustle and prosperity. It was Minuit who purchased the island of Manhattan from the Indians, buying it for goods valued at about sixty guilders—or some forty dollars in modern American money. . . .

ECONOMIC AND SOCIAL GROWTH

The colony of New Netherland was never a very profitable venture for the Dutch West India Company. But as a community it grew, slowly but surely, and laid the foundations for later prosperity. The farmers near the fort at New Amsterdam found that wheat and rye flourished in the good soil and equable climate of Manhattan Island, with the result that 45,000 guilders' worth of grain was exported in 1626, and by 1632 this amount rose to 125,000 guilders. As the country was heavily forested, lumbering and shipbuilding became important parts of the colony's economy. The company had a monopoly of the export of furs and for a time the fur trade proved to be the most important single economic activity of the colony. . . .

In 1633 Walter Van Twiller came to the colony as its governor to succeed Peter Minuit, and his five-year tenure of the governorship is notable for the growth of the liquor traffic. Under him the brewery business expanded rapidly and the commerce in drink came to be second only to the fur trade in its economic importance to the colony. Drunkenness had come to be so bad by 1638 that the residents in the town of New Amsterdam began to lose their rest by reason of the caroling of drunken sailors, and it became necessary to regulate the sale of liquor and to require that "sea faring persons" be aboard their ships before dark. It also became necessary to prohibit the sale of liquor to the Indians because of the Indian tendency to become rough and disorderly when under the influence of drink; but this regulation failed.

Van Twiller was succeeded in 1638 by William Kieft. Kieft made himself notorious on account of his unpleasant relations with the Indians. He tried to tax them and took their lands without their consent. He distrusted them and they distrusted him. By 1641 there was a serious danger of war with the natives, so Governor Kieft called a council of twelve men to advise him on the situation. This gave the twelve men an opportunity to demand a democratic government for the colony, but Kieft dismissed them and nothing was done about it. In 1643 actual war broke out with the Indians and Kieft again called a group of men, this time eight, to advise him. They took advantage of the opportunity and protested against the taxes, demanded a more democratic form of government and sent a request home to the Dutch West India Company for a new governor. On the other hand, they did organize a campaign against the Indians and with the aid of the English from New Haven defeated them. In 1647 their request for a new governor was granted in the person of Peter Stuyvesant. . . .

Stuyvesant was an ex-soldier who had brought his military

habits to his duties as governor of New Netherland. He hesitated to lay more taxes on the colonists without their approval and called together a group of nine prominent colonists to aid him in government. These men quarreled with him on many issues, but this body is to be distinguished from the two groups called together by William Kieft, since it was a semi-permanent group of advisors constituting a loose sort of council rather than a legislature. On account of their quarrels with Stuyvesant the nine men petitioned the government of Holland for direct control. This was not granted them, but certain reforms in their local government did take place. In 1652 the government of New Amsterdam was revised and a "schout" or sheriff was appointed to govern with the aid of two burgomasters and five aldermen appointed by the governor. As for the colony as a whole, in 1653 Stuyvesant called a meeting of representatives from the towns that sent in a remonstrance against the arbitrary appointment of magistrates by the governor, the promulgation of laws without their consent and against the interests of the people, and the manipulation of the lands of the colony for the benefit of the governor's friends. This meeting petitioned for a larger share in the control of their political affairs. The only result, however, was that the schout of each town and those appointed to assist him in government were thereafter generally appointed from the residents of the town concerned; thus, while the governor still did all the appointing, the local officials represented in large measure the desires of the people. In addition to this each town was allowed to have a local excise or tax for its own local purposes. This was as near as New Netherland ever came to self-government under the Dutch regime. . . .

LIFE IN NEW NETHERLAND

The colony established by the Dutch along the Hudson and Delaware rivers is one of the most interesting of all the early European settlements in America. It was composed of people from a variety of nations, and as early as 1664 it was reported that eighteen different languages were spoken in the town of New Amsterdam. The population was chiefly Dutch, but there were Walloons, Swedes, Englishmen from New England, Frenchmen, Germans, and many others who had straggled into the colony from one place or another and who gave this settlement from the earliest decade of its history the cosmopolitan character that it has retained ever since. Naturally these emigrants brought with them various religions and various social customs, and except for one or two sporadic bursts of religious persecution, the general atmosphere of the colony was one of religious toleration.

There was little or no life that could be called cultural. The Dutch West India Company was not particularly interested in education, although it did send over a school teacher about 1637. That poor man, however, was forced to take in washing to supplement the meager income that he received from his scholarly activities. In 1649 the nine men complained that there was still no school building and in 1652 Governor Stuyvesant received authority from the company to use the funds derived from the city tavern for the purpose of erecting a school. A school building appeared in 1655, and in 1658 there was established a Latin School.

The progress of New Amsterdam nevertheless is marked by certain notable civil improvements, and by 1657 there had been established a fire patrol that was maintained appropriately enough by a tax on chimneys, and in 1658 a police force was organized. Certain of the streets of this little Dutch town had been paved, the first of which, we are told, was the street of the breweries. In general, this was a frontier village of a stolid, satisfied Dutch people, without self-government, to be sure, but enjoying a large measure of religious and social tolerance. In many ways it was a more urbane, cosmopolitan, and secular society than had appeared in any of the European establishments thus far located on the shores of the New World.

AMERICAN HISTORY BY ERA

The Pilgrims and the Puritans

CHAPTER 2

THE ORIGINS OF THE PURITANS

ALAN TAYLOR

A professor of history at the University of California in Davis, Alan Taylor won the 1996 Pulitzer Prize in American history for his book *William Cooper's Town: Power and Persuasion on the Frontier of the Early American Republic.* In the following selection from his book *American Colonies*, he traces the roots of Puritanism in England during the late sixteenth and early seventeenth centuries.

According to Taylor, the Puritans were religious reformers who sought to change the official Church of England (also called the Anglican Church) because they felt that it retained too many vestiges of Catholicism. Most Puritans intended to reform the Church of England from the inside, he explains, but some radical Puritans—called Separatists—left the church to establish their own independent congregations. The monarchs of England, who headed the Anglican Church, increasingly viewed Puritanism as a dangerous threat to their authority and began to persecute both the Puritan clergy and laypeople. Eventually, Taylor writes, some Puritans decided to escape persecution by immigrating to the New World.

C hurch and state were united in early modern England. Law demanded that everyone support the official Church of England with taxes and regular attendance. A seventeenth-century aristocrat noted that "the ecclesiastical and civil state" were so "interwoven together, and in truth so incorporated in each other, that like Hippocrates' twins they cannot but laugh and cry together." During the 1530s, Queen Elizabeth's father, King Henry VIII, had rejected the Catholic pope to become the head of an independent Church of England. Thereafter, the English monarch appointed and commanded a hierarchy of two archbishops, twenty-six bishops, and approximately 8,600 parish clergy in England and Wales. Because the monarch led the official church, religious dissent smacked of treason as well as heresy. One clergyman preached that "no subject may, without hazard of his own damnation in rebelling against God, question or disobey the will and pleasure of his sovereign." King James I pithily declared that the entire social order hinged upon the preservation of the church hierarchy: "No Bishop, no King, no nobility."

The crown employed the Anglican Church to promote political as well as religious conformity. A system of church courts (without juries) gave the crown a vehicle to extort revenue and to punish dissidents. The monarch also frequently ordered the bishops to instruct the parish ministers to preach in support of particular policies. In 1620, King James I demanded sermons against "the insolency of our women and their wearing of broad-brimmed hats, pointed doublets, their hair cut short or shorn." In 1626 his son and successor, King Charles I, dictated that the clergy preach that Parliament sinned when it denied new taxes demanded by the monarch. Charles noted, "People are governed by the pulpit more than the sword in time of peace."

A DIVERSE MOVEMENT OF DISSIDENTS

The merger of church and state in service to a hierarchical social order gave political significance to every religious issue. The combination obliged dissidents to express their social and political grievances in religious rhetoric, and it made social and political critics of those seeking religious purity. Especially devout reformers, known as Puritans, wanted to change both the Church of England and the larger society.

Begun as an epithet, "Puritan" persists in scholarship to name the broad movement of diverse people who shared a conviction that the Protestant Reformation remained incomplete in England. Because the monarchs favored religious compromise and inclusion, the Anglican Church was, in the horrified words of one Puritan, "a mingle-mangle" of Protestant and Catholic doctrines and ceremonies. The ecclesiastical structure of bishops and archbishops remained Catholic except for the substitution at the top of the king for the pope.

In seeking reform, Puritans divided over the details. Most remained within the Anglican Church, seeking to capture and reform it, preserving the link between church and state. The more radical Puritans, however, became "Separatists," determined immediately to withdraw into their own independent congregations. Without any larger authority to enforce orthodoxy, the many autonomous Separatist congregations steadily splintered in their beliefs and practices, forming many distinct sects.

Disdaining the legacy of medieval Catholicism, the Puritans sought to recover the original, pure, and simple church of Jesus Christ and his apostles. In a "Reformed Church" individual souls could nurture a more direct relationship with God. Rejecting the intercession of priests administering ceremonial sacraments, the Puritans instead urged every believer to seek God by reading the Bible, forming prayer groups, and heeding learned and zealous ministers who delivered evangelical sermons. Puritans wished to strip away church ceremony and formulaic prayers as legacies of papacy. They also wanted to eliminate or reduce the authority of the bishops by increasing the authority of local congregations.

GRACE AND GOOD WORKS

Puritans longed to experience the "New Birth": a transforming infusion of divine grace that liberated people from profound anxiety over their spiritual worthlessness and eternal fate. By moral living, devout prayer, reading the Bible, and heeding sermons, the hopeful Puritan prepared for the possibility of God's saving grace. But not even the most devout could claim conversion and salvation as a right and a certainty, for God alone determined. He saved selectively and arbitrarily, rather than universally or as a reward for good behavior. In this belief in God's complete power over grace and salvation, the Puritans elaborated upon the "Calvinist" doctrines of the sixteenth-century Swiss theologian Jean Calvin.

Nonetheless, Puritans were incorrigible doers, seeking out the preached word, reading the Scriptures, perfecting their morality, and proposing radical schemes for improving society and disciplining the unruly and indolent. To satirize Puritanism, the seventeenth-century dramatist Ben Jonson aptly named a Puritan character Zeal-of-the-Land Busy. Their prodigious energy expressed their conviction that godly doing manifested itself in those God had elected for salvation. One Puritan subtly explained, "We teach that only Doers shall be saved, and by their doing though not for their doing." Because diligence and discipline honored God, Puritans labored ever harder to perfect their morality and worship—and to extend both to others.

PURITAN VALUES

The Puritan movement especially appealed to residents of the most commercialized area in England: the southeast, particularly London, East Anglia, and Sussex. Puritans came from all ranks of English society, including a few aristocrats, but most belonged to the "middling sort" of small property holders: farmers, shopkeepers, and skilled artisans. The Puritan tended to be the self-employed head of a household, of whom Robert Reyce said that "though hee thriveth ordinarily well, yett he laboreth much." Their own modest property put them a leg up on the impoverished and underemployed half of the English population.

Puritanism reinforced the values of thrift, diligence, and delayed gratification that were essential to the well-being of the middling sort. Puritans held that men honored God and proved their own salvation by working hard in their occupation—which they deemed a "calling" bestowed by God. A Puritan explained, "God sent you unto this world as unto a Workhouse, not a Playhouse." Offering a strict code of personal discipline and morality, Puritanism helped thousands of ordinary people cope with the economic and social turmoil that afflicted England during the early seventeenth century. Puritanism liberated people from a sense of helplessness by encouraging effort, persistence, study, and purpose.

Taking on a demanding tension, the Puritans strove to live in the world, without succumbing to worldliness. On the one hand, Puritans hinted that God would reward the diligent and godly with prosperity. On the other hand, they cautioned that wealth must not be an end unto itself lest carnal temptations overwhelm the ultimate purpose of human life: preparation for salvation in the next world. Puritans denounced conspicuous consumption and covetousness and urged generous donations to spread the Gospel. But the godly could never escape worldly temptation, because Puritan virtues helped them to accumulate money.

Puritans felt sorely afflicted by the many English people who

Attempting to escape religious persecution in their homeland, many English Puritans sought refuge in the New World.

possessed neither their virtues nor their zeal. Puritan rhetoric depicted England as awash in thieves, drunks, idlers, prostitutes, and blasphemers. The godly blamed the unruly and the indolent—and indulgent authorities—for all the social and economic troubles of the realm. Puritans advanced the radical notion that England could be cleansed of poverty and crime if godly men and women united to take charge of their churches and local governments, introducing moral rigor to both.

This Puritan vision appealed to many pious and propertied people weary of the economic upheaval, crime, and poverty of the late sixteenth and early seventeenth centuries. Puritan magistrates strictly enforced the long-neglected laws against gambling, blasphemy, adultery, public drunkenness, and Sabbath-breaking. And Puritans longed to purify the churches by ousting all conspicuous sinners and by inviting members to monitor one another for consistent morality and sound theology. This zeal, however, dismayed most English people, who preferred Anglicanism and the traditional culture characterized by church ales, Sunday diversions, ceremonial services, inclusive churches, and deference to the monarch.

THE ROYAL REACTION TO THE PURITANS

The Puritan rigor also alarmed the seventeenth-century kings, who wanted a united and quiet realm of unquestioning loyalty. They recognized the subversive potential in Puritanism's insistence on the spiritual equality of all godly men and on their superiority to all ungodly men—who, in Puritan eyes, included most of the king's bishops. In 1604, King James I declared that Puritanism "as well agreeth with a monarchy as God and the devil. Then Jack and Tom and Will and Dick shall meet, and at their pleasures censure me and my council and all our proceedings." If the Puritans did not conform to his authority and church, he threatened to "harry them out of the land."

They indifferently conformed, and James reluctantly tolerated their persistence within the realm. Indeed, during his reign dozens of Puritan ministers continued to serve Anglican parishes, and hundreds of lay Puritans retained royal commissions as local magistrates. Purging the pulpits and courts of Puritans was difficult, for the crown depended upon propertied and educated men to keep and preach order in the counties, and such men were often Puritans.

That grudging accommodation between Puritans and most church hierarchy eroded late in James's reign and collapsed in 1625 upon the accession of his son as King Charles I. Married to a Catholic princess, Charles hoped to reconcile English Catholics by restoring some church ceremonies previously suspended to mollify the Puritans. Charles elevated William Laud, the greatest champion of ceremonies, to bishop in 1628 and to archbishop in 1633. In return, Laud and his allies preached the Christian duty, of Parliament and taxpayers to submit to the king.

During the late 1620s and early 1630s, Laud and most other bishops enforced the new Anglican orthodoxy, dismissing Puritan ministers who balked at conducting the high church liturgy. Church courts also prosecuted growing numbers of Puritan laypeople. Laud strictly censored Puritan tracts and had pilloried, mutilated, and branded three Puritans who illegally published their ideas. Puritan hopes of securing redress dissipated after 1629, when Charles I dissolved Parliament and proceeded to rule arbitrarily for the next eleven years. Faced with the growing power of the king and his bishops, some despairing Puritans considered emigrating across the Atlantic to a New England.

THE ARRIVAL OF THE PILGRIMS

ALLAN KELLER

On September 16, 1620, a group of Puritan Separatists called the Pilgrims set sail for the New World, where they hoped to find refuge from religious oppression. The Pilgrims arrived at Cape Cod in November, landing much farther north than they had intended, with little time to prepare for the onslaught of winter. In the following excerpt from his book *Colonial America: A Compact History*, Allan Keller describes the hardships of the early years at Plymouth and the Pilgrims' determination in the face of sickness and starvation. Keller worked for many years as a newspaper reporter and a professor at Columbia University's journalism school in New York City. His books include *Life Along the Hudson* and *Thunder at Harper's Ferry*.

W ith considerable justice, it can be said that England's second successful colony, Plymouth, began in an ancient Yorkshire inn beside the royal road leading from London to Scotland. Here William Brewster, between serving food and ale and supplying fresh horses for stagecoaches, risked his life to support the spread of religious freedom.

In the Manor House at Scrooby, which he rented with the profits from his little tavern, Brewster held services for those who believed in a complete separation of church and state. He found ministers to preach the new concept of religion, organized those Puritans who were so eager to worship in their own way that they were willing to leave their homeland, and eventually led them to Holland. There, with other English Separatists, they settled in Leyden, took the name Pilgrims, and dreamed of a day when they could establish their own home far from repression and hatred.

THE VOYAGE TO AMERICA

For several years the Pilgrims enjoyed the freedom and enlightenment that marked the Netherlands, but time was running out. The truce between Holland and Spain, mortal enemies for years, was about to end. Brewster and his supporters drew up plans to emigrate to the New World. One of the directors of the Virginia Company lent the Pilgrims enough money, without interest, to charter two ships, the *Speedwell* and the *Mayflower*. After a false start, leading to the abandonment of the former vessel, the *Mayflower* sailed on September 16, 1620, from Plymouth, England. On board were 101 passengers willing to risk everything for their faith and the hope of establishing a new and better world. Storms buffeted the little sailing vessel. One of the main timbers of the frame was twisted out of place, nearly wrecking the ship, but a jackscrew was used to force it back. Open seams were calked, sails were patched, and the voyage continued.

On the day before they landed, the Pilgrims signed a set of laws known as the Mayflower Compact. It was a unique document. For the first time a group of people organized themselves from within, by mutual agreement, rather than accept laws from higher authority. It was effrontery, of course, because King James I of England was supposed to be the seat of all power, but these stout-hearted men covenanted with one another to make their own laws.

A DEADLY WINTER

In November they made a landfall at the tip of Cape Cod, having been carried far north of their intended destination by the Gulf Stream. The Jamestown colonists had discovered dogwood in bloom. The Pilgrims found a barren shore, little vegetation, and bitter winds blowing down from the northwest. A few days later, on the twenty-first, they crossed the bay and landed on a beach they called New Plymouth. The women and children remained aboard the *Mayflower* until the men could build cabins, a meetinghouse, and a fort. By January 1621 the common house was roofed and immediately turned into an infirmary. Scurvy struck down whole families, consumption decimated the little band, and by February, when the *Mayflower* finally set sail for home, nearly half the Pilgrims were dead. Nothing dampened their faith, however; not one survivor elected to return with her.

What remained of the winter was a fearsome time for the hungry, emaciated colonists. They had no hope of help from England or Holland for months to come, a recent plague had wiped out the Indian tribes that normally roamed the Massachusetts coast near Plymouth, and not even a fishing boat from the Grand Banks came by to give them food. But these staunch Puritans did not fight and brawl as the colonists at Jamestown had. They read their Bibles, prayed often and long, and survived. In the spring Indians came by, showed them how to plant corn with a fish in each hill to fertilize the plants, and brought in venison and other game. The women gathered greens with which to counter scurvy.

Governor John Carver died, and William Bradford was named in his place. The crops flourished, everyone worked diligently, and for a while the Indians remained friendly. When fall came the Pilgrims decided to give thanks for their survival. Bradford sent out five men to shoot wild turkeys, and Indian braves brought in venison, ducks, and geese. The squaws showed Pilgrim housewives how to cook squash, pumpkin, and corn pudding. When, on November 25, 1621, white settlers and red natives sat down to a bountiful feast, Thanksgiving Day was born.

The early years at Plymouth were hard ones. The colonists fought famine, drought, cold, locusts, and snakes. At first it was a communal undertaking, noble in concept but impractical in fact. Healthy men, laboring in the fields, became disgruntled to see the elderly and weak receiving equal shares. Married men disliked the idea of their wives cooking for bachelors. It was an old problem, and one that has recurred many times since. Governor Bradford cured it the only way he knew how: each family was granted its own plot of land and dissension died down.

COURAGE, FAITH, AND REBELLIOUS ACTS

New groups of settlers came from Leyden and Amsterdam and from England, eager to escape the oppression that was steadily worsening as James I bickered with his enemies. Yet the colony grew slowly, deaths often offsetting the gain in numbers from Europe. The Pilgrims arrived with little but hope and an abiding faith in God. After the communal arrangement had been set aside, everyone willingly helped one another. Women cared for the ill, served as midwives, and gathered clams and mussels. Men fashioned the crude pine boxes in which their friends were laid to rest on Burial Hill, prayed over the open graves, and went back to tilling the fields, building homes, and cutting down the forest for new settlers.

Raw courage and deep faith saw the Pilgrims through those first years. So fervent was their devotion to the church that women rose from their beds within a few days of childbirth and walked through blizzards to the meetinghouse so their offspring could be baptized. According to early historians of the colony, the sacramental bread froze and rattled on the plates at communion and infants shuddered in the cold. Lips blue, hands and feet aching from chilblains, the mothers watched the icy water fall on their babies' brows and sang their hymns of praise to God. Yet beneath the austerity and religious zeal that was almost fanaticism, life in the Plymouth colony was not entirely devoid of pleasure. Love bloomed, families grew, and word went back to Europe that New England, if not a Garden of Eden, was still preferable to Amsterdam or London.

If any one factor is responsible for the survival of the colony, other than the indomitable courage of the members themselves, it was the plague that had wiped out so many Indians shortly before the *Mayflower* landed: unlike Jamestown, Plymouth had no problems with the natives until it was fairly well established.

The Pilgrims had drafted the Mayflower Compact with the sure knowledge that they were affronting royal prerogative. The Church of England held that no marriage was sacred unless a minister officiated. Edward Winslow, destined to be a leading light of the colony, lost his wife during the first winter, and Susanna White, who on the voyage from England had given birth to Peregrine White, the first child of the colony, lost her husband. The Pilgrims said Winslow and Susanna could be married "as were Boaz and Ruth, in the presence of the people," and so they were. William Brewster preached each Sunday—not because he had been ordained, for he hadn't been—but because the people themselves delegated to him the authority to preach. These were rebellious acts that cast long shadows ahead. Democracy was already taking shape on Plymouth Bay.

SQUANTO'S RELATIONSHIP WITH THE PILGRIMS

BERND C. PEYER

During their arduous first year at the Plymouth colony, the Pilgrims were befriended by a Native American man named Squanto, who helped them survive by teaching them to grow corn and other indigenous crops. As Bernd C. Peyer explains, Squanto was able to communicate with the Pilgrims in their own language because he had been captured by an English explorer and had spent several years overseas before returning to his homeland. The author examines Squanto's precarious position as an intermediary between the Pilgrims and the Wampanoag tribe in the following excerpt from *The Tutor'd Mind: Indian Missionary-Writers in Antebellum America*. Peyer teaches at the Center for North American Studies at the University of Frankfurt in Germany, where he specializes in American Indian cultures.

Squanto's biography, or what little is known of it, is exemplary for the experience of involuntary Indian voyagers to sixteenth- and seventeenth-century Europe. His nigh incredible odyssey was not unique, however, as it was preceded by the adventures of Assacomit (Sassacomoit), one of five Abenakis abducted by Captain George Weymouth in 1605. Assacomit and his companions were brought to England, where they were taken up by Sir Walter Raleigh's associates, Sir John Popham and Ferdinando Gorges. En route to Maine as a guide

Bernd C. Peyer, *The Tutor'd Mind: Indian Missionary-Writers in Antebellum America*, Amherst: University of Massachusetts Press, 1997. Copyright © 1997 by The University of Massachusetts Press. Reproduced by permission.

and interpreter for another English expedition (probably with Henry Challoung in 1606), he was captured by the Spanish along with the rest of the crew and taken to Spain. Assacomit returned to England after being ransomed by Gorges and from there sailed again to New England in 1614 as a guide for the Nicholas Hobson expedition.

SQUANTO'S TRAVELS

Nothing is known about Squanto (Tisquantum) prior to his kidnapping by Thomas Hunt in 1614, or of the three years he spent in Spain after he had been taken there by Hunt to be sold as a slave along with about twenty other Indian captives. There is even some uncertainty about the exact date of his capture, as the aging Ferdinando Gorges reported that he was brought to England by Weymouth along with Assacomit and the other Abenakis in 1605, and Captain John Smith claims to have put a certain "Tantum" ashore at Cape Cod in 1614. If this is so, then he may have traveled to England repeatedly before he was captured by Hunt. He is thought to have been a member of a Pawtuxet community living in the vicinity of the Plymouth site and may have been twenty or thirty years of age at the time of his capture. Judging from his subsequent display of diplomatic talent, historian Neal Salisbury concludes that he may well have had some previous standing in his own community, perhaps as a spiritual war leader (*pniese*), before his involuntary transatlantic travels began. By 1617 he had apparently also accomplished the astonishing feat of escaping slavery in Spain and making his way back to England, because he is reported to have been a resident at the London home of John Slany, treasurer of the Newfoundland Company.

In 1618 Squanto was sent on an English expedition to Newfoundland, where he became acquainted with Thomas Dermer and sailed back to England with him that same year. He gave such a glowing account of his homeland in New England that Dermer finally asked Ferdinando Gorges for a commission to explore the area. Upon his return to New England with Dermer in 1619, Squanto discovered that his native village had been devastated by a wave of smallpox epidemics in 1617–19. Those who had managed to survive were scattered among neighboring Indian communities. Then, when the Indians mounted a devastating attack on Dermer's party, Squanto found himself a prisoner of the Wampanoags (Pokanokets). The fact that he was

not immediately dispatched by the war party for being allied to
the hated English and was turned over instead to Massasoit, the
Wampanoag sachem [chief], speaks for both his own skills as a
diplomat and the political farsightedness of Massasoit.

MEETING THE PILGRIMS

At the time of the Separatists' arrival in Plymouth in 1620 the
Wampanoags were in the humiliating position of tributaries to
the Narragansetts, who had somehow managed to remain unaffected by the 1617–19 epidemics and consequently were able to
dominate their decimated neighbors. Massasoit, himself the paramount leader of a once powerful confederacy of tribes, thus regarded the English as welcome allies against the Narragansetts.
The presence of a bilingual Indian with knowledge of European
ways was, of course, a most opportune coincidence, even if his
status among the Wampanoags was merely that of a lowly captive. In keeping with tribal decorum and plain common sense,
however, Massasoit first appointed Samoset, a trusted sachem
from the Pemaquid River region in Maine who had been trading
with the English for years and could also communicate in their
language, to open up negotiations with the settlers. Only after
contact had thus been officially established did Samoset introduce Squanto, who obviously had better command of English,
allowing him to mediate in the conclusion of the first treaty of
friendship between the Wampanoags and the Puritans. Massasoit thereupon released Squanto to the Pilgrims, perhaps as a reward for his services as mediator. Squanto soon proved to be of
invaluable service to the English colonists. He taught them how
to cultivate Indian staple foods like maize, instructed them in local hunting and fishing techniques, acted as guide for inland explorations, and functioned as interpreter in the colonists' subsequent endeavors to establish relations with other tribes of the
area—in short, all of those services which have earned him a permanent place of honor at Thanksgiving celebrations.

Brushing aside all mythic-propagandistic fantasies, Squanto
clearly had no moral obligations toward the Wampanoags or
the English, both of whom had merely sought to impress his
services to their own advantage. The fact that he "sought his
own ends and played his own game," as William Bradford put
it and which some historians have disparaged as manifestations
of an "irrational" or a "childish" form of behavior that ultimately threatened the delicate peace between New England

colonists and Indians, can also be interpreted as the survival tactics of a highly capable and well-traveled individual, who was as adept at the art of diplomacy as any of his adversaries. Since Squanto's prestige among other tribes of the region was steadily increasing and he was also busy trying to establish good relations between the English and the powerful Massachusetts, Massasoit had very good reason to feel threatened by his former captive. In the summer of 1621 he sent another bilingual emissary to the Pilgrims, a ranking Wampanoag *pniese* named Hobbamock, who presumably had orders to keep an eye on Squanto's doings.

The strained relations between Squanto and Massasoit finally came to a head when general hysteria broke out among the colonists following the news of Opechancanough's insurrection in Virginia in 1622, and both men accused each other of intriguing against the Puritans. Massasoit demanded that Squanto be turned over to him for punishment, as was his prerogative according to one of the stipulations of the treaty of friendship, but the English, who obviously still had good use for his talents, simply refused to comply. As John Smith conceded, "he [Squanto] speaking our language we could not well be without him." On the other hand, by having thus invoked Massasoit's enmity, Squanto in turn became entirely dependent upon the colonists' goodwill as he now had to remain as close to their settlements as possible if he wanted to stay alive. When he did finally venture out again in the company of a trading expedition led by William Bradford to the remote southeastern shore of Cape Cod in October of 1622, Squanto suddenly took ill with what Bradford diagnosed as "an Indian fever" and died within a few days. According to Bradford, just before his death Squanto requested the governor "to pray for him that he might go to the Englishman's God; and bequeathed sundry of his things to sundry of his English friends as remembrances of his love; of whom they had a great loss." Whether his death was caused by some infectious disease (as is likely) or, as Bradford implied, induced by Indian witchcraft, it certainly occurred at a most opportune moment for Massasoit. With the assistance of the faithful Hobbamock, the Wampanoag leader resumed his diplomatic relations with the Pilgrims and, after turning them against the Massachusetts with repeated implications of an impending insurrection, temporarily restored the supremacy of his own confederacy.

LIMITED CHOICES

The conflict between Squanto and Massasoit can be regarded as an example of traditional competitive leadership among Coastal Algonquians, with the incumbent Squanto representing a legitimate alternative to Massasoit as an intertribal leader because of his linguistic skills and intimate knowledge of English ways. Since his native community had been disbanded by the effects of disease while he was away in England, Squanto really had no choice but to find an application for his newly acquired talents elsewhere. Perhaps, as Salisbury has suggested, he even envisioned a reconstituted Pawtuxet band with himself as its paramount leader.

THOMAS MORTON OF MERRY MOUNT

WILLIAM BRADFORD

Although the Pilgrims sought religious freedom for themselves, they were not tolerant of those settlers whose beliefs and lifestyles contradicted their Puritan values. One such colonist was Thomas Morton, an Anglican lawyer who came to Massachusetts in 1625 and established a trading post just a few miles south of Plymouth. In 1627, Morton and his fellow settlers at Merry Mount decided to celebrate May Day by carousing around an eighty-foot maypole. News of the revel infuriated the Pilgrims, who opposed May Day and similar celebrations that had their origins in the pagan beliefs of ancient Europe. They also objected to Morton's selling guns, ammunition, and whiskey to the local Indians. William Bradford, the governor of Plymouth, describes the conflict between Morton and the Pilgrims in the following excerpt from *History of Plymouth Plantation*, his chronicle of the events that occurred in the early years of the colony.

There came over one Captain Wollaston, (a man of pretty parts,) and with him three or four more of some eminency, who brought with them a great many servants, with provisions and other implements for to begin a plantation; and pitched themselves in a place within the Massachusetts, which they called, after their captain's name, Mount Wollaston. Amongst whom was one Mr. Morton, who, it should seem, had some small adventure (of his own or other men's) amongst them; but had little respect amongst them, and was slighted by

William Bradford, *History of Plymouth Plantation*, Boston: Little, Brown, 1856.

the meanest servants. Having continued there some time, and not finding things to answer their expectations, nor profit to arise as they looked for, Captain Wollaston takes a great part of the servants, and transports them to Virginia, where he puts them off at good rates, selling their time to other men; and writes back to one Mr. Rassdall, one of his chief partners, and accounted their merchant, to bring another part of them to Virginia likewise, intending to put them off there as he had done the rest. And he, with the consent of the said Rassdall, appointed one Fitcher to be his Lieutenant, and govern the remains of the plantation, till he or Rassdall returned to take further order thereabout. But this Morton above-said, having more craft than honesty, (who had been a kind of pettifogger, of Furnefell's Inn,) in the other's absence, watches an opportunity, (commons being but hard amongst them,) and got some strong drink and other junkets, and made them a feast; and after they were merry, he began to tell them, he would give them good counsel. "You see," saith he, "that many of your fellows are carried to Virginia; and if you stay till this Rassdall return, you will also be carried away and sold for slaves with the rest. Therefore I would advise you to thrust out this Lieutenant Fitcher; and I, having a part in the plantation, will receive you as my partners and consociates; so may you be free from service, and we will converse, trade, plant, and live together as equals, and support and protect one another," or to like effect. This counsel was easily received; so they took opportunity, and thrust Lieutenant Fitcher out of doors, and would suffer him to come no more amongst them, but forced him to seek bread to eat, and other relief from his neighbors, till he could get passages for England. After this they fell to great licentiousness, and led a dissolute life, pouring out themselves into all profaneness. And Morton became lord of misrule, and maintained (as it were) a school of Atheism. And after they had got some goods into their hands, and got much by trading with the Indians, they spent it as vainly, in quaffing and drinking both wine and strong waters in great excess, and, as some reported, ten shillings worth in a morning. They also set up a May-pole, drinking and dancing about it many days together, inviting the Indian women, for their consorts, dancing and frisking together, (like so many fairies, or furies rather,) and worse practices. As if they had anew revived and celebrated the feast of the Roman goddess Flora, or the beastly practices of the mad Bacchanalians. Morton likewise (to show his poetry) composed sundry rhymes and verses, some tending to lasciviousness, and others to the detraction and scandal of some persons, which he affixed to this idle or idol May-pole. They changed also the name of their place, and instead of calling it Mount Wollaston, they call it Merry Mount, as if this jollity would have lasted ever. But this continued not long, for after Morton was sent for England, (as follows to be declared,) shortly after came over that worthy gentleman, Mr. John Endicott, who brought over a patent under the broad seal, for the government of the Massachusetts, who visiting those parts caused that May-pole to be cut down, and rebuked them for their profaneness, and admonished them to look there should be better walking; so they now, or others, changed the name of their place again, and called it Mount Dagon.

GIVING GUNS TO THE INDIANS

Now, to maintain this riotous prodigality and profuse excess, Morton, thinking himself lawless, and hearing what gain the French and fishermen made by trading of pieces, powder, and shot to the Indians, he, as the head of this consortship, began the practice of the same in these parts; and first he taught them how to use them, to charge and discharge, and what proportion of powder to give the piece, according to the size or bigness of the same; and what shot to use for fowl, and what for deer. And having thus instructed them, he employed some of them to hunt and fowl for him, so as they became far more active in that employment than any of the English, by reason of their swiftness of foot, and nimbleness of body, being also quick-sighted, and by continual exercise well knowing the haunts of all sorts of game. So as when they saw the execution that a piece would do, and the benefit that might come by the same, they became mad, as it were, after them, and would not stick to give any price they could attain to for them; accounting their bows and arrows but baubles in comparison of them.

And here I may take occasion to bewail the mischief that this wicked man began in these parts, and which since base covetousness prevailing in men that should know better, has now at length got the upper hand, and made this thing common, notwithstanding any laws to the contrary; so as the Indians are full of pieces all over, both fowling pieces, muskets, pistols, etc. They have also their moulds to make shot, of all sorts, as musket bullets, pistol bullets, swan and goose shot, and of smaller sorts; yea, some have seen them have their screw-plates to make screw-pins themselves, when they want them, with sundry other implements, wherewith they are ordinarily better fitted and furnished than the English themselves. Yea, it is well known that they will have powder and shot, when the English want it, nor can not get it; and that in a time of war or danger, as experience hath manifested, that when lead hath been scarce, and men for their own defence would gladly have given a groat a pound, which is dear enough, yet hath it been bought up and sent to other places, and sold to such as trade it with the Indians, at twelve pence the pound; and it is like they give three or four shillings the pound, for they will have it at any rate. And these things have been done in the same times, when some of their neighbors and friends are daily killed by the Indians, or are in danger thereof, and live but at the Indians' mercy. Yea, some (as they have acquainted them with all other things) have told them how gunpowder is made, and all the materials in it, and that they are to be had in their own land; and I am confident, could they attain to make saltpetre, they would teach them to make powder. Oh, the horribleness of this villany! how many both Dutch and English have been lately slain by those Indians, thus furnished; and no remedy provided, nay, the evil more increased, and the blood of their brethren sold for gain, as is to be feared; and in what danger all these colonies are in is too well known. Oh! that princes and parliaments would take some timely order to prevent this mischief, and at length to suppress it, by some exemplary punishment upon some of these gain-thirsty murderers, (for they deserve no better title,) before their colonies in these parts be overthrown by these barbarous savages, thus armed with their own weapons, by these evil instruments, and traitors to their neighbors and country. But I have forgot myself, and have been too long in this digression; but now to return: This Morton having thus taught them the use of pieces, he sold them all he could spare; and he and his consorts determined to send for many out of England, and had by some of the ships sent for above a score; the which being known, and his neighbors meeting the Indians in the woods armed with guns in this sort, it was a terror unto them, who lived stragglingly, and were of no strength in any place. And other places (though more remote) saw this mischief would quickly spread over all, if not prevented. Besides, they saw they should keep no servants, for Morton would entertain any, how vile soever,

and all the scum of the country, or any discontents, would flock
to him from all places, if this nest was not broken; and they
should stand in more fear of their lives and goods (in short
time) from this wicked and debauched crew, than from the savages themselves.

BANISHMENT

So sundry of the chief of the straggling plantations, meeting together, agreed by mutual consent to solicit those of Plymouth
(who were then of more strength than them all) to join with
them to prevent the further growth of this mischief, and suppress Morton and his consorts before they grew to further head
and strength. Those that joined in this action (and after contributed to the charge of sending him for England) were from
Pascataway, Namkeake, Winisimett, Weesagascusett, Natasco,
and other places where any English were seated. Those of Plymouth being thus sought too by their messengers and letters,
and weighing both their reasons, and the common danger, were
willing to afford them their help; though themselves had least
cause of fear or hurt. So, to be short, they first resolved jointly
to write to him, and in a friendly and neighborly way to ad-
monish him to forbear these courses, and sent a messenger with
their letters to bring his answer. But he was so high as he
scorned all advice, and asked who had to do with him; he had
and would trade pieces with the Indians in despite of all, with
many other scurrilous terms full of disdain. They sent to him a
second time, and bade him be better advised, and more tem-
perate in his terms, for the country could not bear the injury he
did; it was against their common safety, and against the king's
proclamation. He answered in high terms as before, and that the
king's proclamation was no law; demanding what penalty was
upon it. It was answered, more than he could bear, his majesty's
displeasure. But insolently he persisted, and said the king was
dead and his displeasure with him, and many the like things;
and threatened withal that if any came to molest him, let them
look to themselves, for he would prepare for them. Upon which
they saw there was no way but to take him by force; and having so far proceeded, now to give over would make him far
more haughty and insolent. So they mutually resolved to proceed, and obtained of the Governor of Plymouth to send Captain [Myles] Standish, and some other aid with him, to take
Morton by force. The which accordingly was done; but they

found him to stand stiffly in his defence, having made fast his doors, armed his consorts, set divers dishes of powder and bullets ready on the table; and if they had not been overarmed with drink, more hurt might have been done. They summoned him to yield, but he kept his house, and they could get nothing but scoffs and scorns from him; but at length, fearing they would do some violence to the house, he and some of his crew came out, but not to yield, but to shoot; but they were so steeled with drink as their pieces were too heavy for them; himself with a carbine (overcharged and almost half filled with powder and shot, as was after found) had thought to have shot Captain Standish; but he stepped to him, and put by his piece, and took him. Neither was there any hurt done to any of either side, save that one was so drunk that he ran his own nose upon the point of a sword that one held before him as he entered the house; but he lost but a little of his hot blood. Morton they brought away to Plymouth, where he was kept, till a ship went from the Isle of Shoals for England, with which he was sent to the Council of New-England; and letters written to give them information of his course and carriage; and also one was sent at their common charge to inform their Honors more particularly, and to prosecute against him. But he fooled of the messenger, after he was gone from hence, and though he went for England, yet nothing was done to him, not so much as rebuked, for aught was heard; but returned the next year. Some of the worst of the company were dispersed, and some of the more modest kept the house till he should be heard from. But I have been too long about so unworthy a person, and bad a cause.

A City upon a Hill

John Winthrop

Encouraged by the successful establishment of Plymouth, other English Puritans began to investigate the possibility of founding colonies in New England. During the spring and summer of 1630, an expedition of more than one thousand Puritans sailed to Massachusetts Bay, where they built a settlement that would become the city of Boston. The arrival of this fleet marked the beginning of an immense wave of Puritan migration to Massachusetts between 1630 and 1640.

John Winthrop, the governor of the Massachusetts Bay Company, was the leader of the first four ships that sailed from England in the spring of 1630. Unlike the Pilgrims, Winthrop and his followers were not Separatists; they believed that they could reform the Church of England through the example of the holy community they planned to establish in America. During the ocean crossing, Winthrop delivered the following sermon, entitled "A Modell of Christian Charity," in which he outlined the guiding principles that should govern the colony. He called on the Puritans to create "a city upon a hill" to serve as a beacon of hope and a tangible sign of their special covenant with God.

God Almighty, in His most holy and wise providence, has so disposed of the condition of mankind, as in all times some must be rich; some poor; some high and eminent in power and dignity; others mean and in subjection.

The Reason Hereof: first, to hold conformity with the rest of His works, being delighted to show forth the glory of His wisdom in the variety and difference of the creatures and the glory of His power, in ordering all these differences for the preservation and good of the whole; and the glory of His greatness in that,

John Winthrop, "A Modell of Christian Charity," *The Winthrop Papers*, vol. 2, edited by Allyn B. Forbes, Boston: Massachusetts Historical Society, 1931. Reproduced by permission.

as it is the glory of princes to have many officers, so this Great King will have many stewards, counting Himself more honored in dispensing His gifts to man by man than if He did it by His own immediate hand.

Second, that He might have the more occasion to manifest the work of His spirit; first, upon the wicked in moderating and restraining them, so that the rich and mighty should not eat up the poor, nor the poor and despised rise up against their superiors and shake off their yoke; second, in the regenerate in exercising His graces in them, as in the great ones their love, mercy, gentleness, temperance, etc.; in the poor and inferior sort, their faith, patience, obedience, etc.

Third, that every man might have need of others, and from hence they might be all knit more nearly together in the bond of brotherly affection. From hence it appears plainly that no man is made more honorable than another or more wealthy, etc., out of any particular or singular respect to himself, but for the glory of his Creator and the common good of the creature, man. Therefore, God still reserves the property of these gifts to Himself, as [in] Ezek. 16:17; He there calls wealth His gold and His silver, etc.; [in] Prov. 3:9 He claims their service as His due "Honor the Lord with thy riches," etc. All men are thus (by Divine Providence) ranked into two sorts, rich and poor; under the first are included all men such as are able to live comfortably by their own means duly improved; and all others are poor according to the former distribution.

Two Rules and Two Laws

There are two rules whereby we are to walk one toward another: *justice and mercy*. These are always distinguished in their act and in their object, yet may they both concur in the same subject in each respect, as sometimes there may be an occasion of showing mercy to a rich man in some sudden danger of distress; and also doing of mere justice to a poor man in regard of some particular contract, etc. There is likewise a double law by which we are regulated in our conversation one toward another: in both the former respects, the law of nature and the law of grace, or the moral law or the law of the gospel (we may omit the law of justice as not properly belonging to this purpose otherwise than it may fall into consideration in some particular case). By the first of these laws, man . . . is commanded to love his neighbor as himself. Upon this ground stands all the precepts of the moral law which concerns our dealings with men. To apply this to the works of mercy, this law requires two things: first, that every man afford his help to another in every want or distress; second, that he perform this out of the same affection which makes him careful of his own good, according to that of our Savior, (Matt. 7: 12) "Whatsoever ye would that men should do to you. . . ."

The law of grace or the gospel has some difference from the former as in these respects: First, the law of nature was given to man in the estate of innocence; the law of the gospel in the estate of regeneracy. Second, the law of nature propounds one man to another, as the same flesh and image of God, the law of

John Winthrop

gospel as a brother in Christ also, and in the communion of the same spirit, and so teaches us to put a difference between Christians and others. . . . The law of nature could give no rules for dealing with enemies, for all are considered as friends in the state of innocence, but the gospel commands love to an enemy. . . . "If thine enemy hunger, feed him; love your enemies; do good to them that hate you" (Matt. 5:44).

This law of the gospel propounds, likewise, a difference of seasons and occasions. There is a time when a Christian must sell all and give to

the poor as they did in the apostles' times. There is a time also when Christians (though they give not all yet) must give beyond their ability. . . . Likewise, community of perils calls for extraordinary liberality and so does community in some special service for the Church. Lastly, when there is no other means whereby our Christian brother may be relieved in this distress, we must help him beyond our ability, rather than tempt God in putting him upon help by miraculous or extraordinary means. . . .

Having already set forth the practice of mercy according to the rule of God's law, it will be useful to lay open the grounds of it; also being the other part of the Commandment, and that is the affection from which this exercise of mercy must arise. The apostle tells us that this love is the fulfilling of the law (Rom. 13:10). Not that it is enough to love our brother and no more. . . . Just as, when we bid a man to make the clock strike, he does not lay his hand on the hammer, which is the immediate instrument of the sound, but sets to work the first manner or main wheel, knowing that it will certainly produce the sound which he intends, so the way to draw men to the works of mercy is not by force of argument on the goodness or necessity of the work, for though this course may persuade a rational mind to some present act of mercy (as is frequent in experience), yet it cannot work the habit of mercy into a soul so that it will be prompt on all occasions to produce the same effect except by framing the affections of love in the heart, which will as natively bring forth mercy as any cause produces an effect.

THE BONDS OF SPIRITUAL LOVE

The definition which the Scripture gives us of love is this: love is the bond of perfection (Col. 3:14). First, it is a bond, or ligament. Second, it makes the work perfect. There is no body that does not consist of parts, and that which knits these parts together gives the body its perfection, because it makes each part so contiguous to the others that they mutually participate with each other, both in strength and infirmity, in pleasure and in pain. To instance the most perfect of all bodies: Christ and His church make one body. The several parts of this body considered apart before they were united were as disproportionate and as much disordered as so many contrary qualities or elements, but when Christ came and by His spirit and love knit all these parts to Himself and to each other, it became the most perfect and best proportioned body in the world. . . .

Among members of the same body, love and affection are reciprocal in a most equal and sweet kind of commerce. . . . In regard to the pleasure and content that the exercise of love carries with it, we may see in the natural body that the mouth receives and minces the food which serves to nourish all the other parts of the body, yet it has no cause to complain. For first, the other parts send back by secret passages a due proportion of the same nourishment in a better form for the strengthening and comforting of the mouth. Second, the labor of the mouth is accompanied by pleasure and content which far exceed the pains it takes, so it is all a labor of love.

Among Christians, the party loving reaps love again, as was shown before, which the soul covets more than all the wealth in the world. Nothing yields more pleasure and content to the soul than when it finds that which it may love fervently, for to love and be loved is the soul's paradise, both here and in heaven. In the state of wedlock there are many comforts to bear out the troubles of that condition, but let those who have tried the most say whether there is any sweetness . . . comparable to the exercise of mutual love. . . .

APPLYING THESE PRINCIPLES

Now to make some application of this discourse to the situation which gave the occasion of writing it. Herein are four things to be propounded: the persons, the work, the end, the means.

First, for the persons, we are a company professing ourselves fellow members of Christ. . . . Though we are absent from each other by many miles, and have our employments at far distance, we ought to account ourselves knitted together by this bond of love, and live in the exercise of it, if we would have the comfort of our being in Christ. This was common in the practice of Christians in former times; they used to love any of their own religion even before they were acquainted with them.

Second, the work we have in hand is by mutual consent with a special overruling Providence, with a more than ordinary mandate from the churches of Christ to seek out a place to live and associate under a due form of government both civil and ecclesiastical. In such cases as this the care of the public must hold sway over all private interests. To this not only conscience but mere civil policy binds us, for it is a true rule that private estates cannot exist to the detriment of the public.

Third, the end is to improve our lives to do more service to the Lord and to comfort and increase the body of Christ of which we are members, so that ourselves and our posterity may be better preserved from the common corruptions of this evil world in order to serve the Lord and work out our salvation under the power and purity of His holy ordinances.

Fourth, the means whereby this must be effected are twofold. First, since the work and end we aim at are extraordinary, we must not content ourselves with usual ordinary means. Whatsoever we did or ought to have done when we lived in England, we must do that and more also wherever we go. That which most people in their churches only profess as a truth, we must bring into familiar and constant practice. We must love our brothers without pretense; we must love one another with a pure heart and fervently; we must bear one another's burdens; we must not look only on our own things but also on the things of our brethren. Nor must we think that the Lord will bear with such failings at our hands as He does from those among whom we have lived, for three reasons: (1) Because of the closer bonds of marriage between the Lord and us, wherein He has taken us to be His own in a most strict manner, which makes Him more jealous of our love and obedience, just as He told the people of Israel, "You only have I known of all the families of the Earth; therefore will I punish you for your transgressions" (Amos 3:2); (2) Because the Lord will be sanctified in those who come near Him. We know that there were many who corrupted the service of the Lord, some setting up altars to other gods before Him, others offering both strange fires and sacrifices; yet no fire came from heaven, or other sudden judgment upon them . . . ; (3) When God gives a special commission He wants it strictly observed in every article. . . .

A Sacred Covenant

Thus stands the case between God and us. We are entered into covenant with Him for this work. We have taken out a commission. The Lord has given us leave to draw our own articles; we have promised to base our actions on these ends, and we have asked Him for favor and blessing. Now if the Lord shall please to hear us, and bring us in peace to the place we desire, then He has ratified this covenant and sealed our commission, and will expect strict performance of the articles contained in it. But if we neglect to observe these articles, which are the ends we have propounded, and—dissembling with our God—shall embrace this present world and prosecute our carnal intentions, seeking great things for ourselves and our posterity, the Lord will surely break out in wrath against us and be revenged of such a perjured people, and He will make us know the price of the breach of such a covenant.

Now the only way to avoid this shipwreck and to provide for our posterity is to follow the counsel of Micah: to do justly, to love mercy, to walk humbly with our God. For this end, we must be knit together in this work as one man; we must hold each other in brotherly affection; we must be willing to rid ourselves of our excesses to supply others' necessities; we must uphold a familiar commerce together in all meekness, gentleness, patience, and liberality. We must delight in each other, make others' conditions our own and rejoice together, mourn together, labor and suffer together, always having before our eyes our commission and common work, our community as members of the same body.

So shall we keep the unity of the spirit in the bond of peace. The Lord will be our God and delight to dwell among us as His own people. He will command a blessing on us in all our ways, so that we shall see much more of His wisdom, power, goodness, and truth than we have formerly known. We shall find that the God of Israel is among us, and ten of us shall be able to resist a thousand of our enemies. The Lord will make our name a praise and glory, so that men shall say of succeeding plantations: "The Lord make it like that of New England." For we must consider that we shall be like a City upon a Hill; the eyes of all people are on us.

If we deal falsely with our God in this work we have undertaken and so cause Him to withdraw His present help from us, we shall be made a story and a byword throughout the world; we shall open the mouths of enemies to speak evil of the ways of God and all believers in God; we shall shame the faces of many of God's worthy servants and cause their prayers to be turned into curses upon us, till we are forced out of the new land where we are going.

ANNE BRADSTREET: AMERICA'S FIRST POET

FRANCIS MURPHY

Born to a well-to-do family in England, Anne Dudley Bradstreet was still in her teens when she sailed to the New World in 1630 as part of the first Puritan expedition to the Massachusetts Bay Colony. Despite the rigors of colonial life, Bradstreet managed to find time to write poems, which she circulated privately among her friends and family members. In 1650, Bradstreet's brother-in-law arranged to have a collection of her poems printed in London without her knowledge, making her the first published American poet. As Francis Murphy explains in the following essay, Bradstreet's poetry has held up to the test of time; while her works are steeped in the traditions of her seventeenth-century Puritan environment, they also address ideas and feelings that resonate with modern readers. Murphy is a professor of English language and literature at Smith College in Northampton, Massachusetts.

Anne Bradstreet (c. 1612–1672) was the second of six children born to Thomas Dudley and Dorothy Yorke. We know very little about her mother, but her father's career as manager of the estate of the Earl of Lincoln and, later, as governor of Massachusetts four times and thirteen times deputy governor, is well documented. He came to America in 1630 aboard the flagship *Arbella* as one of the founders of the Massachusetts Bay Colony. His daughter and her husband, Simon

Francis Murphy, "Anne Bradstreet and Edward Taylor," *The Columbia History of American Poetry*, edited by Jay Parini, New York: Columbia University Press, 1993. Copyright © 1993 by Columbia University Press. Reproduced by permission.

Bradstreet, were with him. Together they established formidable households, with both men well trained in business and law. Simon was himself to serve as secretary to the colony and governor for ten years. Thomas Dudley was something of a poet and, for this period, unusual in his encouragement of his daughter's literary appetite. It seems fitting that she should dedicate her most ambitious literary effort (her "Quaternions," or poems on groups of four: the four elements, the four humors, the four ages of man, the four seasons of the year, and the four monarchies—the Assyrian, the Persian, the Grecian, and the Roman) to him. In her dedication she acknowledges her debt to the example of Guillaume Du Bartas (a writer now almost forgotten, but whose *Divine Weeks* as translated by Joshua Sylvester in 1641 was one of the most popular poems in seventeenth-century England) as her model, but she hopes her father will recognize his daughter's particular voice in that crowd of voices which constitutes the music of any beginning poet's work:

> I honor him, but dare not wear his wealth,
> My goods are true (though poor), I love no stealth,
> But if I did, I durst not send them you,
> Who must reward a thief, but with his due.
> I shall not need my innocence to clear,
> These ragged lines will do't, when they appear.
> On what they are, your mild aspect I crave,
> Accept my best, my worst vouchsafe a grave.
> ("To Her Most Honored Father")

FIRST PUBLICATION

When Bradstreet wrote these lines she must have done so with some future publication in mind. She shared her poems with friends and relatives and was sensitive to the fact that her reputation as wife and mother and slave to the Muses was the subject of gossip. It is characteristic of her in "The Prologue" to these poems to handle this criticism with forthrightness and a determination to proceed with her writing.

> I am obnoxious to each carping tongue
> Who says my hand a needle better fits,
> A poet's pen all scorn I should thus wrong,
> For such despite they cast on female wits:
> If what I do prove well, it won't advance,
> They'll say it's stol'n, or else it was by chance.

Bradstreet's brother-in-law, Rev. John Woodbridge, decided, without Bradstreet's permission, to let New England audiences determine this matter for themselves. On a trip to London in 1647 he brought with him a manuscript including thirteen Bradstreet poems. They were published in 1650 by Stephen Bowtell "at the sign of the Bible in Popes Head-Alley," and entitled *The Tenth Muse Lately sprung up in America*, written "By a Gentlewoman in those parts." Bradstreet's name first appears at the close of the dedicatory poem to her father. The poems have rarely been out of the public eye since. Bradstreet said the book's publication caught her by surprise and made her "blush." By the year 1666 she was anticipating a new edition:

> I cast thee by as one unfit for light,
> Thy visage was so irksome in my sight;
> Yet being mine own, at length affection would
> Thy blemishes amend, if so I could:
> I washed thy face, but more defects I saw,
> And rubbing off a spot still made a flaw.
>   ("The Author to her Book")

No manuscript exists, but the publication by John Foster of Boston, Massachusetts, in 1678 of *Several Poems* "By a Gentlewoman in New England . . . Corrected by the Author and enlarged by an Addition of several other Poems found amongst her Papers after her Death," clearly represents our first genuine poet at her best. Most of the poems she added to *The Tenth Muse*—"Contemplations," "The Flesh and the Spirit," "Before the Birth of one of her Children," and three poems on her grandchildren, for example—are those works upon which Anne Bradstreet's present literary reputation rests. For, in contrast to the ingenious and often gnarled efforts of her male contemporaries, she speaks artfully but directly from her pages:

> If ever two were one, then surely we.
> If ever man were loved by wife, then thee;
> If ever wife was happy in a man,
> Compare with me, ye women, if you can.
> I prize thy love more than whole mines of gold
> Or all the riches of the East doth hold.
> My love is such that rivers cannot quench,
> Nor ought but love from thee, give recompense.
> Thy love is such I can no way repay,
> The heavens reward thee manifold, I pray.

Then while we live, in love let's so persevere
That when we live no more, we may live ever.
					("To My Dear and Loving Husband")

"Contemplations" remains her best long poem. It is a work full
of the wonder of the creation:

Under the cooling shadow of a stately elm
Close sat I by a goodly river's side,
Where gliding streams the rocks did overwhelm,
A lonely place, with pleasures dignified.
I once that loved the shady woods so well,
Now thought the rivers did the trees excel,
And if the sun would ever shine, there would I dwell.

For all the attraction of the landscape, however, Bradstreet is no
romantic. She knows that winter always follows summer and
age takes its toll of beauty. What makes the poem so pleasing is
the way in which the reader, like the writer, takes the lure—only
to get caught:

Silent alone, where none or saw, or heard,
In pathless paths I lead my wand'ring feet,
My humble eyes to lofty skies I reared
To sing some song, my mazed Muse thought meet.
My great Creator I would magnify,
That nature had thus decked liberally,
But Ah, and Ah, again, my imbecility!

What she had forgotten is the petty reward of the temporal
when viewed in eternity's perspective. Knowing the conven-
tions of Renaissance moral verse, one might have anticipated
the turn of her ending without having anticipated the power of
her last lines and the striking use she makes of Biblical allusion:

O Time the fatal wrack of mortal things,
That draws oblivion's curtains over kings;
Their sumptuous monuments, men know them not,
Their names without a record are forgot,
Their parts, their ports, their pomp's all laid in th' dust,
Nor wit nor gold, nor buildings scape time's rust;
But he whose name in graved in the white stone
Shall last and shine when all of these are gone.

BRADSTREET'S CONFESSIONS

In 1867 John Harvard Ellis published *The Works of Anne Bradstreet in Prose and Verse.* In doing so he provided modern read-

ers with not only Bradstreet's "Meditations when my Soul hath been refreshed with the Consolations which the world knows not," but a remarkable spiritual autobiography addressed to her "dear children":

> This Book by Any yet unread,
> I leave for you when I am dead,
> That being gone, here you may find
> What was your living mother's mind.

Puritan men and women were in the habit of keeping diaries and making notes on their spiritual histories, but those that survive are often predictable and confess nothing more alarming than disobedience to their parents. Bradstreet's is notable for her frank confession that although she has "sometimes tasted of that hidden manna that the world knows not," she has just as often been perplexed because her spiritual pilgrimage has not been one of "constant joy." Instead, there have been "times of sinkings and droopings"; she has doubted the truth of the Scriptures and wondered "whether there was a God." "I never saw any miracles to confirm me," she adds, "and those which I read of how did [I] know but they were feigned." It seems fitting that she finally settled on a poet's rather than a theologian's way of resolving her doubts.

> That there is a God my reason would soon tell me by the wondrous works that I see, the vast frame of the heaven and the earth, the order of all things, night and day, summer and winter, spring and autumn, the daily providing for this great household upon the earth, the preserving and directing of all to its proper end.

Puritans were not indifferent to the things of this world. Some of the most eloquent passages about the American landscape can be found in the writings of Samuel Sewall and Jonathan Edwards. But Puritan men and women were constantly reminded of the difference between this fleeting world and the city of heavenly light:

> The city where I hope to dwell,
> There's none on earth can parallel;
> The stately walls both high and strong,
> Are made of precious jasper stone;
> The gates of pearl, both rich and clear,
> And angels are for porters there;
> The streets thereof transparent gold,

Such as no eye did e'er behold;
A crystal river there doth run,
Which doth proceed from the Lamb's throne.

("The Flesh and the Spirit")

Yet knowing something intellectually and living it are two quite
different things. Bradstreet's poetry is attractive to us because
she is so honest about her affections. Her ultimate love is for
Christ—"upon this rock Christ Jesus will I build my faith, and if
I perish, I perish"—but the here and now has its charms. In her
delight in her marriage, in the sadness that followed the burning of her house, in the rewards of parenting, and in the heart-
breaking loss of children she explores a tension between this
world and the next that transcends the age in which she lived.

Colonial Expansion

CHAPTER 3

THE ESTABLISHMENT OF MARYLAND AS A CATHOLIC REFUGE

ANTHONY MCFARLANE

Anthony McFarlane is a professor in the School of Comparative American Studies at the University of Warwick in England, where he specializes in the pre-Columbian and colonial history of Latin America. In the following excerpt from his book *The British in the Americas, 1480–1815*, McFarlane examines the founding of Maryland in 1634 as a sanctuary for Catholics escaping religious oppression in England. While Maryland was not exclusively limited to Catholic settlers, the author notes, it was the first British colony in North America to attract a substantial number of non-Protestants. He also describes the failed attempts of the Maryland founders to create a feudal social order similar to that of medieval England and the gradual establishment of a more democratic system.

A significant development in the Chesapeake Bay region during the 1630s was the creation of an entirely new colony north of Virginia, in Maryland. In its conception and early development, Maryland differed from Virginia. The colony originated with George Calvert, the first Baron Baltimore, who, after an abortive attempt to found a colony in Newfoundland in 1627, had visited Virginia in 1629 and conceived the idea of an American refuge for English Catholics. His son, Cecilius Calvert, second Baron Baltimore, was given a grant of territory north of the Potomac River, and, calling it 'Mariland' in honour of Queen Mary of England, he sent two hundred people, led by his younger brother Leonard, to plant the first colony at St Mary's in 1634.

A UNIQUE COLONY

In fact, the colony was not exclusively reserved for Catholics; more Protestants than Catholics settled in its territory, and its government made a conscious effort at religious tolerance. Maryland was, nonetheless, a unique colony, with a political and legal status that differed substantially from those of other North American colonies. Baltimore's royal charter not only made him the proprietor and governor of the territory, but also endowed him with the powers of a medieval English frontier lord, able to dispense justice and administration independently of the King, and to grant land in feudal style. By using these powers, Baltimore intended to create a strongly hierarchical social order, based on a system of manors and manorial courts of a kind long in decay in England. Thus Maryland was something of a utopian project, designed to remake in the New World a society and religion which were rapidly being effaced in the mother country.

To underpin his social design, Baltimore sought to avoid the 'starving time' which had been experienced in early Virginia. He insisted that the small groups of first settlers should produce for their own subsistence and maintain good relations with the local Indians. When they had secured their own food supply, the settlers were then able to turn to tobacco planting, so that they might sustain trade with England. Baltimore's plans to create a feudal social order were, however, largely frustrated. Large landed estates were created, with lords of the manor and manorial courts, but they were rarely cultivated as single units and the idea of an aristocracy of great landowners did not survive amidst the realities of pioneering development in a new land.

CHANGES IN THE COLONY

In 1640, the population of Maryland consisted of only about 500 settlers; to induce immigration, land had to be made widely available and allocated in small parcels which poor migrants could afford. Thus, despite the programme of privilege planned by its proprietor, the characteristic unit of the Maryland economy soon became the small farm. Furthermore, with the move

towards tobacco cultivation, Maryland increasingly came to resemble Virginia, on a smaller scale. Migrants and settlers sought
to become independent farmers as soon as possible, and spread
out over the surrounding riverbanks and estuaries of the Chesapeake region, raising their own food and growing tobacco for
sale to the merchants who came to the Bay.

The political order in Maryland also eventually followed patterns established in Virginia, in spite of the peculiarities of the
charter granted to Lord Baltimore and his determination to in-
stall a feudal form of government. In 1635, Baltimore was forced
to concede an informal assembly to Protestants at Kent Island,
and to allow the assembly to conduct itself in the manner of a
local parliament when it first met in 1638. When more Protestants from Virginia entered the region, Maryland's Catholic proprietor came under mounting attack; indeed, during and after
the English Civil War, Baltimore lost control of his colony to Puritan opponents. Although Baltimore was reinstated as proprietor in 1657, Maryland came increasingly to resemble Virginia,
as a tobacco-producing colony of tidewater plantations, with its
feudal 'hundreds' replaced by counties and parishes. In some
respects, however, Maryland remained very different from the
other colonies, including its near neighbour in Virginia: English
Catholic emigrants established a network of families which in-
termarried with each other, sustained communications with
their co-religionists in England or in exile in Europe, and provided a niche in English Protestant America where the Catholic
church established its first ecclesiastical presence.

Religious Freedom in Rhode Island

Franklin Folsom

In the following passage from *Give Me Liberty: America's Colonial Heritage*, freelance writer Franklin Folsom traces the beginnings of the colony of Rhode Island, unique among the early settlements for its insistence on complete religious freedom. He focuses on Rhode Island's founder, Roger Williams, who first arrived in the Massachusetts Bay Colony as a Puritan clergyman but eventually broke with the Puritan leaders over theological differences and the treatment of Native Americans. Williams stirred up enough controversy that he was banned from Massachusetts, the author explains; fleeing to Rhode Island, he established a community based on the tenets of religious freedom and welcomed followers of a variety of beliefs. Among Folsom's numerous publications are the books *Beyond the Frontier, The Explorations of America,* and *Indian Uprising on the Rio Grande: The Pueblo Revolt of 1680.*

A date to mark on the calendar of liberty is 1631. In that year a very gentle, very pleasant, and also very uncompromising young man named Roger Williams came to the small Puritan village of Boston and began a lifetime of agitation. Almost from his first day in the year-old settlement in Massachusetts Bay Colony he talked, argued, split hairs, and suffered for a cause—the separation of church and state—which was finally achieved by the American Revolution.

Williams, twenty-eight years old when he landed, was a qualified clergyman. Although Boston had only about three hundred residents, he was offered a post as a kind of assistant minister in the town's one church. To the chagrin of the elders, the young man turned them down. The Boston Church, he said, was too closely tied to the Church of England, which he thought so corrupt as to be beyond reform. Williams left both employment and the town of Boston behind him and moved on up the coast to Salem, another Puritan village. There he found a congregation more independent in spirit, and he agreed to accept their offer of a post. But he was not allowed to keep it for long. The leaders of the Boston Church, annoyed by his independence, now brought pressure to bear on the Salem congregation. And Williams moved on again. This time he left Massachusetts Bay Colony and went to Plymouth Colony, which was not controlled by Puritan ministers and magistrates. In Plymouth he found a church that he regarded as really independent—that is, separate from the Church of England—and here the energetic young man mixed pastoral duties with activities as a trader and missionary among the Indians on Cape Cod.

This association with Indians produced unexpected results.

QUESTIONS ABOUT LAND RIGHTS

In the course of his trading and preaching, Williams learned a good deal of the Algonkian language, spoken by the Wampanoag Indians on Cape Cod and by other tribes elsewhere in Massachusetts. (He had a talent for languages and could already read and speak Latin, Greek, Hebrew, French, and Dutch, in addition to English.) Along with Algonkian words, Williams also learned something of Indian attitudes. The Wampanoag, he discovered, were upset by the increasing number of white men in their midst and by the notions these men had about the fields and forests that Indians had been using for millenia. Almost all Europeans, Protestant and Catholic alike, believed that a Christian sovereign had divine right to claim ownership of any lands they entered, if the people who lived there were not themselves Christian. Royal ownership by what was called "the right of discovery" took precedence over the Indians' ownership by right of possession and use. In 1607 English settlers did not doubt that the king of England had proper title to Virginia and that he could transfer title to them. In Massachusetts, beginning in 1620, householders and farmers felt sure that what was called the King's Patent to the land was legally valid and, accordingly, that they had every right to live there.

Now it happened that Roger Williams knew a surprising amount about the legalities of land titles and about law generally. Before coming to the New World he had served as a court stenographer and was a personal friend of Sir Edward Coke, one of the leading lawyers in London. All this legal experience in England came to Williams' mind when he contemplated the land titles of the Plymouth settlers. One question especially bothered him: Did the English colonists really own this land on which they lived? Did they have any right to it? Although he himself was the most ardent of Christians, Williams began to doubt that the religion of kings should have anything to do with ownership of any portion of this earth. On the contrary, it seemed to him that title to land was a civil matter and should be quite separate from religious beliefs. The proper way for a Christian to get land from non-Christians was to buy it or arrange to get it by treaty. Neither the king of England nor the settlers at Plymouth had bought their townsite from the Indians. To Williams this meant that the Pilgrims were guilty of trespass and the same was also true of most Puritans.

As usual, Williams did not keep his ideas to himself, and at the request of Plymouth's Governor William Bradford, he put into writing this disturbing theory about land. At that time William Brewster, now nearing seventy years old, was still a leading spirit in Plymouth. Predictably the younger man's arguments alarmed him. This new doctrine challenged the very right of Plymouth to exist.

STIRRING UP TROUBLE

Brewster and others now began to pay close attention to what Williams said in his sermons. Some of his religious theories, they found, were extreme, even for the Separatist church, which in turn seemed extreme to the Puritans in Boston and other Puritan towns. Altogether Williams was being a troublesome sort of fellow. Brewster thought that Plymouth and its assistant minister should part company. It is not clear whether Brewster and others now took the initiative and dismissed him or whether Williams asked for release from his pastoral post. At any rate, in 1633 he left Plymouth and returned to Salem.

Soon the same kind of trouble started all over again. No one in Salem—or Boston—could feel secure if Roger Williams was right about the King's Patent. In addition, many people were disturbed by Williams' relentless attacks on what he regarded as survivals among them of doctrines or practices that came from the Church of England. All of the New England settlers had grown up in the Anglican church, which was itself a direct descendant of the Roman Catholic church. It was not surprising that traces of Catholicism persisted in Anglican services, and to Williams anything that smacked of Catholicism smacked of the Devil.

The Salem authorities now became concerned about Williams. So did the authorities in Boston. The latter insisted that Williams come to Boston to stand trial. In court he spoke out as he did in church, and took back none of his fiery sermonizing. This was bad enough. But underneath the arguments about doctrine, the court magistrates sensed that Williams held an even more threatening belief: that religious and civil affairs should be kept separate. The church should not control civil institutions, and government should not have any control over men's faith.

This alarming idea had never been part of the thinking of either Pilgrims or Puritans. Both groups merely wanted a governmental arrangement—a state—that would protect and support their kind of church. Neither the Pilgrims nor the Puritans, in fact, allowed any churches except their own to operate in their communities.

Standing before the court in Boston, the devout young minister, now aged thirty-three, listened while the following was read to him:

> Whereas Mr. Roger Williams, one of the elders of the church of Salem, hath broached & dyvulged dyvers newe & dangerous opinions, against the aucthoritie of magistrates, as also writt l[ett]res of defamacon, both of the magistrates & churches here, & that before any conviccon, & yet mainetaineth the same without retraccon, it is therefore ordered, that the said Mr. Williams shall dep[ar]te out of this jurisdiccon within sixe weekes nowe nexte ensueing, wch if he neglect to p[er]forme, it shalbe lawfull for the Govnr & two of the magistrates to send him to some place out of this jurisdiction, not to returne any more without licence from the Court.

This order did not close the dissenter's mouth. When he returned to Salem, he continued to speak his mind, whereupon the court in Boston sent representatives to seize him so they could ship him back to England. But Williams had been warned they were coming. Before they arrived, he escaped into the wilderness, although he was ill and the weather was bitter cold. However he did not go into country that was unknown to him. He had often traveled along the wilderness trails and had dreamed of establishing a trading post and of doing missionary work among the Narraganset Indians in the area now known as Rhode Island. In preparation he had already bought land from the Indians. What he paid for it is not known. It couldn't have been much. Indeed, Williams at one point said he paid mainly in love. But at least he had been consistent and had arranged to get title from the Indians themselves, not from the king.

Now Roger Williams, city bred, college trained, a linguist and theologian, began the precarious existence of a farmer and Indian trader in the wilderness. With him were his children and his wife (who, curiously, remained illiterate while his own knowledge of language continued to increase). Not only she but other women were his devoted followers—in spite of his insistence at one stage that, according to the Bible, all women should wear veils in church.

In the course of time, several English communities grew up near the area where Williams settled. All of the newcomers, he insisted, should buy equal-sized tracts, and of course their land titles had to come ultimately from the Indians. With this egalitarian measure—and in other democratic ways—he had decisive influence in the policies of the newcomers. He continued to believe that church and state should be separate, and he persuaded his neighbors that he was right. Their wilderness settlement, known as Providence Plantations, became a laboratory in which to test the workability of Williams' new theories.

TRUE FREEDOM OF RELIGION

Providence at that time was the only place in the Christian world where real freedom of religion existed, and this freedom led to greater democracy than was known elsewhere. Any adult male could vote, if he owned land and was head of a family. In Massachusetts, by contrast, only adult, male members of the Puritan and Separatist churches could vote, and church members were likely to vote as their ministers directed. A theocracy had developed in Massachusetts, where no church could exist without government approval. Any church at all could exist in Providence. In Massachusetts Bay Colony and in Plymouth Colony the state provided economic support for the ministers of the approved churches. In Providence Plantations, no minister received any state support whatsoever. In Boston and surrounding towns, it was a punishable offense to speak disrespectfully of religious leaders. In Providence, anyone could speak his mind about any minister or about his theories without fear of harsh punishment.

All kinds of dissidents availed themselves of the new freedom offered in Providence. Separatists, of whom Williams was one at the time, were the first to come. Later there were Baptists, whom Williams joined for a while. Antinomians and Seekers came. So did Sephardic Jews and Quakers. Not only did Williams, on principle, insist that the followers of these religious sects be admitted, he also as a matter of principle spoke out vigorously against any of their doctrines with which he disagreed. He attacked the Quakers, for example, with unrestrained language. But he never wavered in his insistence that, wrong though he thought they were, they had full right to live and worship in Providence.

SEEKING PROTECTION

No sooner did the freedom-seeking settlers start to develop their farms than they had knotty political problems to solve. The firstcomers, who were refugees from Massachusetts, had obtained their land directly from the Indians or from Roger Williams, who had it from the Indians. But none of them had any authority from anyone except themselves to establish a government on their land. It may be asked why rebellious souls felt they needed authorization from anyone to organize community life. The reason lay in their weakness. To the north and east of them were Massachusetts Bay and Plymouth colonies, which had no desire to see Providence turn into a successful experiment in freedom of religion. To the west, Puritan settlers were building up Connecticut. They, too, presented a threat to Providence. And Indians were all around, none too pleased at the steady increase of Englishmen who insisted on appropriating the country's resources.

The Providence colonists understandably felt they needed support from a strong center of power. One obvious source of support was the head of the English government, to which all the first settlers had strong emotional ties. Twice Roger Williams journeyed to London to petition for a charter—a document giving official sanction to the colony, which came to be called

Rhode Island. Williams did not sense any inconsistency here. Although, to his mind, the land itself belonged originally to the Indians, the right to organize and direct colonies belonged to his mother country. This right could be granted in a charter, but in addition to the usual clauses, the charter Williams sought would guarantee religious freedom in the colony.

In the end he got what he wanted. While England went through a revolution led by Puritans and then a counter-revolution led by anti-Puritans, Williams kept insisting that the Rhode Island colonists must have freedom of conscience. Finally King Charles II agreed.

AN ESSENTIAL CONTRIBUTION TO DEMOCRACY

Now, alone in America, Rhode Islanders, living on land they had bought from its true owners, could worship—or not worship—in any way they wanted, and for a while they enjoyed this privilege under a government headed by Williams. Nowhere else in the entire Christian world in the seventeenth century was such freedom possible. . . .

The separation of church and state which Williams advocated was an attack on tyranny and later became part of the United States Constitution. There is no mention of God or religion in the original text of that document, and the First Amendment to the Constitution specifically began, "Congress shall make no law respecting an establishment of religion, or prohibiting the free exercise thereof. . . ." This amendment—an achievement of the American Revolution—is an enduring monument to the exile who succeeded more than a century earlier in establishing religious freedom in Rhode Island.

A prominent minister in Boston, who may have been embarrassed by the banishment of Roger Williams, called his expulsion an "enlargement." Williams did enlarge liberty, his own and others', when he was forced to live outside Massachusetts, and he became a part of the whole enlarging, expanding process of revolution that would shape a new nation.

MIGRATIONS FROM MASSACHUSETTS

BRUCE CATTON AND WILLIAM B. CATTON

Best known for his widely acclaimed histories of the U.S. Civil War, journalist Bruce Catton also served as the editor of *American Heritage* magazine for many years. His book *The Bold and Magnificent Dream: America's Founding Years, 1492–1815* was cowritten with his son William B. Catton, a retired professor and historian in residence at Middlebury College in Vermont. In the following excerpt, the Cattons provide a brief overview of the new colonies that arose during the 1630s and 1640s in the present-day states of Maine, New Hampshire, and Connecticut. They pay particular attention to Connecticut, which was primarily settled by dissatisfied Puritans who left Massachusetts due to political and religious disagreements.

T he government set up by the community of Saints in the Massachusetts Bay Colony proved enduringly workable. But it is hardly surprising that a society based upon so complex and powerful a doctrine, inhabited by such strong-willed believers, and subject to the pressures of population growth as hundreds of new migrants arrived each year, proved unable to contain so many people and so much doctrine within a single body politic. Massachusetts became subject to disaffected out-migrations, or hivings off, less than five years after the first settlers arrived, and the process continued until by the 1640s a whole cluster of small New England colonies had come into existence.

The string of little fishing villages stretching north and east from Salem along the coast were all drawn into the Bay Colony's orbit. The old Council for New England, whose existence consisted mainly of a series of futile gestures, protested during the 1630s that Massachusetts was infringing upon its territory. It granted the land north of the Merrimack to a pair of would-be lords proprietor, who in turn divided the region into the separate grants of New Hampshire and Maine. But their efforts to exploit these territories made no headway against the expanding Bay Colony, which dominated the former area until the 1670s and the latter until the early nineteenth century.

DIVISIVE TENDENCIES

Expansion southward was another matter. The Plymouth settlements discreetly minded their own business and maintained a separate existence until 1691, when the Bay Colony absorbed them. But Massachusetts found itself boxed in along the rest of its southern border, chiefly because this region was settled by folk who were there because Massachusetts could not hold them, and who were as strong-minded and resolute as the people they had left. Two clusters of settlements became the centers of new colonies in the 1630s—one around Hartford, in the lower Connecticut Valley, and the other around New Haven, on Long Island Sound. These departures from Massachusetts arose from differences that were political rather than doctrinal; both the Connecticut and New Haven settlements (they were not merged until the 1660s) were communities of Puritan Saints with religious and political institutions patterned closely after those of the Bay Colony. The Reverend Thomas Hooker and his flock took off to found Hartford in 1636 because they found John Winthrop's government too arbitrary, and the Reverend John Davenport took off to found New Haven in 1637 because he considered the Winthrop government too lax.

It is also possible that both of these eminent divines found the religious atmosphere in Massachusetts a shade too stifling because it was so completely subject to the influence of the Reverend John Cotton. Cotton had a powerful personality and a good mind and a large following (many of whom, Roger Williams caustically observed, "could hardly believe that God would suffer Mr Cotton to err"). The process here at work demonstrated one of Puritanism's inherently divisive tendencies, on the purely personal level, in that the strong wills required to master and stay on top of such a body of beliefs often found it difficult to stay on top of them together.

In any case, both the Connecticut and the New Haven out-migrations proceeded on the basis of no authority save their own, into regions to which neither they nor Massachusetts held title. And like the *Mayflower* pilgrims and other groups of Englishmen in like situations, they drew up their own covenant-charters to serve as a basis for government and authority until higher validation could be obtained. Since England was itself entering the stormy period of the Civil War, when final authority had no agreed-upon location, this validation proved impossible to get until the dust settled with the Stuart Restoration in 1660.

THE CONSTITUTION OF THE UNITED COLONIES OF NEW ENGLAND

THE NEW ENGLAND CONFEDERATION

On May 19, 1643, the Puritan colonies of Massachusetts Bay, Plymouth, Connecticut, and New Haven joined together to form the New England Confederation. The details of their pact were stipulated in the following constitution, in which the four colonies pledged mutual aid in case of outside attack, established a governing body for the confederation, and provided a procedure for settling disputes between the member colonies. This loose union, which lasted for forty years, had no power to enforce its decisions. However, it created a sense of self-government and solidarity among the New England colonies. The confederation also served as an important harbinger of later American experiments with federalism.

W hereas we all came into these parts of America with one and the same end and aim, namely, to advance the Kingdom of our Lord Jesus Christ and to enjoy the liberties of the Gospel in purity with peace; and whereas in our settling (by a wise providence of God) we are further dispersed upon the sea coasts and rivers than was at first intended, so that we can not according to our desire with convenience

The New England Confederation, "Union Against Outside Attack," *Settlements to Society: 1584–1763*, edited by Jack P. Greene, New York: McGraw-Hill, 1966.

communicate in one government and jurisdiction; and whereas we live encompassed with people of several nations and strange languages which hereafter may prove injurious to us or our posterity. And forasmuch as the natives have formerly committed sundry insolence and outrages upon several Plantations of the English and have of late combined themselves against us: and seeing by reason of those sad distractions in England which they have heard of, and by which they know we are hindered from that humble way of seeking advice, or reaping those comfortable fruits of protection, which at other times we might well expect. We therefore do conceive it our bounden duty, without delay to enter into a present Consociation amongst ourselves, for mutual help and strength in all our future concernments: That, as in nation and religion, so in other respects, we be and continue one according to the tenor and true meaning of the ensuing articles: Wherefore it is fully agreed and concluded by and between the parties or Jurisdictions above named, and they jointly and severally do by these presents agree and conclude that they all be and henceforth be called by the name of the United Colonies of New England.

2. The said United Colonies for themselves and their posterities do jointly and severally hereby enter into a firm and perpetual league of friendship and amity for offence and defence, mutual advice and succor upon all just occasions both for preserving and propagating the truth and liberties of the Gospel and for their own mutual safety and welfare. . . .

PROVIDING FOR WARFARE

4. It is by these Confederates agreed that the charge of all just wars, whether offensive or defensive, upon what part or member of this Confederation soever they fall, shall both in men, provisions, and all other disbursements be borne by all the parts of this Confederation in different proportions according to their different ability in manner following, namely, that the Commissioners for each Jurisdiction from time to time, as there shall be occasion, bring a true account and number of all their males in every Plantation, or any way belonging to or under their several Jurisdictions, of what quality or condition soever they be, from sixteen years old to three-score, being inhabitants there. And that according to the different numbers which from time to time shall be found in each Jurisdiction upon a true and just account, the service of men and all charges of the war be borne

by the poll: each Jurisdiction or Plantation being left to their own just course and custom of rating themselves and people according to their different estates with due respects to their qualities and exemptions amongst themselves though the Confederation take no notice of any such privilege: and that according to their different charge of each Jurisdiction and Plantation the whole advantage of the war (if it please God so to bless their endeavors) whether it be in lands, goods, or persons, shall be proportionably divided among the said Confederates.

5. It is further agreed, that if any of these Jurisdictions or any Plantation under or in combination with them, be invaded by any enemy whomsoever, upon notice and request of any three magistrates of that Jurisdiction so invaded, the rest of the Confederates without any further meeting or expostulation shall forthwith send aid to the Confederate in danger but in different proportions; namely, the Massachusetts an hundred men sufficiently armed and provided for such a service and journey, and each of the rest, forty-five so armed and provided, or any less number, if less be required according to this proportion. . . .

THE COMMISSIONERS

6. It is also agreed, that for the managing and concluding of all affairs proper, and concerning the whole Confederation two Commissioners shall be chosen by and out of each of these four Jurisdictions: namely, two for the Massachusetts, two for Plymouth, two for Connecticut, and two for New Haven, being all in Church-fellowship with us, which shall bring full power from their several General Courts respectively to hear, examine, weigh, and determine all affairs of our war, or peace, leagues, aids, charges, and numbers of men for war, division of spoils and whatsoever is gotten by conquest, receiving of more Confederates for Plantations into combination with any of the Confederates, and all things of like nature, which are the proper concomitants or consequents of such a Confederation for amity, offence, and defence. . . .

8. It is also agreed that the Commissioners for this Confederation hereafter at their meetings, whether ordinary or extraordinary, as they may have commission or opportunity, do endeavor to frame and establish agreements and orders in general cases of a civil nature, wherein all the Plantations are interested, for preserving of peace among themselves, for preventing as much as may be all occasion of war or differences

with others, as about the free and speedy passage of justice in every Jurisdiction, to all the Confederates equally as to their own, receiving those that remove from one Plantation to another without due certificate, how all the Jurisdictions may carry it towards the Indians, that they neither grow insolent nor be injured without due satisfaction, lest war break in upon the Confederates through such miscarriages. It is also agreed that if any servant run away from his master into any other of these confederated Jurisdictions, that in such case, upon the certificate of one magistrate in the Jurisdiction out of which the said servant fled, or upon other due proof; the said servant shall be delivered, either to his master, or any other that pursues and brings such certificate or proof. And that upon the escape of any prisoner whatsoever, or fugitive for any criminal cause, whether breaking prison, or getting from the officer, or otherwise escaping, upon the certificate of two magistrates of the Jurisdiction out of which the escape is made, that he was a prisoner, or such an offender at the time of the escape, the magistrates, or some of them of that Jurisdiction where for the present the said prisoner or fugitive abideth, shall forthwith grant such a warrant as the case will bear, for the apprehending of any such person, and the delivery of him into the hands of the officer or other person who pursues him. And if there be help required, for the safe returning of any such offender, then it shall be granted to him that craves the same, he paying the charges thereof.

9. And for that the justest wars may be of dangerous consequence, especially to the smaller Plantations in these United Colonies, it is agreed that neither the Massachusetts, Plymouth, Connecticut, nor New Haven, nor any of the members of them, shall at any time hereafter begin, undertake, or engage themselves, or this Confederation, or any part thereof in any war whatsoever (sudden exigencies, with the necessary consequents thereof excepted), which are also to be moderated as much as the case will permit, without the consent and agreement of the forementioned eight Commissioners, or at least six of them, . . . and that no charge be required of any of the Confederates, in case of a defensive war, till the said Commissioners have met, and approved the justice of the war, and have agreed upon the sum of money to be levied, which sum is then to be paid by the several Confederates. . . .

11. It is further agreed that if any of the Confederates shall

hereafter break any of these present articles, or be any other ways injurious to any one of the other Jurisdictions; such breach of agreement or injury shall be duly considered and ordered by the Commissioners for the other Jurisdictions, that both peace and this present Confederation may be entirely preserved without violation.

THE CONQUEST OF NEW SWEDEN AND NEW NETHERLAND

LOUIS B. WRIGHT

In the following excerpt from *The American Heritage History of the Thirteen Colonies*, Louis B. Wright explores the rapid transference of power that took place in the region between the Delaware River and the Hudson River during the 1650s and 1660s. As the author relates, the Delaware Valley was first claimed by the Swedes, who founded the small colony of New Sweden there. However, he notes, the Dutch colonists conquered New Sweden in 1655 and incorporated it into New Netherland. Less than a decade later, the English took control of New Netherland and renamed the colony New York.

An expert in the English Renaissance and the American colonial period, Wright was the director of the Folger Shakespeare Library in Washington, D.C., for twenty years. He also taught at the University of North Carolina in Chapel Hill and served as a history consultant for the National Geographic Society. Among his extensive publications are the books *The Colonial Search for a Southern Eden*, *Everyday Life in Colonial America*, *The First Gentlemen of Virginia: Intellectual Qualities of the Early Colonial Ruling Class*, *The Dream of Prosperity in Colonial America*, and *The Atlantic Frontier: Colonial American Civilization, 1607–1763*.

Louis B. Wright, *The American Heritage History of the Thirteen Colonies*, New York: American Heritage Publishing Co., 1967. Copyright © 1967 by American Heritage Publishing Co. Reproduced by permission.

The Swedes first entered the Delaware Valley under the leadership of the same Peter Minuit who had purchased Manhattan Island for the Dutch. In the 1630's, Sweden, then leading a crusade against the power of Catholic Spain, determined to create a base for attacking Spanish possessions in the New World. At the same time, she hoped to reap some of the profits of colonial trade. To that end, Sweden chartered in 1637 the New Sweden Company, modeled after the Dutch West India Company, and sent Minuit with a party of Swedes and Dutchmen to make a settlement on the Delaware. Minuit selected a spot where the city of Wilmington now stands and called it Fort Christina after the Swedish princess and later queen.

Sweden, like Holland, had no surplus population or dissident groups of citizens who wished to emigrate, and enlisting settlers for New Sweden was difficult. Since the Finns, a minority group in Sweden, were skilled in forest crafts, the New Sweden Company induced a few to settle on the Delaware to help clear the forests. But try as she might, Sweden could not arouse any enthusiasm for emigration to America. The New Sweden Company found the fur trade sufficiently profitable to maintain its bases on the lower Delaware, but it could not develop the back country. So the Dutch retained a tenuous hold on the upper Delaware with a few soldiers at Fort Nassau and watched with misgivings as the Swedes established themselves lower on the river. Since both were threatened by the infiltration of English settlers from neighboring colonies, they made common cause against the English invaders and in 1642 burned one of their villages on the Schuylkill.

In the same year, the New Sweden Company sent Johan Printz to be director of the colony. Printz, like New Netherland's director-general Peter Stuyvesant a veteran soldier, had fought for King Gustavus Adolphus and was a man of courage and competence (because of his huge girth, the Indians called him "Big Guts"). For the ten years from 1643 until 1653, Printz labored to make something of the Swedish colony. By fair dealings with the Indians, he kept the peace and increased the profits from the fur trade. His continued efforts induced the company to send over a few more farmers and artisans. So impressed were some of the English who had become squatters in the valley that they swore allegiance to Sweden in order to live under Printz's rule in the Delaware Valley. As the little colony grew to something approaching two hundred inhabitants, Printz moved a few settlers up the river and built two forts there.

CONFLICT WITH THE DUTCH

So long as the Swedish colony was merely a small trading post with little prospect of growing, Stuyvesant tolerated it, but when Printz established additional bases on the Delaware and began to recruit colonists, the Dutch director-general acted. Moving two hundred men to the Delaware, he established Fort Casimir between Printz's new fortresses and Fort Christina, thus dividing and neutralizing the Swedish strength, all too little in any case.

Stuyvesant had served notice that he would not permit Swedish expansion. Although Printz strove to recruit fresh settlers and to induce the New Sweden Company to send aid, little was forthcoming. An insurrection among his own people so discouraged him that he left the colony to settle its own quarrels and went to New Amsterdam to await a ship bound for Europe. With Printz's departure, the best days of New Sweden ended. Though the Swedes in 1654 sent over another vigorous director, Johan Rising, with additional settlers, he made the fatal mistake of taking Fort Casimir from the Dutch, an affront that Stuyvesant would not tolerate. Consequently, in the summer of 1655, Stuyvesant sent to the Delaware troops who forced the capitulation of the Swedes and thus ended any effective development of a rival colony.

Although the Swedish population was never greater than two hundred, the Swedes helped establish the Lutheran Church in America. They also contributed a technique of building that became enormously useful on the frontier, the use of notched logs to make cabins. Only the Swedes—and later the Germans—originally used this type of construction, which their example taught other frontiersmen to adopt.

The days of Dutch rule in New Netherland were also numbered. After the Restoration of Charles II as king of England, his courtiers began a systematic search for means of recouping losses they had suffered during the long years of Puritan domination. One source of wealth lay in lands across the seas and in trade with the colonies already established there. Charles was ready to make grants of vaguely defined territory in America, grants that required merely a stroke of the king's pen, for nei-

To monopolize the slave trade, British forces took over the Dutch colony of New Netherland, which they called New York.

ther he nor his counselors knew or cared much about existing boundaries. If these grants stored up trouble for the future, the Merry Monarch showed very little concern about it.

THE ENGLISH TAKEOVER

One vast territory known to English traders was the region claimed by the Dutch between the Hudson and the Delaware, and it was this region that the king's own brother, James, Duke of York, fancied. The Duke of York was head of the Royal African Company, which was intent upon monopolizing the slave trade with the New World, and their most energetic rival was the Dutch West India Company. As it happened, the Duke of York was also Lord High Admiral in command of Charles II's navy.

The upshot of all this was that the Duke of York in 1664 dispatched a fleet to American waters to protect English interests against violations of the Navigation Acts and to assert English authority over trespassers on English territory. The worst offender, it turned out, was the West India Company, and at the end of August the English fleet anchored off New Amsterdam and summoned Peter Stuyvesant to surrender. This was not an act of war against a friendly nation, the duke made clear, but merely a police action to clear trespassers from land rightfully English.

Stuyvesant's rage knew no bounds. He mounted the ramparts of the fort and threatened to open fire upon the enemy, but his chief gunner informed him that the powder was so scanty and damp that no proper defense was possible. Stuyvesant then offered to lead his men, in spite of his peg leg, in an assault upon the English. The parson pleaded with him to be calm, and a petition from the women and children of New Amsterdam begged him to surrender without exposing them to destruction. Though the old director declared that he himself would rather be carried out dead, he agreed to capitulate. The English commander, Colonel Richard Nicolls, who had been named deputy governor, promised to respect all property rights of the Dutch inhabitants and to give them a voice in the government. The prospects for the average citizen looked better under Nicolls than under Stuyvesant. Although old Peter Stuyvesant was bitter at having to surrender to the English, he was not so heartbroken that he could not return to New York and live out his days there. He had a farm in the Bowery and a fine house near the site of St. Mark's Episcopal Church. There he died in 1672 and was buried in a chapel on his farm.

With the exception of a period from July 30, 1673, until November 10, 1674, when the Dutch temporarily regained control, the English henceforth occupied the former Dutch territory and consolidated their possession of the Atlantic seaboard from Maine to Florida. Thereafter, the city on the Hudson and the province would be called New York. The Dutch left their mark, however, on the architecture, on customs, on business habits, on the language, and on the legendary history of New York. Perhaps the most pervasive commercial contribution they made was to introduce Santa Claus to the American people.

The greatest benefit to the English of the Dutch occupation of the Hudson Valley was a gift of time. The Dutch and their Indian allies served as a shield against the French until the English themselves were strong enough to resist French attempts to seize this vital and strategic territory.

The Founding of the Carolinas

Oliver Perry Chitwood

Oliver Perry Chitwood served as a professor of history at West Virginia University in Morgantown for nearly forty years. His books include *Justice in Colonial Virginia, A Short History of the American People*, and *The United States: From Colony to World Power*. In the following selection from *A History of Colonial America*, Chitwood describes the early years of North and South Carolina. Initially, this region was known collectively as Carolina, the author explains, but almost from the beginning it was clear that the northern and southern sections were very different from one another. According to Chitwood, South Carolina grew far more quickly than North Carolina, which had trouble attracting colonists due to its unfavorable geography. He also explores South Carolina's ties to the West Indies, a factor that had considerable influence on the type of slavery practiced on the plantations of South Carolina.

W hen Charles II became king of England in 1660 a few bold pioneers were living on the Chowan River, near Albemarle Sound in present-day North Carolina, and in this same year some New Englanders made a temporary settlement on the Cape Fear River. These frontiersmen were the only white people then to be found in all that vast region lying between the present state of Virginia and the Spanish possessions in the south. It was hardly to be expected that a monarch who was so much interested in imperial expansion as was the younger Charles would overlook so fruitful a field for colo-

Oliver Perry Chitwood, *A History of Colonial America*, New York: Harper & Row, 1961.

nization. Even had he been blind to the opportunities offered by this favored region, there were plenty of courtiers around him who would not be slow to point out the possibilities for gain both to themselves and to the empire that would result from the exploitation of this wide area of unappropriated land. Spain claimed this territory, but for more than three-quarters of a century had made no effort to settle it. England had already staked off for herself most of this region, and it had been at the disposal of the king since the charter of the Virginia Company was annulled in 1624.

In 1629 Charles I granted to Sir Robert Heath, the attorney-general, all the land between the thirty-first and thirty-sixth degrees of north latitude. To this region was given the name Carolina, in honor of the king. Sir Robert failed to support his title by settlement, and Charles II gladly availed himself of this as an excuse to regain this princely domain. He could now reward with land grants in America some prominent men who had remained faithful to him in his exile or who had helped him back to his throne.

It was in keeping with this policy that he gave Carolina to a group of eight of his favorites (1663) and made them proprietors of this vast territory with all the rights and privileges that Lord Baltimore was enjoying in Maryland. These grantees included in their number some of the leading statesmen and politicians of the day. Among them were Edward Hyde, Earl of Clarendon, Lord High Chancellor of England; George Monk, the Duke of Albemarle; Anthony Cooper, Lord Ashley, Chancellor of the Exchequer; and Sir William Berkeley, Governor of Virginia. The proprietors were given authority to govern the settlers, dispose of the land, and confer titles of nobility, provided they did not employ titles then in use in England. Their power over the settlers was limited by the important provision that laws were to be made with the consent of the freemen or their delegates or deputies. . . .

Two years later (1665) a second charter was granted to the same proprietors, extending the limits of the province on the north to the parallel of 36° 30' and on the south to the twenty-ninth parallel. The northern extension was made to include the settlement on the Chowan River, which was outside of the first Carolina patent.

Before the proprietors received their charter, colonization had begun in the northern portion of their grant, the region now known as North Carolina. The first settlement was the one on the Chowan River, near Albemarle Sound, and was made about 1653 by adventurers from Virginia, who had pushed into the wilderness in search of new home sites. The land on which the colony was planted was level and fertile, and there were a number of large navigable rivers, which abounded in fish and also served as an easy means of communication.

Despite these favorable circumstances, however, the colony grew slowly, and by 1677 the population was only about three thousand. One of the main reasons for its backwardness was its isolation, being separated from the Virginia settlements by wide areas of swamp lands. The rivers, although they promoted communication within the colony, discouraged intercourse with neighboring provinces, for many of them were too wide to be forded and as they flowed eastward it was impossible to construct roads of any length to the north and south. The roads were, therefore, very poor even as measured by colonial standards. Besides, the harbors were too shallow for large ocean vessels, and so the settlers had little or no trade with the mother country. . . .

The colony on the Chowan River was slow in expanding southward, and it was not until 1690 that there was any permanent occupation of that portion of North Carolina that lies south of Albemarle Sound. The first settlement permanently established in this region was the one made on the Pamlico River (1690) by French Huguenots from Virginia. Other adventurers soon found their way into this section from Albemarle, Virginia, and Europe, many of the European emigrants being French Huguenots. In 1704 a group of the last-named foreigners planted a settlement on (or near) the Pamlico River, which they called Bath and which enjoyed the distinction of being the first incorporated town in North Carolina, though it never became anything more than a sleepy village. . . .

THE EARLY HISTORY OF SOUTH CAROLINA

In the first attempts at colonization in North Carolina the initiative was taken by the settlers without any assistance from the proprietors. But it was not long before the latter began to take an active interest in the colonization of their province. As a result of their efforts, which included the expenditure of about four thousand pounds in money, three vessels were fitted out and sent from England (1669), carrying a considerable number of emigrants with a liberal supply of guns, ammunition, tools, and provisions. The expedition sailed to Barbados, where it picked up a few recruits. It then proceeded to the Carolina coast under the command of William Sayle, a Bermudian planter, who became the first governor of the new colony. The emigrants touched at Port Royal, a short distance above the mouth of the Savannah River, as that was the place designated for the settlement. But as they were not favorably impressed with this location, they sailed farther northward and entered Charleston Harbor in April, 1670. They chose for their settlement a location on the Ashley River, a short distance above its mouth, which they named Albemarle Point. . . . The colony endured some of the hardships incident to pioneer life, but it did not pass through a period of famine and suffering like that experienced by Virginia and Plymouth. They did not have to depend upon the mother country for their outside food supplies, as did the first settlers in the older colonies, but received them from Virginia and Barbados. The site of the original settlement was not healthful, and soon some of the colonists went over and settled at the point where the Ashley and Cooper rivers unite to form Charleston Harbor. There were, however, only a few houses at the new site until 1680, when by order of the proprietors it became the seat of government and was given the name of Charlestown. The new town grew rapidly, having a hundred houses in two years, and the old settlement at Albemarle Point began to be abandoned. . . . The rapid growth of the new town was due in large measure to its fine location on the best harbor on the Atlantic coast south of Virginia. It was protected from the sea by sandbars, but these did not impede access to the harbor by the small vessels of that day. Charleston was, therefore, fitted by nature to be the center of commerce for all the region south of Norfolk, Virginia, and during the eighteenth century it enjoyed the distinction of being the most important city in the South. . . .

South Carolina, more than any other continental colony, was influenced by the social ideals of the West Indian planters. Indeed, the founding of this colony was a sort of westward movement from the British island colonies. The lands in the English sugar islands had begun to wear thin, and the planters there were looking to the Carolina mainland as a virgin field for their industry. Barbados especially was interested in this westward expansion, as the little island was overcrowded with her numerous population, and so took a prominent part in the colonization of South Carolina. Several of the leading men in the early settlements and many of the first colonists came from this island. The connection between South Carolina and the West Indies was strengthened by the fact that in 1670 the Carolina proprietors had the Bahama Islands added to their land grant, and so they were now interested in the development of trade between these islands and their province on the mainland.

It was largely due to this influence that slavery soon became firmly established in South Carolina. At the time Charleston was settled, Barbados had a large slave population—about two Negroes to one white man—and a very rigid slave code was deemed necessary to keep the blacks under proper subjection. The Barbadian attitude toward slavery was brought over to the Ashley River colony, where conditions of soil and climate favored its perpetuation. For this reason and the additional one that in South Carolina the slaves also became more numerous than the freemen, this province imposed greater restraints on its Negroes than did any other continental colony. . . .

TWO DISPARATE REGIONS

All the territory on the mainland owned by the proprietors was in the early years designated under the term Carolina. They at first distinguished the two divisions of their province by calling the northern portion "our colony northeast of Cape Fear," and the southern "our colony southwest of Cape Fear." By the end of the seventeenth century the term North Carolina, as applied to the northern settlements, had come into use. North Carolina had a separate executive up until 1691, at which time Philip Ludwell became governor of the whole province of Carolina. He resided at Charleston and appointed a deputy for the northern province. Ludwell and his successors, however, paid little or no attention to their deputies in North Carolina. The bonds that held the northern and southern communities together were very slight. This nominal union of the two provinces continued until 1712, when a governor was appointed for North Carolina, and from that time until the end of the proprietary period the northern colony remained a separate province.

There was really no reason why these two distinct centers of colonization should ever have been united. For not only were they separated by a vast expanse of tractless forest, but the economic and social life in the two sections was quite different. In the southern province slavery took deep root quite early, while it developed slowly in the northern settlements. South Carolina carried on trade with the West Indies and Europe and had few dealings with the other English colonies on the mainland. The introduction of rice culture in South Carolina drew it into closer relations with Europe. North Carolina, on the other hand, traded with her sister colonies to the northward, and for a long time had hardly any commercial relations directly with the Old World. In South Carolina there was a prosperous town which was the center of life for the whole province; whereas in North Carolina there were no towns for a long time, and even as late as 1709 the only place that was called a town was a hamlet of twelve houses. In the former province, the social ideals were aristocratic; in the latter they were democratic.

FRENCH EXPANSION IN THE INTERIOR OF THE CONTINENT

DAVID HAWKE

Until the 1670s, the French presence in North America was primarily confined to present-day Canada and the Great Lakes region. According to David Hawke, a former history professor at the City University of New York, during this decade the French colonists began to send expeditions into the interior of the continent. Their objective, Hawke relates, was to claim the great inland basin of North America for their king and establish a profitable fur-trading business with the Indians. French explorers traveled the length of the Mississippi River to Louisiana, he writes, building a series of forts along the way. Hawke's numerous books include *Everyday Life in Early America, Those Tremendous Mountains: The Story of the Lewis and Clark Expedition,* and *The Colonial Experience,* from which the following selection is taken.

L ouis XIV came to the throne of France in 1661 determined, like Charles II of England, to rule, and he brought with him a young man named Jean Baptiste Colbert to help realize that ambition. Louis and Colbert together made France the greatest power in Europe, and at the same time they transformed Canada from a feeble colony into an enemy potentially capable of conquering the English empire in America. (Canada embraced that part of New France that bordered the

David Hawke, *The Colonial Experience*, Indianapolis: Bobbs-Merrill Company, Inc., 1966.
Copyright © 1966 by The Bobbs-Merrill Company, Inc. Reproduced by permission.

St. Lawrence River. It contained 3,418 white settlers in 1666, less than the population of Rhode Island.) Colbert assumed that French strength in Europe was related to her resources overseas. Canada played the key role in his precise plan to develop those resources. She would turn out ships, iron, and naval stores for France and produce food for the French West Indies, leaving those islands free to concentrate on tobacco, sugar, and indigo for the home market. The fur trade of New France would be extended to meet the costs of developing the American empire. Colbert's plan differed from England's fuzzy version of mercantilism in that one man was imposing his conception on the empire's development rather than allowing it to mature haphazardly, and the full strength of the French monarchy stood behind this plan, where in England the crown gave only half-hearted direction. Colbert never succeeded in making Canada a profitable enterprise for France—in the 1740's the crown was spending over two million livres to maintain the colony and receiving in import duties and taxes less than a quarter of a million—but when he died in 1683, New France loomed as a threat to the well-being of English America.

RUMORS OF A GREAT RIVER

Louis XIV and Colbert invigorated New France first by sending competent leaders. Jean Talon was dispatched as intendant. (Two royal officers shared between them all power over the affairs of New France. Military matters and Indian relations were vested in the governor general. The intendant controlled everything else, which meant mainly financial affairs and all local administration. The two officials supposedly checked, as well as helped, one another; but when strong men occupied the posts, the clash of wills often frustrated the sure direction of New France's affairs.) Talon was a man of force, imagination, and boldness. He centered his attention on the west, where the French advance had stopped after Jean Nicolet's trip to Green Bay in 1634 and where the Jesuits, whom Talon disliked, were the sole authority. In 1670 Talon sent an emissary to take possession of the great inland basin of North America for Louis with all the pomp possible to muster in a wilderness. One of the missionaries who went along returned with a report from Indians of a great river, which he assumed flowed to "the sea of Florida [the Gulf of Mexico] or that of California [the Pacific]." Talon feared that the English, either from the outpost they had erected on Hudson Bay or from Virginia, might reach the great river first, and he persuaded Frontenac, the recently arrived governor general, to send out an exploratory party at once.

Louis de Buade, Count Frontenac, was the second powerful personality Louis XIV sent to the colony. (So powerful, indeed, that Talon left for France not long after Frontenac arrived; he got along no better with Talon's replacement.) He arrived in 1672 at the age of fifty-two, a man of vigor, vision, and strong mind, three virtues that helped to balance but did not cancel out two failings. First, he came to Canada determined to reap profit for himself as much as for New France. (A 2 per cent cut on all beaver pelts exported by the company that monopolized New France's fur trade offered one among several ways that the governor general might line his pockets.) His ego, the size of a mountain, revealed a less tolerable failing. "He could not endure a rival," says a friendly biographer. "Opposition maddened him, and when crossed or thwarted, he forgot everything but his passion." He detested Talon, but instructions from the king reminded him that "after the increase of the colony of Canada, nothing is of greater importance for that country and for the service of his Majesty than the discovery of a passage to the South Sea." And with those words in mind, he backed Talon's suggestion that the Indian rumor of a great river be investigated. The task was given in May 1673 to Louis Jolliet, a onetime priest turned fur trader, and Father Jacques Marquette, a Jesuit who had long lived in the western country and knew a number of Indian dialects.

Jolliet and Marquette, with five men, left Green Bay in mid-June, paddled along the Wisconsin River and from there into the Mississippi, where they swept southward into a world unlike anything they had known. The outsize prevailed—prairies that stretched farther than the eye could see, catfish huge enough to upset canoes, cougars the size of tigers. They flushed a band of Indians who rode in dugouts and eyed their birchbark canoes with wonder. They swept past the noisy, muddy, and turbulent Missouri—"I have seen nothing more dreadful," Marquette wrote—and after a talk with Indians decided this was the route to California. Below the Ohio they met Indians who carried English guns. . . . A short while later they met natives who made them understand that the great river emptied into the Gulf of Mexico and that the Indians who lay below were ferocious. In mid-July, though still some seven hundred miles from the mouth, they turned back. The slow, upriver trip lasted until the end of September, when they reached Green Bay after an absence of four months on a trip of some twenty-five hundred miles.

DREAMS OF EMPIRE

The king's desire to follow Jolliet's and Marquette's explorations was frustrated for nearly a decade, for in 1672 he had launched a series of wars in Europe that left little energy to spare for New France. Fortunately, the exploration had fired the imagination of René-Robert Cavelier, Sieur de La Salle, a man of large dreams who had sailed for Canada in 1666 to make his fortune. La Salle, then twenty-three years old, began as a fur trader and quickly mastered the business. He learned several Indian languages and soon knew more about inland America than any man alive. He set out to revolutionize the fur business by controlling it from a central point, and because the plan had the double virtue of promoting the fortunes of both Frontenac and New France it was put into operation. Fort Frontenac went up on Lake Ontario at a spot designed to check Iroquois forays into the western country and to prevent the drifting of furs from that country southward into the hands of the English. La Salle ran the fort until 1677, when he sailed for France to win royal backing for a larger dream, for he now saw that the fur trade revealed only a small part of the wealth the interior of North America had to offer. Here, he realized, could be created the greatest agricultural and commercial empire in the world. Colbert caught the brilliance of La Salle's vision, and on his urging the king granted a patent to erect all the forts necessary to secure the Mississippi Basin for France.

La Salle returned to Canada late in 1678 accompanied by his able second-in-command, Henri de Tonty, an Italian who had lost an arm fighting in Sicily. First, a fort was built at the mouth of the Niagara River, a spot through which nearly all western trade had to funnel on its way east. Next came a series of forts along the Chicago, St. Joseph, and Illinois Rivers and on Lake Peoria. La Salle used his skill of persuasion with the Indians to bring order among the Western tribes. He taught them to settle close by his forts, where they could bring their furs for trade and come for protection if the Iroquois invaded the country. Once he had secured this territory, he set out in the winter of 1682 to explore the Mississippi to its mouth. On April 9, not far from the present site of New Orleans, La Salle claimed Louisiana, as he called it, and "all the nations, peoples, provinces, cities, towns, villages, mines, minerals, fisheries, streams, and rivers" that comprised the vast watershed of the Mississippi for King Louis XIV and France.

DISASTER IN TEXAS

La Salle fired others with his vision of a great inland empire for France, but in the end the dream came to nothing. The king gave him ships and men to establish a settlement at the mouth of the Mississippi. In 1685 he sailed into Spain's great "lake," the Caribbean, but missed the mouth of the river and landed with four hundred men in Texas at Matagorda Bay. The settlement had dwindled to forty-five by 1687 when La Salle made a desperate overland attempt to reach Fort St. Louis on the Illinois, where Tonty awaited him. On the way, however, he was murdered. He died at forty-three, "one of the greatest men of his age," said Tonty, certainly one of the greatest explorers of any age. His dreams exceeded his grasp, but they "ultimately proved to be so apt and shrewd that history has been right in elevating him to greatness, even though he carried to completion almost nothing of what he essayed."

The Quaker Settlements

George Brown Tindall and David E. Shi

George Brown Tindall is a professor emeritus of history at the
University of North Carolina in Chapel Hill. David E. Shi is a
history professor and the president of Furman University in
Greenville, South Carolina. In the following excerpt from their
book *America: A Narrative History*, Tindall and Shi provide an
account of the colonies settled by the Society of Friends, more
commonly known as the Quakers. The authors write that
William Penn, a prominent English Quaker, established the
colony of Pennsylvania as a religious sanctuary for Quakers and
members of other persecuted faiths. Furthermore, they state,
English Quakers also settled large portions of the territories that
would eventually become New Jersey and Delaware.

S hortly after the conquest of New Netherland in 1664, the
duke of York granted his lands between the Hudson and
the Delaware rivers to Sir George Carteret and Lord John
Berkeley (brother of Virginia's governor), and named the territory for Carteret's native island of Jersey. The New Jersey pro-
prietorship then passed through a sequence of incredible com-
plications. In 1674 Berkeley sold his share to a Quaker leader,
whose affairs were so encumbered that their management fell
to three trustees, one of whom was William Penn, another
prominent Quaker. In 1676, by mutual agreement, the colony
was divided by a diagonal line into East and West New Jersey,
with Carteret taking the east. Finally in 1682 Carteret sold out
to a group of twelve, including Penn, who in turn brought into

George Brown Tindall and David E. Shi, *America: A Narrative History*, New York: W.W.
Norton & Company, Inc., 1996. Copyright © 1984 by W.W. Norton & Company, Inc. Reproduced by permission.

partnership twelve more proprietors, for a total of twenty-four! In East New Jersey, peopled at first by perhaps 200 Dutch who had crossed the Hudson, new settlements gradually arose: some disaffected Puritans from New Haven founded Newark, Carteret's brother brought a group to found Elizabethtown (Elizabeth), and a group of Scots founded Perth Amboy. In the west, which faces the Delaware River, a scattering of Swedes, Finns, and Dutch remained, soon to be overwhelmed by swarms of English Quakers. In 1702 East and West New Jersey were united as a royal colony.

THE "HOLY EXPERIMENT"

The Quaker sect, as the Society of Friends was called in ridicule, was the most influential of many radical groups that sprang from the turbulence of the English Civil War. Founded by George Fox in about 1647, the Quakers carried further than any other group the doctrine of individual inspiration and inter-pretation—the "inner light," they called it. Discarding all for-mal sacraments and formal ministry—all spoke only as the spirit moved them—they refused deference to persons of rank, used the familiar "thee" and "thou" in addressing everyone, re-fused to take oaths because that was contrary to Scripture, and embraced pacifism. Quakers were subjected to intense perse-cution—often in their zeal they seemed to invite it—but never inflicted it on others. Their toleration extended to complete re-ligious freedom for all, of whatever belief or disbelief, and to the equality of sexes and the full participation of women in reli-gious affairs.

In 1673 George Fox had returned from an American visit with the vision of a Quaker commonwealth in the New World and had enticed others with his idea. The entrance of Quakers into the New Jersey proprietorships had encouraged Quakers to mi-grate, especially to the Delaware River side. And soon, across the river, arose Fox's "Holy Experiment," William Penn's Quaker commonwealth, the colony of Pennsylvania. Penn was the son of Admiral Sir William Penn, who had supported Par-liament in the Civil War and had led Oliver Cromwell's con-quest of Jamaica but later helped in the Restoration of the king. Young William was reared as a proper gentleman, but as a stu-dent at Oxford he had turned to Quakerism. His father dis-owned him, then after a reconciliation sent him off to France to get his mind on other things. It worked for a while, but Penn later came back to the Quaker faith.

Upon his father's death Penn inherited the friendship of the Stuarts and a substantial estate, including a claim of £16,000 his

William Penn

father had lent the crown. Whether in settlement of the claim or out of simple friendship he got from Charles II in 1681 proprietary rights to a tract extending westward from the Delaware River for 5 degrees of longitude and from the "beginning" of the 43rd degree on the north of the "beginning" of the 40th degree on the south. The land was named, at the king's insistence, for Penn's father: Pennsylvania (literally Penn Woods). The boundary overlapped lands granted to both New York and Maryland. The New York boundary was settled on the basis of the duke of York's charter at 42° North, but the Maryland boundary remained in question until 1767 when a compromise line (nineteen miles south of the 40th parallel) was surveyed by Charles Mason and Jeremiah Dixon—the celebrated Mason-Dixon line.

THE CHARACTER OF EARLY PENNSYLVANIA

When Penn assumed control of the area there was already a scattering of Dutch, Swedish, and English settlers on the west bank of the Delaware, but Penn was soon making vigorous efforts to bring in more settlers. He published glowing descriptions of the colony, which were translated into German, Dutch, and French. They were favorably received, especially by members of Pietist sects whose beliefs paralleled those of the Quakers. By the end of 1681 Penn had about 1,000 settlers in his province, and in October of the next year arrived himself with 100 more. By that time a town was growing up at the junction of the Schuylkill and Delaware Rivers. Penn called it Philadelphia (the City of Brotherly Love). Because of the generous terms on which Penn offered land, because indeed he offered aid to emigrants, the colony grew rapidly.

The relations between the Indians and the Quakers were cordial from the beginning, because of the Quakers' friendliness and because of Penn's careful policy of purchasing land titles from the Indians. Penn even took the trouble to learn the language of the Delawares, something few colonists even tried. For some fifty years the settlers and the natives lived side by side in peace, in relationships of such trust that Quaker farmers sometimes left their children in the care of Indians when they were away from home.

The government, which rested on three Frames of Government promulgated by Penn, resembled that of other proprietary colonies, except that the freemen (taxpayers and property owners) elected the councilors as well as the assembly. The governor had no veto—although Penn, as proprietor, did. "Any government is free . . . where the laws rule and the people are a party to the laws," Penn wrote in the 1682 Frame of Government. He hoped to show that a government could run in accordance with Quaker principles, that it could maintain peace and order without oaths or wars, and that religion could flourish without an established church and with absolute freedom of conscience. Because of its tolerance, Pennsylvania became a refuge not only for Quakers but for a variety of dissenters—as well as Anglicans—and early reflected the ethnic mixture of Scotch-Irish and Germans that became common to the middle colonies and the southern backcountry. Penn himself stayed only two years in the colony. Although he returned in 1699 for two more years, he continued at home the life of an English gentleman—and Quaker.

DELAWARE

In 1682 the duke of York also granted Penn the area of Delaware, another part of the Dutch territory. At first Delaware became part of Pennsylvania, but after 1701 it was granted the right to choose its own assembly. From then until the American Revolution it had a separate assembly, but had the same governor as Pennsylvania.

Religious Persecutions and Enthusiasms

—| CHAPTER 4 |—

ANNE HUTCHINSON AND THE ANTINOMIAN CONTROVERSY

MARILYN WESTERKAMP

During the first decade of its existence, the Massachusetts Bay Colony underwent a religious crisis that later became known as the Antinomian controversy. At the center of the controversy was Anne Hutchinson, a recent arrival from England who had quickly gained prominence in the colony as a religious lay leader. Hutchinson and her adherents were called Antinomians (literally, "above the law") because they argued that those who had been saved were above the rule of earthly ministers. This challenge to the authority of the colony's leaders created an upheaval that eventually resulted in Hutchinson's banishment.

In the following essay, Marilyn Westerkamp examines the theological, political, and social implications of the Antinomian controversy. A history professor at the University of California in Santa Cruz, Westerkamp is the author of *Women and Religion in Early America, 1600–1850: The Puritan and Evangelical Traditions* and *Triumph of the Laity: Scots-Irish Piety and the Great Awakening, 1625–1760.*

I n November 1637, Anne Hutchinson was banished from the colony of Massachusetts Bay. The sentence concluded her two-day trial before the General Court and resolved the most serious crisis that had threatened the colony during its first decade. . . .

The hostility surrounding Hutchinson at that moment starkly contrasted with the vast popularity she had enjoyed as a religious leader only eighteen months before. Intellectually gifted and personally charismatic, she had welcomed many to her home for private prayer and study. Her guests included men as well as women; many were among the highest leaders in the colony. Between sixty and eighty persons came weekly to hear her expound upon the week's sermons and advise them in their spiritual journeys, and she had, according to leading minister John Cotton, greatly helped many women of the town. "I doubt not but some of you [women] have also received much good from the Conference of this our Sister and by your Converse with her: and from her it may be you have received help in your spiritual Estates." Yet by November, she seemed almost friendless and powerless as she fought for her freedom, her own beliefs, and her status as a spiritual leader called by God. Who was this woman who attracted so many disciples? And why did government officials of this colony less than eight years old, a colony in the wilderness, find it necessary to throw her out?

Anne Marbury Hutchinson lived during an era of rising Puritan power, a time when the Puritan movement was growing in both numerical size and political strength. . . .

Like most Reformed Protestants of this era, Puritans were followers of John Calvin's theology. They believed in the total depravity of humanity, the inability of people to save themselves, and the gracious mercy of God in lifting a few chosen, or the elect, out of their evil pathways and bringing them to salvation. The atonement of Christ, through his Crucifixion, was a miracle, and the elect were able to accept Christ's love in faith through the intervention of divine grace, a grace that was irresistible. In other words, God empowered those few elect to have faith; the rest were left to the terrifying punishment they so justly deserved. Puritans believed that, from the beginning of time, all individuals had been predestined to either salvation or damnation. They knew that their destiny had been decided by God's arbitrary will, and no amount of virtuous acts or evildoing could change a believer's ultimate fate. Oddly enough, this lesson did not destroy hope or create anarchic pleasure-seeking. Instead, most Puritans, who were generally convinced of the real potential for their own salvation, struggled to convince themselves and others that they were indeed among the elect. . . .

HUTCHINSON'S BACKGROUND

Anne Marbury was born in 1591, the second of thirteen children. Her childhood was spent in the Puritan stronghold of Lincolnshire, East Anglia. Her parents, Bridget Dryden and Francis Marbury, were among the lesser gentry in England. As a girl, Anne Marbury would not have been formally educated, but from what is known about her parents, it might safely be supposed that she was well educated by them. Bridget Dryden was connected to a well-placed family network that would produce the poet laureate John Dryden in 1631. Francis Marbury seems to have been an obstreperous clergyman and a published theological writer who was deeply committed to the value of education. . . .

At twenty-one, Anne Marbury married William Hutchinson, a successful merchant living in her hometown—Alford, England. There the Hutchinsons prospered for twenty-two years, and during those years Anne bore fourteen children, all but two of whom survived into adulthood. Very little is known about the Hutchinsons during this central period of their lives. Alford seems to have been a good choice for business as William's trade increased with his family, and his reputation and status rose accordingly. But it was also a good choice for a clergyman's daughter who was deeply interested in the affairs of the soul and who embraced the cultural critique and spiritual intensity of the Lincolnshire Puritan community. Some twenty miles south, in the larger city of Boston, St. Botolph's Church was pastored by the renowned John Cotton. Although the Hutchinsons could travel there only occasionally, Anne found his preaching so inspiring that she attended his services whenever the long journey could be made. It is difficult to ascertain whether this was Anne's or William's desire. If the Hutchinsons' New England years fairly reflected their marriage, William pursued his economic and political callings while Anne attended to the spiritual side. Although a believer himself—William would become a member of the congregation after he had arrived in Massachusetts—he left religious leadership to his wife. In any case, Cotton so impressed Anne with his theological understanding and his experience of grace that she and her family followed him to New England and joined his congregation there. . . .

In 1634, Anne Hutchinson landed in Boston, one year after John Cotton was established as the teacher of the Boston congregation. There she found a colony scarcely four years old and

a town that was little more than a village with great ambitions. . . . As the wife of a prominent merchant, Anne would
have found a respectable position among Boston's matrons. Beyond this, . . . her biblical knowledge and theological sophisti-
cation also were soon greatly admired. Such skills and abilities
increased her reputation independently of William, but her rise
to prominence, and ultimate downfall, inexorably tied her husband's stature to her own.

For a while there were no problems. In the same month that
the Hutchinsons joined the church, the Reverend John Wilson
sailed for England to try, for a third and final time, to persuade
his wife to come to Massachusetts. People had been quite clear
about this matter. It was a scandal that Wilson was here without his family; and if his wife still refused to sail, he should remain in England. In Wilson's absence, Cotton served as the sole
pastor, and Hutchinson instituted her private religious meetings. Her superior intellect and charisma made her a natural
leader, and she quickly moved beyond explicating his sermons
to preaching her own. At some point, women began to bring
their husbands, and soon Hutchinson was holding two weekly
meetings, one for women only and one for both women and
men. . . . In 1635, Wilson, with his wife, returned to Massachusetts and the pulpit at the Boston Church; so, too, did the hot-
tempered minister John Wheelwright, Hutchinson's brother-in-
law, arrive. These two rigid, uncompromising personalities
would become key performers as the controversy took hold,
and the presence and activities of each one would stir his rival
to greater exertions in the cause of truth.

DISPUTES OVER THEOLOGY

Trouble when it first arose concerned neither of those men but
Cotton's dissatisfaction with the theology of his colleagues, including Wilson. Anne Hutchinson and her followers agreed
with Cotton's opinion and promoted his views, but the early
(and private) dispute occupied Cotton and a few ministers. One
theological issue involved the relationship between human effort and salvation. The Calvinist principles of predestination
and election placed salvation completely in the hands of God.
Believers could have no responsibility for their salvation because they had no ability to effect it. Grace extended to the elect
transformed their thoughts and actions, and such saints became
recognizable through their sanctified, or godly, behavior.

Cotton and the Hutchinsonians emphasized God's free, unconditional offer of divine grace and thus stressed the futility of human action and the value of an absolute, passive dependence upon an all-powerful God. While most New England ministers did not deny the twin truths of predestination and election, they thought that undue emphasis upon these two principles might lead to irreligion and anarchy. They understood the anxiety of believers desperate for some sign of their salvation and emphasized the hope that lay in the evidence of sanctification. Moreover, many promoted an idea that the potential saint could prepare for grace. Although acknowledging that human effort had no impact upon God, ministers encouraged people to study Scripture, attend services, watch their conduct, and pray so that they would be ready to receive divine grace. Such efforts may have kept believers from feeling desperate and lost, but Cotton found in this "preparationism" disturbing hints of salvation through works—earning your way into Heaven. Because Cotton enjoyed a gentle, conciliatory personality, he might well have been able to resolve quietly his differences with those colleagues had not Hutchinson and her followers become involved. In her meetings she had apparently condemned those who preached sanctification and preparationism, which challenged most ministers, and her disciples expressed those misgivings publicly and aggressively.

A second dispute involved the question of the union of the Holy Spirit with the saint. While most theologians rejected outright any idea of a persistent divine presence within the soul, Cotton embraced a belief in the indwelling of the Spirit, although he did not mean that any divine properties were communicated or granted to the believer. This question was not merely academic. Here was lodged the center of Hutchinson's charisma. She spoke and preached out of an authority that came not from a university education or a congregation's call (of course, women could not be called to ordination), but from the authority of the Spirit within. One disciple described her as "a Woman that Preaches better Gospel than any of your black-coats that have been at the Ninniversity, a Woman of another kind of spirit, who hath had many Revelations of things to come, and . . . I had rather hear such a one that speaks from the mere motion of the spirit, without any study at all, than any of your learned Scholars, although they may be fuller of Scripture."

In 1636, in response to the continuing strife, Puritan authorities held conferences, one in October and a second in December. Ostensibly, the clergy met to discuss their disagreements with Cotton, Wheelwright, and Hutchinson. How extraordinary that Hutchinson, a layperson and a woman, would attend such a conference! This reveals much about the situation in Massachusetts. The problem was not with Cotton questioning the preaching of other clergy, but with Hutchinson doing so. It might be argued that by bringing her to what was essentially a clerical conference, the clergy acknowledged her leadership. While they certainly denied her any legitimate claim to such a role, their actions unconsciously confirmed the strength of her spiritual authority. Any person suspected of heretical views, particularly a laywoman, could have been dealt with privately, but Hutchinson had so many followers that she had become a public figure. However, they could not afford to deal with her publicly because they might lose. At this point she was quite powerful; she had the support of Cotton, three magistrates, several deputies to the General Court, the majority of the congregation of the Boston Church, including the two lay elders, and the current governor of the colony, Henry Vane. . . . John Cotton remembered the first conference as fairly successful at achieving a common theological understanding, but the events of that autumn and the following year demonstrated that a final confrontation had merely been delayed.

CHANGES IN LEADERSHIP

A series of public confrontations began in the last months of 1636. Since these were the actions of men, Hutchinson was not directly involved. However, both the clergy and magistrates would later work on the assumption that Hutchinson was privately directing the charge. Boston's Hutchinsonians challenged the authority of Wilson by calling John Wheelwright as a third minister to the Boston Church; the effort was derailed by a small minority led by Deputy Governor John Winthrop, who invoked a technical rule that a pastoral call must be unanimous. Wilson then delivered a sermon on the sadly divided condition of the churches, pointing to the rise of new, dangerous opinions and further irritating his congregation. The General Court called for a "Day of Fasting" to pray for reconciliation, and Cotton invited Wheelwright to preach. He delivered an outrageous sermon that revived the theological controversy, attacked the concept of the fast itself, and argued that any who strove to do God's work were hypocrites pretending to salvation through their own merits. Encouraged by Wheelwright's sermon, the Hutchinsonians took their struggle into the outlying towns, heckling preachers, irritating their congregations, and refusing to serve in the militia organized to fight the Pequot, a local Indian nation, because the militia's chaplain was John Wilson.

The Hutchinsonians may have dominated Boston, but their influence ended there. When the General Court met in March 1637, a strong anti-Hutchinson coalition was evident. They approved Wilson's sermon, charged Wheelwright with sedition, and refused to consider petitions filed by Wheelwright's supporters. At Winthrop's recommendation, they moved the June elections to Newtown, effectively disenfranchising most Bostonians because they could not travel so far. At the June session, before petitions for Wheelwright could be read, Winthrop's faction called for elections, and the new majority elected Winthrop as governor and threw the two Boston magistrates and Henry Vane out of office. . . . The tide had turned, and Winthrop spent the rest of the summer dismantling the coalition and preparing for Anne Hutchinson's trial. . . .

Because Hutchinson's trial could end in her banishment, she could only be tried by the General Court. It was neither a criminal court moderated by a justice nor a supreme court with a panel of justices but rather the entire colonial government of governor, magistrates, and town representatives. While usually functioning as a legislature, the General Court did serve as the highest judiciary in the colony. In this incredible confrontation with the amassed political authority of the colony, Hutchinson revealed her formidable intellectual prowess. For one and one-half days she ran circles around her opponents. They quoted Scripture; she quoted back. They interpreted a verse against her; she responded with an alternative text. Winthrop began with a lengthy, condemnatory, rather frightening speech accusing her of disturbances, errors, and discord; he then demanded a response. She replied that she could not answer charges until she knew precisely what they were. She put Winthrop immediately on the defensive, for he had very few specific charges, and those he did have were supported only by hearsay.

THE ACCUSATIONS

He first said that she broke the Fifth Commandment—Honor thy father and thy mother—because she countenanced those who had signed the Wheelwright petitions and challenged the authority of the General Court, that is, their parents. She responded that she might entertain persons as children of God without approving their transgression. After a quick verbal thrust and parry, a frustrated Winthrop asserted that she did adhere to the petitioners' cause, she did endeavor to promote their faction, and thus she dishonored the magistrates, who stood as her parents, breaking the Fifth Commandment. Further, the Court did "not mean to discourse with those of your sex." Undoubtedly, Winthrop hoped to silence her, and perhaps calm the uneasiness of the General Court, by dismissing the right and ability of a woman to hold, maintain, and debate a dissenting opinion. However, such flourishes did not change the fact that debates with this woman continued.

Winthrop moved on to her private meetings. The Scriptures clearly forbade women to teach publicly, but, answered Hutchinson, her home was not public, and the Bible taught the duty of elder women to instruct younger ones. When questioned about men attending these meetings, she insisted that at mixed ones only the men spoke, and Winthrop had no evidence to countermand her assertion. When Winthrop refused to acknowledge that her biblical citations provided a rule for her leadership, she asked whether she must "shew my name written therein?" In a second outburst of frustrated authority, Winthrop announced that the meetings must end because he said so. "We are your judges, and not you ours and we must compel you to it." She agreed to accept the court's order.

However, her acquiescence did not satisfy the magistrates. They wanted her gone, for, as Deputy Governor Thomas Dudley complained during the trial, three years before the colony had been at peace, but from the moment that Hutchinson arrived, she had ignited great disturbances. Knowing that she was the primary problem, they sought weightier charges in order to banish her, and so they turned to her criticism of the clergy. If she had argued that the clergy were not preaching the true pathway to salvation, she implied that the colony's spiritual guides were beneath the regard of an ordinary congregant. The clergy believed, and the magistrates agreed, that such a view had to be curtailed and condemned, but Winthrop had to prove that Hutchinson had delivered such derogatory opinions. Initially, the magistrates' complaints sounded like hearsay and rumor. Magistrates had certainly heard the uncomplimentary opinions held by some Hutchinsonians about certain clergymen, but the magistrates had apparently never heard Hutchinson herself utter any such statements. Nor could they expect her followers to testify against her. Instead, Dudley and Winthrop opened a third fruitless dialogue, accusing Hutchinson of making statements that she then denied. Finally, cleric Hugh Peters, who hoped that he and other ministers "may not be thought to come as informers against the gentlewoman," proceeded to inform against her. At the December conference, Peters reported, Hutchinson had discounted their abilities and spirituality. She had said that they preached a Covenant of Works, that is, salvation through human endeavor, and so argued that they were not true ministers of the Gospel. Several clerics testified to their own memory of her statements, providing corroboration for each other's accounts. Hutchinson challenged her clerical accusers, at one point asking John Wilson for the notes that he took at the conference. The day ended with yet another standoff.

On the following morning, Hutchinson brilliantly redirected and enlivened the proceedings by demanding that those clergymen testifying against her swear an oath. In this request, she invoked standard legal procedure. She had read Wilson's notes and she asserted that she remembered the conversations differently. This obvious affront to the clergymen's veracity ignited a self-righteous defense of the reliability and sincerity of the ministers, but doubt had been raised, and the clergy proved reluctant to swear, lending credence to Hutchinson's challenges. She then asked that three witnesses be called. Although supporter John Coggeshall was frightened into silence, and church elder Thomas Leverett proved able to utter only three sentences before he was rebuffed by Winthrop, a third witness delivered his troubling testimony in full. John Cotton had not wanted to testify, but his own memory of the conference agreed with Hutchinson's account. He regretted that he and his colleagues should be compared, but he did recall mild disagreements, and the difference was not then "so ill taken as it is [now] and our brethren did say also that they would not so easily believe reports as they had done and withall mentioned that they would speak no more of it, some of them did; and afterwards some of them did say they were less satisfied than before." He also asserted that he "did not find her saying they were under a covenant of works, nor that she said they did preach a covenant of works."

By this point, the trial was proving a disaster for Winthrop.

Hutchinson had responded to the initial charges with skill and finesse. She outmaneuvered her opponents in scriptural argument and then graciously agreed to their demands. The later, more serious charge of sedition against the ministry held great promise, but it had to be substantiated with ministers' reports of a private conference held a year before. Just as the momentum seemed strongest, Hutchinson derailed the prosecution with the reasonable demand for sworn testimony, underlining the weakness of the prosecution's evidence. In the midst of the procedural discussion, three witnesses challenged the clerical version of the conference; and, while two were easily silenced, Cotton's personal authority and prestige demanded the court's attention. Winthrop was running out of arguments. Hoping to invoke the law to legitimate proceeding against Hutchinson, Winthrop found that she could use the trial to expose him and his government.

PROPHETIC REVELATIONS

Hutchinson chose this moment to proclaim her vision. Turning to her own spiritual conversion, she told the court of her early religious experiences: her doubts, her ultimate dependence upon God, and God's response to her pleas. She granted that she had become "more choice" in selecting a minister, for God had led her to distinguish the voices of truth.

> MR. NOWELL: How do you know that that was the spirit?
>
> MRS. H.: How did Abraham know that it was God that bid him offer his son, being a breach of the sixth commandment?
>
> DEP. GOV.: By an immediate voice.
>
> MRS. H.: So to me by an immediate revelation.
>
> DEP. GOV.: How! an immediate revelation.
>
> MRS. H.: By the voice of his own spirit to my soul.

Pouncing upon her testimony, Winthrop and other accusers pursued this question of revelation. They believed that any claim to a miraculous revelation was blasphemy, for the age of miracles had long passed. . . .

Many historians have judged Hutchinson weak in proclaiming her revelations. Surely a woman who displayed such intelligence during her trial knew better than to open this door. However, the moment might also be seen as one of exceptional strength. She began by warning, "Now if you do condemn me for speaking what in my conscience I know to be truth I must commit myself unto the Lord." She seemed to revel in her prophetic moment, as the court remained riveted upon her words. . . .

Long suspected of charisma grounded in her prophetic revelations, Hutchinson undermined the authority of secular and sacred leaders with her own spiritual power. At last she had openly claimed her own spiritual authority, for which her opponents were profoundly grateful, but they remained unable to convince many people, including Cotton, that her pronouncements were blasphemous. Winthrop and the clergy returned to charges of sedition and procedural rules of evidence, winning her banishment with the agreement of all but three participants. Winthrop must indeed have been satisfied.

Following this trial, the Hutchinsonian community divided. Some acknowledged their fault and remained in Massachusetts; some followed Wheelwright to a new colony in what would become New Hampshire; others, including the Hutchinson family, settled in Rhode Island. . . .

Anne's husband William served in the leadership of the new community, and the two grew frustrated at the bickering among the residents. After William died in 1642, Hutchinson and her seven younger children moved to Long Island where, in August 1643, she and six of the seven children were killed by Indians. In this violent end, some New Englanders found the divine vindication of Winthrop's work and judgment. . . .

Looking back over those three years during the first decade's settlement, the Hutchinsonians represented many threats to the governing elite. Personally, Winthrop had lost support among Boston's leadership and his premier position, sitting as deputy under twenty-two-year-old Governor Vane. The Hutchinsonian crisis also involved competition between Boston and the outlying towns that would support Winthrop against his own community. The theological differences were problematic, though initially resolvable, since both sides agreed that divine grace was freely granted, human effort had no impact upon salvation, and sanctified behavior was evidence of election. The involvement of the laity in the debates, and its criticism of the standing clergy, exacerbated the situation as people on each side, both clerical and lay, began to oversimplify issues and stereotype their opponents.

THE THREAT POSED BY A WOMAN

Still, the Hutchinsonian crisis involved more than politics, social conflict, and theological disputes. Under the trial and all of the accounts ran a current of male fury at the audacity of a woman to challenge the patriarchal magisterium. At her November trial, magistrates grieved that in leading these private meetings she was stepping outside her prescribed role. Winthrop would later say that she was more husband than wife, and he described William as "a man of very mild temper and weak parts, and wholly guided by his wife.". . .

Overall, it really is not surprising that the Puritan ministers and magistrates, committed as they were to their own patriarchal authority, would do everything possible to destroy her. She was a powerful woman who had attracted a significant community of female followers, and her example as a religious leader could have brought women to question their own acceptance of a subordinate domestic role. Her punishment certainly served as a deterrent to any other woman who might step outside the household. What is astonishing, however, is the trouble that she caused. If this truly had been an unbending patriarchal society, if Puritans truly felt that women had no authority and no power, they would not have worried about her. Rather than simply ignore her, or quietly censure her in church, the leadership brought her into clerical conferences and banished her from the colony, but not before further destroying her credibility through excommunication. Obviously, women could have power in this society in one of the colony's most important arenas—religion. Anne Hutchinson heard the voice of the Holy Spirit and said so. That is, she believed that God spoke through her, and so did many Bostonians. To women and men of influence, she spoke as a prophet.

Seventeenth-century Massachusetts was a paradoxical society that embraced an intense, personal spirituality and yet valued an ordered hierarchy as outlined in the Bible. People embraced the voice of the Holy Spirit, for it offered personal assurance of salvation and privileged community efforts to establish an exemplary biblical commonwealth. Still, Puritan leaders knew that God did not respect earthly inequalities of wealth, class, education, and gender. They knew that the ignorant, the poor, and women could be touched by the Spirit, and they did not want to share their civil or spiritual power with any women. The charismatic Hutchinson, whose experience of the Holy Spirit was revealed in prophetic speeches, undermined the established secular and sacred authority. An intellectually powerful woman who criticized clergymen represented a threat to order at many levels. During the state trial, Anne Hutchinson successfully countered biblical arguments and acceded to all demands that she cease public activity, yet she was still dangerous to the leaders. Even in silence, a woman claiming an authority from God that was recognized by the majority of her community represented a threat to the standing order. A woman who received revelations from God was under no civil or clerical control. In the end, although the ostensible cause for her banishment was sedition, the primary factors that drove her accusers were her leadership of women and men, her claims to prophetic revelations, and the challenge that these threats represented to their own magistracy and patriarchal power.

THE SALEM WITCHCRAFT TRIALS

PAULA A. TRECKEL

The village of Salem, Massachusetts, experienced an outbreak of witchcraft hysteria during 1692. Several girls and young women of the town began to behave strangely, falling into violent fits; they claimed that they had been hexed by witches and named a number of citizens as their assailants. By the time the frenzy ended, fourteen women and five men (including a minister) had been hanged for the crime of witchcraft. One man had died while being tortured to force a confession, and at least two of the accused had perished in prison while awaiting trial.

Historians and other experts have suggested many factors that may have contributed to the tragic events in Salem, including mass hysteria, physical illnesses that could have caused the young accusers to hallucinate about witches, and social tensions between various factions in the village. Paula A. Treckel, a professor of history at Allegheny College in Meadville, Pennsylvania, explores several possible reasons for the witch craze in the following selection from her book *To Comfort the Heart: Women in Seventeenth-Century America*.

W itchcraft was a capital offense in the law codes drawn up in all the colonies. Although it was perceived as a crime against God, it was considered a crime against the state, and witchcraft trials took place in civil courts. In the colonies, as in Europe, witchcraft was a crime identified with middle-aged and married women. Of the 344 people accused of witchcraft in New England during the seventeenth century,

Paula A. Treckel, *To Comfort the Heart: Women in Seventeenth-Century America*, New York: Twayne Publishers, 1996. Copyright © 1996 by Twayne Publishers. Reproduced with the permission of Macmillan Library Reference USA, a division of Ahsuog, Inc.

nearly 80 percent were women. Most accused women were 40 years of age or older, although only 18 percent were more than 60 years old. Nearly three-quarters of those accused of witchcraft before the Salem outbreak were women. Around half of the men accused of witchcraft were suspect by virtue of their relationship to accused women.

Witchcraft accusations were often preceded by years of gossip about a woman's character and behavior. As long as she had a male family member to defend her name in a court of law, such gossip could be deflected before it culminated in accusations of witchcraft. Some men sued their daughters' or wives' accusers for slander or defamation of character to protect them from further charges. Turning the tables—taking the offensive— men shielded their womenfolk from attack. Once a woman's male protector died, she was defenseless against her neighbors' gossip. Single, widowed, divorced, or deserted women without the direct protection of a male relative were especially vulnerable to witchcraft accusation. Although some women sued their accusers for slander themselves, this was risky; if the accuser's case appeared credible, the accused further jeopardized her position. Although a woman might win her slander suit, her reputation usually suffered. By taking action against her accuser, she had to be aggressive and assertive, defying the Puritan ideal of the submissive goodwife.

Women accused of witchcraft in New England came from all levels of society, but most were of the "middling sort." Although the courts tended to dismiss allegations against wealthy women from prominent families, poorer women did not fare so well. They were disproportionately represented among those convicted of witchcraft in colonial New England. Another factor that made some women especially vulnerable to witchcraft accusation in New England was the Puritans' inheritance laws, designed to keep property in men's hands, and the restrictions they placed on women's property rights. Women who were their parents' sole heir, had no sons of their own, or were childless stood to inherit and control more property than many men in the region. In a culture where property meant power, these women were especially threatening. They were looked on with suspicion by their neighbors and accused of using occult powers to acquire their wealth. . . .

Wars with Native Americans, the Antinomian and Quaker Controversies, the Restoration of Charles II, and the Glorious

Revolution challenged the Puritan's mission in New England. By the end of the seventeenth century the values that united the original colonists had changed. The earliest years of settlement were characterized by a sense of community and cooperation—values that enabled the first generation of settlers to survive the wilderness and create God's "citee upon a hill." But economic success soon supplanted concerns about salvation, individualism emerged as the avenue for advancement, and competition replaced cooperation as the way to achieve success. The early social hierarchy based on church membership and service to the community gave way to a new one based on wealth and generated by self-interest. These changes had unfortunate consequences. Frustrated ministers preached powerful sermons, "Jeremiads," claiming that God was displeased with the people of New England and was punishing them. As people's sense of guilt, coupled with feelings of resentment and jealousy, grew, they looked for someone on whom to blame their problems. Satan, they claimed, was in their midst, bringing God's wrath down upon them. And who were Satan's handmaidens? Witches!

The witchcraft hysteria that swept New England and culminated in the trials at Salem, Massachusetts, in 1692 was a sad expression of women's involvement in the region's religious life. As both accusers and the accused, women gave voice to the beliefs of their day. Their powerlessness and despair were emblematic of deeper anxieties that infected the entire culture and fueled the witchcraft craze. And they were its principle victims.

Despite the religious orthodoxy of New England, many colonists—even "Saints"—believed in magic. Religious belief supposes a supernatural authority that may be influenced only through prayer. Magic, on the other hand, permits one to harness supernatural forces for his or her own ends. But the boundaries between what a culture defines as religion and magic are fragile and blurred. Although Puritan theologians tried to purge the Anglican Church of its "magical" symbols and eliminate forever the belief in magic, they failed. Despite their claims that religious and magical traditions were antithetical, the common people refused to surrender "folk" beliefs—the charms, spells, superstitions, and traditions—that gave them a sense of control over their lives. A pregnant woman, for example, might earnestly pray to God for a safe delivery, yet consult the village "wise woman" for a charm to ensure her good health or to dis-

Often falling into violent fits, "afflicted" women testified against accused witches during the Salem witchcraft trials in 1692.

cover the sex of her unborn child. Even the most learned Puritan men blamed unusual natural phenomena on ghosts and specters or saw them as portents of things to come. Plagues of locusts, comets, earth tremors, and mighty storms were signs that in both the visible and the invisible world God was at war with Satan. Although some ministers warned women and men that they were helpless to control their fate, even they protected themselves and their families with magic.

"White magic," the use of the occult to achieve positive ends, was relatively common in seventeenth-century America and viewed by most colonists as harmless. Potions and charms used to divine the future, ward off spells, and cure physical ailments, bore close resemblance to the medicines—homemade cordials, liquors, and poultices—made by women to remedy their families' ills. Virtually every New England town also had a "wise woman" known for her ability to treat the sick or her skill as a midwife. Some of them probably crossed the tenuous boundary between medicine and the occult. . . .

Many women accused of witchcraft in the colonies prior to the Salem outbreak were healers or midwives. . . .

Since maternity was the focus of most women's lives, women

whose childbearing experience was "exceptional" were also regarded with suspicion. Anne Hutchinson and Rebecca Nurse of Salem, Massachusetts, had remarkable success in the bearing and rearing of children and were suspected of practicing witchcraft to ensure their good fortune. Women plagued by miscarriage or the death of a child were also viewed with trepidation by their neighbors; those accused of practicing witchcraft were twice as likely as their peers to be childless. Thus, women suspected of somehow interfering with birth and death, especially those recognized as nurses or midwives, were vulnerable to witchcraft accusation. Many accused women were from the lower classes, but more from the middle and upper classes were "cried out" as the century progressed. The disintegration of the value system that bound Puritan communities together and the restructuring of the social hierarchy contributed to this change in who was "blamed" for the region's problems.

The Salem Village witchcraft trials of 1692 marked the climax of witchcraft belief in colonial New England. Late in the winter of 1691, a group of young girls met secretly in the Salem Village home of the Reverend Samuel Parris. Among them were Parris's daughter Elizabeth and his niece Abigail Williams. The girls wished to know who they would marry and "what trade their sweethearts should be of." To divine their fate, they created a primitive crystal ball from egg whites and a glass of water. But when their magic crystal revealed images of coffins, they were frightened. These daughters of Puritans knew that what they had done was wrong.

Early in 1692 young Elizabeth Parris and her cousin Abigail fell ill with "odd postures," "distempers," and "fits." When the physician could not diagnose their disturbing behavior, he attributed it to witchcraft. And as rumors of the girls' affliction spread throughout the village, other girls involved in their fortune-telling exhibited strange behavior, too. Finally, on 29 February 1692, warrants were issued for three Salem Village women whom the girls claimed had bewitched them.

A TALE OF TWO FAMILIES

Had events at Salem followed the pattern of earlier witchcraft accusations, the incident would most likely have ended with the imprisonment and trial of these three women. But the circumstances of Salem Village distinguished this outbreak from others. Deep-seated divisions in the community—embodied by the Putnam and Porter families—reflected the very different values battling for primacy in late seventeenth-century New England. This conflict fueled the outbreak of witchcraft at Salem.

John Putnam and John Porter came to Salem during the 1640s. Both prospered as farmers, but a half-century later the fortunes of their descendants diverged. The Putnams continued to farm the rocky lands around Salem, but watched helplessly as their wealth and political influence declined. The Porters diversified, participated in trade with surrounding communities, and prospered. The corporate values espoused by the earliest Puritan settlers, and embodied by the Putnams, gave way to the competition and individualism of a new, commercial age, represented by the Porters; while the Putnams held fast to the old, the Porters embraced the new. The Putnams fought hard to retain their influence in the Salem Village church—the traditional heart of their community. They championed the selection of the Reverend Samuel Parris in the face of the Porters' opposition. Thus, beneath the surface of Salem Village life, an intense battle raged between two families—two value systems—for the future of New England.

Within this family conflict, the experiences of Ann Carr Putnam and her daughter Ann Putnam illustrate how women's powerlessness and dependence fed the hysteria at Salem. The daughter of George Carr, one of the wealthiest men in Salisbury, Massachusetts, Ann Carr married Thomas Putnam, Jr., in 1678. The young couple had every reason to expect their fortunes would increase. But when George Carr died, he willed the bulk of his estate to his widow and his sons; Ann received only a modest cash settlement, much to her husband's disappointment. Thomas Putnam's widowed father remarried a younger woman and fathered a son, Joseph. When Putnam died in 1686, he left the best part of his estate to his widow and Joseph, naming them joint executors. Thomas challenged the wills of his father and his father-in-law to no avail. He was further angered when Joseph married into the Porter family, taking with him the wealth he inherited from their father. As Thomas witnessed his wealth and influence decline through no fault of his own, he felt powerless to control his fate. He attributed his bad fortune to witchcraft.

Ann Carr Putnam was embittered by the actions of her father and helpless to assuage her husband's anger. She witnessed her family's decline with a sense of frustration, outrage, and jealousy, but as a dutiful goodwife was prohibited from expressing these emotions. At the same time, she harbored a sense of guilt: she was a disappointment to her husband, who had married her in hopes of advancing himself. Following their marriage, Ann gave birth to four sons and six daughters, including her namesake, Ann. While sons were an asset to a farming family, daughters were a liability, especially in an era of declining opportunity. Because a girl's future as a wife depended on the size of her dowry, it is little wonder that young Ann was among the girls divining their fates at the Reverend Parris's house. Most of Salem's "afflicted girls," like young Ann Putnam, were actually young single women over the age of 16. Many had lost one or more of their parents in the Indian wars that plagued New England's frontier and had been taken in by relatives. Few of these penniless young women had any real hope of marrying. Anxious about their futures, yet powerless to control them, they sought answers from a crystal ball.

The outrageous behavior of Salem's afflicted girls and women immediately thrust them into the public eye. Ordinarily, they would have been punished severely for their actions, but these were extraordinary times in Salem. Important men examined them and concluded that they were possessed. When asked who afflicted them, the girls were slow to identify their tormenters. When pressed, however, they named three women: Tituba, a West Indian slave owned by the Reverend Parris, Sarah Good, and Sarah Osborne. All were arrested and imprisoned in Boston to await trial.

THE ACCUSED

Tituba was an outsider. A native of Barbados, possibly of both African and West Indian ancestry, she was probably exposed to Native American and African religions on this Caribbean island. Although she came to Salem as the Reverend Parris's slave, it is unlikely that she was a baptized Christian. Whether Tituba practiced what the English colonists called witchcraft or merely worshipped her God or gods as she saw fit, she was an easy target for accusation in Salem.

Imprisoned with Mary Black, another slave accused during the witchcraft hysteria, Tituba testified that in Barbados she learned how to discover a witch and prevent bewitchment. And she admitted making a cake of meal and the afflicted girls' urine "to find out the Witch," an age-old method used by English folk to ward off enchantment. She argued that she was not a witch, although "her Master did beat her and otherways abuse her to make her confess and accuse (such as he call'd) her Sister-Witches." A slave in a free society, a person of color in a white society, a woman in a society dominated by men, Tituba fulfilled the expectations of her masters by confessing. But, in doing so, she saved her life.

Sarah Good's life was filled with misfortune. The daughter of a wealthy man, Sarah married beneath herself, a penniless indentured servant. When he died, Sarah was held liable for his debts and had to sell her dowry lands. Her second husband, a weaver, was unable to support her. They lost their home and depended on the charity of Salem's residents to survive. A bitter, angry woman, Sarah Good grudgingly accepted assistance for herself and her young daughter, Dorcas. Those who helped her criticized her resentful attitude and feared her muttered curses. Even her husband feared her wrath, testifying at her trial that he was "afraid that she was a witch or would be one very quickly." Pregnant at the time of her arrest, Sarah Good reminded all women of their vulnerability: a bad marriage could propel a woman from wealth to poverty. In Sarah, they saw their own worst fears come to life.

Sarah Price Osborne was neither poor nor an outsider. A long-time Salem resident, she was the wife of a successful village farmer. When her husband died, he left his considerable property to her in trust for their two sons. But village gossips had much to talk about when Sarah married her young Irish indentured servant, Alexander Osbourne, and tried to break her first husband's will. In trying to secure title to her sons' inheritance, Sarah violated the ideal of the selfless goodwife who placed her children's welfare before her own. She also challenged the colony's laws regarding inheritance. Her behavior attracted the censure of both women and men, who saw her as a threat to their own values and well-being. Goody (short for Goodwife) Osborne died of natural causes on 10 May 1692 while imprisoned in Boston.

Tituba, Sarah Good, and Sarah Osborne were women the afflicted girls knew made Salem's adults uncomfortable. Tituba's confession prompted the afflicted girls' inquisitors to ask if there were other witches in the community. At first they named no others, but then young Ann Putnam accused Martha Corey of witchcraft.

Goodwife Corey laughed when told she was accused of

witchcraft. She pointed out that she was a "Gosple-woman"— a church member—and claimed there were no witches in New England. But her accusation marked a major change in whom the girls of Salem "cried out" as witches. The circle of the accused expanded to include married women of property and standing in the community, church members, and even men. Instead of targeting those who violated the norms of their society, the girls "cried out" those whose who embodied the very qualities they were reared to respect and emulate. Martha Corey, a "Gosple-woman," epitomized the ideal Puritan goodwife.

The afflicted girls then named the elderly Rebecca Nurse and middle-aged Elizabeth Procter, both from wealthy families, as their tormenters. Goody Nurse was the daughter of a suspected witch, and her sisters—Mary Easty and Sarah Cloyse—were also accused, tried, and found guilty of witchcraft at Salem. Little Dorcas Good, Sarah Good's daughter, was also accused of witchcraft and confessed, while Elizabeth Procter was the granddaughter of an accused witch. Many who had survived earlier suspicions of witchcraft—Bridget Bishop, Susanna Martin, and Dorcas Hoar—lost their lives at Salem, and even male relatives of the accused were vulnerable. Elizabeth Procter's husband, John, was the first man named at Salem. Giles Corey, Martha's husband, was also accused of witchcraft and died while being tortured to exact a plea.

Of the nearly 200 people accused of witchcraft in the Salem outbreak, 75 percent were women. That so many men were accused probably reflects the underlying political tensions within the community. It is also possible that the afflicted girls, emboldened by community support, directly challenged men's authority by accusing them, as well as their wives, mothers, and daughters, of witchcraft.

By the summer of 1692, the circle of witchcraft accusation widened to include men and women whose "quality . . . did bespeak better things" and whose "blameless and holy lives before did testify for them." Among those accused were Governor William Phips's wife, Lady Mary Phips, and the wife of the Reverend John Hale. When one of the most respected ministers in the colony, the Reverend Samuel Willard, was named, the ministers and magistrates decided to halt the trials. But before the trials ended in October 1692, at least fifty people accused of witchcraft in Salem and surrounding towns had confessed. The majority of confessed witches were women. The authorities' decision to spare those who admitted their guilt probably prompted some of these confessions, for those who did not confess and were found guilty were executed by hanging. . . .

WOMEN AS REBELS AND VICTIMS

The events in Salem in 1692 marked a turning point in women's religious lives in Puritan New England. The afflicted girls' beliefs and fears led them to accuse others in their community of witchcraft. Ministers, magistrates, and townspeople initially encouraged their actions to revitalize religious faith and restore traditional values in their community. Yet even as the afflicted girls reinforced the subordinate position of women in Puritan society through their accusation of other women, they rebelled against the gender norms of their community. When their accusations reached beyond those suspected by their community of sinful, inappropriate behavior, they threatened the very foundations of Puritan patriarchy. The ministers and magistrates had to restrain them to preserve their authority in the community. . . .

That women were chief among both the accusers and the accused at Salem, demonstrates how deeply Puritans' ideas about women's sinful nature were imbedded in the minds of all. Frustration, resentment, fear, and self-loathing led the afflicted girls to turn on other women, the most vulnerable in their society, and blame them for their own powerlessness. Thus, female accusers and the accused, alike, were victims at Salem.

SINNERS IN THE HANDS OF AN ANGRY GOD

JONATHAN EDWARDS

During the eighteenth century, a powerful religious revival known as the Great Awakening swept across Europe, England, and the American colonies. This movement offered an emotionally stirring alternative to the solemn style of worship then typical in most Protestant churches. Many historians consider Jonathan Edwards, a Massachusetts minister, one of the most important and influential theologians of this era. The following selection is excerpted from his famous sermon, "Sinners in the Hands of an Angry God," which was first delivered at Enfield, Massachusetts, on July 8, 1741. In this classic example of a hellfire-and-brimstone sermon, Edwards employs vivid and even frightening imagery to awaken his listeners to the danger of remaining unrepentant of their sins. Emphasizing that each individual can be saved only through the mercy of God, he urges his congregation to make a heartfelt commitment to Christ.

God has laid Himself under no obligation by any promise to keep any natural man out of hell one moment. God certainly has made no promises either of eternal life or of any deliverance or preservation from eternal death but what are contained in the covenant of grace, the promises that are given in Christ, in whom all the promises are yea and amen. But surely they have no interest in the promises of the covenant of

Jonathan Edwards, *Sinners in the Hands of an Angry God: A Sermon Preached at Enfield, July 8th, 1741*, Boston: S. Kneeland and T. Green, 1741.

grace who are not the children of the covenant, who do not believe in any of the promises, and have no interest in the Mediator of the covenant.

So that, whatever some have imagined and pretended about
promises made to natural men's earnest seeking and knocking,
it is plain and manifest that whatever pains a natural man takes
in religion, whatever prayers he makes, till he believes in Christ,
God is under no manner of obligation to keep him a moment
from eternal destruction.

So that, thus it is that natural men are held in the hand of
God, over the pit of hell, they have deserved the fiery pit, and
are already sentenced to it; and God is dreadfully provoked, His
anger is as great towards them as to those that are actually suffering the executions of the fierceness of His wrath in hell, and
they have done nothing in the least to appease or abate that
anger, neither is God in the least bound by any promise to hold
them up one moment; the devil is waiting for them, hell is gaping for them, the flames gather and flash about them, and
would fain lay hold on them, and swallow them up; the fire
pent up in their own hearts is struggling to break out; and they
have no interest in any Mediator, there are no means within
reach that can be any security to them. In short, they have no
refuge, nothing to take hold of; all that preserves them every
moment is the mere arbitrary will, and uncovenanted, un-
obliged forbearance of an incensed God.

WICKEDNESS AND THE PERILS OF HELL

The use of this awful subject may be for awakening unconverted persons in this congregation. This that you have heard
is the case of every one of you that are out of Christ. That world
of misery, that lake of burning brimstone is extended abroad under you. There is the dreadful pit of the glowing flames of the
wrath of God; there is hell's wide gaping mouth open; and you
have nothing to stand upon, nor any thing to take hold of: there
is nothing between you and hell but the air; it is only the power
and mere pleasure of God that holds you up.

You probably are not sensible of this; you find you are kept
out of hell, but do not see the hand of God in it; but look at other
things, as the good state of your bodily constitution, your care
of your own life, and the means you use for your own preservation. But indeed these things are nothing: if God should withdraw His hand, they would avail no more to keep you from

falling, than the thin air to hold up a person that is suspended in it.

Your wickedness makes you as it were heavy as lead, and to tend downwards with great weight and pressure towards hell; and if God should let you go, you would immediately sink and swiftly descend and plunge into the bottomless gulf, and your healthy constitution, and your own care and prudence, and best contrivance, and all your righteousness, would have no more influence to uphold you and keep you out of hell, than a spider's web would have to stop a fallen rock. Were it not for the sovereign pleasure of God, the earth would not bear you one moment; for you are a burden to it; the creation groans with you; the creature is made subject to the bondage of your corruption, not willingly; the sun does not willingly shine upon you to give you light to serve sin and Satan; the earth does not willingly yield her increase to satisfy your lusts; nor is it willingly a stage for your wickedness to be acted upon; the air does not willingly serve you for breath to maintain the flame of life in your vitals, while you spend your life in the service of God's enemies. God's creatures are good, and were made for men to serve God with, and do not willingly subserve to any other purpose, and groan when they are abused to purposes so directly contrary to their nature and end. And the world would spew you out, were it not for the sovereign hand of Him who hath subjected it in hope. There are black clouds of God's wrath now hanging directly over your heads, full of the dreadful storm, and big with thunder; and were it not for the restraining hand of God, it would immediately burst forth upon you. The sovereign pleasure of God, for the present, stays His rough wind; otherwise it would come with fury, and your destruction would come like a whirlwind, and you would be like the chaff of the summer threshing floor.

GOD'S MIGHTY WRATH

The wrath of God is like great waters that are dammed for the present; they increase more and more, and rise higher and higher, till an outlet is given; and the longer the stream is stopped, the more rapid and mighty is its course when once it is let loose. It is true that judgment against your evil works has not been executed hitherto: the floods of God's vengeance have been withheld; but your guilt in the meantime is constantly increasing, and you are every day treasuring up more wrath; the waters are constantly rising, and waxing more and more mighty; and there is nothing but the mere pleasure of God that holds the waters back, that are unwilling to be stopped, and press hard to go forward. If God should only withdraw His hand from the floodgate, it would immediately fly open, and the fiery floods of the fierceness and wrath of God, would rush forth with inconceivable fury, and would come upon you with omnipotent power; and if your strength were ten thousand times greater than it is, yea, ten thousand times greater than the strength of the stoutest, sturdiest devil in hell, it would be nothing to withstand or endure it.

The bow of God's wrath is bent, and the arrow made ready on the string, and justice bends the arrow at your heart, and strains the bow, and it is nothing but the mere pleasure of God, and that of an angry God, without any promise or obligation at all, that keeps the arrow one moment from being made drunk with your blood. Thus all you that never passed under a great change of heart, by the mighty power of the Spirit of God upon your souls, all you that were never born again, and made new creatures, and raised from being dead in sin, to a state of new, and before altogether unexperienced light and life, are in the hands of an angry God. However you may have reformed your life in many things, and may have had religious affections, and may keep up a form of religion in your families and closets, and in the house of God, it is nothing but His mere pleasure that keeps you from being this moment swallowed up in everlasting destruction. However unconvinced you may now be of the truth of what you hear, by and by you will be fully convinced of it. Those that are gone from being in the like circumstances with you see that it was so with them; for destruction came suddenly upon most of them; when they expected nothing of it and while they were saying, peace and safety: now they see that those things on which they depended for peace and safety, were nothing but thin air and empty shadows.

The God that holds you over the pit of hell, much as one holds a spider or some loathsome insect over the fire, abhors you, and is dreadfully provoked: His wrath towards you burns like fire. He looks upon you as worthy of nothing else but to be cast into the fire; He is of purer eyes than to bear to have you in His sight; you are ten thousand times more abominable in His eyes than the most hateful venomous serpent is in ours. You have offended Him infinitely more than ever a stubborn rebel did his prince; and yet it is nothing but His hand that holds you from falling into the fire every moment. It is to be ascribed to nothing else, that you did not go to hell the last night; that you was suffered to awake again in this world, after you closed your eyes to sleep. And there is no other reason to be given, why you have not dropped into hell since you arose in the morning, but that God's hand has held you up. There is no other reason to be given why you have not gone to hell, since you have sat here in the house of God, provoking His pure eyes by your sinful wicked manner of attending His solemn worship. Yea, there is nothing else that is to be given as a reason why you do not this very moment drop down into hell.

THOSE WHO DESERVE DAMNATION

O sinner! Consider the fearful danger you are in: it is a great furnace of wrath, a wide and bottomless pit, full of the fire of wrath, that you are held over in the hand of that God, whose wrath is provoked and incensed as much against you, as against many of the damned in hell. You hang by a slender thread, with the flames of divine wrath flashing about it, and ready every moment to singe it, and burn it asunder; and you have no interest in any Mediator, and nothing to lay hold of to save yourself, nothing to keep off the flames of wrath, nothing of your own, nothing that you ever have done, nothing that you can do, to induce God to spare you one moment. . . .

How dreadful is the state of those that are daily and hourly in the danger of this great wrath and infinite misery! But this is the dismal case of every soul in this congregation that has not been born again, however moral and strict, sober and religious, they may otherwise be. Oh that you would consider it, whether you be young or old! There is reason to think that there are many in this congregation now hearing this discourse that will actually be the subjects of this very misery to all eternity. We know not who they are, or in what seats they sit, or what thoughts they now have. It may be they are now at ease, and hear all these things without much disturbance, and are now flattering themselves that they are not the persons, promising themselves that they shall escape. If they knew that there was one person, and but one, in the whole congregation, that was to be the subject of this misery, what an awful thing would it be to think of! If we knew who it was, what an awful sight would it be to see such a person! How might all the rest of the congregation lift up a lamentable and bitter cry over him! But, alas! instead of one, how many is it likely will remember this discourse in hell? And it would be a wonder, if some that are now present should not be in hell in a very short time, even before this year is out. And it would be no wonder if some persons, that now sit here, in some seats of this meetinghouse, in health, quiet and secure, should be there before tomorrow morning. Those of you that finally continue in a natural condition, that shall keep out of hell longest will be there in a little time! your damnation does not slumber; it will come swiftly, and, in all probability, very suddenly upon many of you. You have reason to wonder that you are not already in hell. It is doubtless the case of some whom you have seen and known, that never deserved hell more than you, and that heretofore appeared as likely to have been now alive as you. Their case is past all hope; they are crying in extreme misery and perfect despair; but here you are in the land of the living and in the house of God, and have an opportunity to obtain salvation. What would not those poor damned hopeless souls give for one day's opportunity such as you now enjoy!

CHRIST IS CALLING

And now you have an extraordinary opportunity, a day wherein Christ has thrown the door of mercy wide open, and stands in calling and crying with a loud voice to poor sinners; a day wherein many are flocking to Him, and pressing into the kingdom of God. Many are daily coming from the east, west, north and south; many that were very lately in the same miserable condition that you are in are now in a happy state, with their hearts filled with love to Him who has loved them, and washed them from their sins in His own blood, and rejoicing in hope of the glory of God. How awful is it to be left behind at such a day! To see so many others feasting, while you are pining and perishing! To see so many rejoicing and singing for joy of heart, while you have cause to mourn for sorrow of heart, and howl for vexation of spirit! How can you rest one moment in such a condition?. . .

Are there not many here who have lived long in the world, and are not to this day born again? and so are aliens from the commonwealth of Israel, and have done nothing ever since they have lived, but treasure up wrath against the day of wrath? Oh, sirs, your case, in an especial manner, is extremely dangerous. Your guilt and hardness of heart is extremely great. Do you not see how generally persons of your years are passed over and left, in the present remarkable and wonderful dispensation of God's mercy? You had need to consider yourselves, and awake thoroughly out of sleep. You cannot bear the fierceness and wrath of the infinite God. And you, young men, and young women, will you neglect this precious season which you now enjoy, when so many others of your age are renouncing all youthful vanities, and flocking to Christ? You especially have now an extraordinary opportunity; but if you neglect it, it will soon be with you as with those persons who spent all the precious days in youth in sin, and are now come to such a dreadful pass in blindness and hardness. And you, children, who are unconverted, do not you know that you are going down to hell, to bear the dreadful wrath of that God, who is now angry with you every day and every night? Will you be content to be the children of the devil, when so many other children in the land are converted, and are become the holy and happy children of the King of kings?

And let every one that is yet of Christ, and hanging over the pit of hell, whether they be old men and women, or middle-aged, or young people, or little children, now hearken to the loud calls of God's word and providence. This acceptable year of the Lord, a day of such great favors to some, will doubtless be a day of as remarkable vengeance to others. Men's hearts harden, and their guilt increases apace at such a day as this, if they neglect their souls; and never was there so great danger of such person being given up to hardness of heart and blindness of mind. God seems now to be hastily gathering in His elect in all parts of the land; and probably the greater part of adult persons that ever shall be saved, will be brought in now in a little time, and that it will be as it was on the great outpouring of the Spirit upon the Jews in the apostles' days; the election will obtain, and the rest will be blinded. If this should be the case with you, you will eternally curse this day, and will curse the day that ever you was born, to see such a season of the pouring out of God's Spirit, and will wish that you had died and gone to hell before you had seen it. Now undoubtedly it is, as it was in the days of John the Baptist, the axe is in an extraordinary manner laid at the root of the trees, that every tree which brings not forth good fruit, may be hewn down and cast into the fire.

Therefore, let everyone that is out of Christ, now awake and fly from the wrath to come.

Relations Between the Colonists and the Native Peoples

CHAPTER 5

THE EFFECTS OF EUROPEAN SETTLEMENT ON NATIVE AMERICAN CULTURES

R.C. SIMMONS

The European settlers had an enormous impact on the Indian nations of North America, as R.C. Simmons relates in the following selection from *The American Colonies: From Settlement to Independence*. The Europeans possessed a vast technological advantage, he explains, which ensured that they would eventually subjugate the native peoples. They introduced new goods and weapons that irrevocably altered Native American cultures, as well as new diseases that devastated many tribes.

Simmons also notes that warfare broke out in the colonies on a regular basis: Most tribes took sides in the violent rivalry between the French and English colonists, while others tried to drive the settlers off their lands. He points out that the various wars caused numerous tribes to abandon their homes and relocate to distant regions, which further disrupted their traditional way of life. Simmons is a professor of American history at the University of Birmingham in England.

R.C. Simmons, *The American Colonies: From Settlement to Independence*, New York: W.W. Norton & Company, Inc., 1976. Copyright © 1976 by R.C. Simmons. Reproduced by permission of the publisher.

The history of Spanish, French, Dutch, and English in North America was tragically intertwined with that of the Indian. From the beginnings of European contact with American Indians, it was obvious that superior European organization and technology would lead to European domination. Sixteenth- and seventeenth-century European society was warlike and aggressive, gearing itself through the development of long-range ocean-going ships, armed with powerful cannons, that would carry military men and materials around the world. At the same time, state bureaucracies and groups of moneyed men financed and encouraged this armed expansion. Technological and scientific advances in the same years often sprang from military developments, and governments became more efficient in response to needs created by the struggle of nation against nation or state against state. No grouping of North American Indians had the technological resources or knowledge, the level of organization or the perception of the world, necessary to resist the European advance. And with rare exceptions, no Europeans had the imagination or sensitivity to transcend the general view of primitive peoples as barbarians, devil worshippers, or noble savages to be sacrificed where necessary to the expansion of white settlement, trade, and power.

THE FUR TRADE

European demand for furs rather than for territory brought the first significant contacts between Indians and whites in North America and suggested the future pattern of relationships. European fur traders in the St. Lawrence river valley and the northeastern regions caused great rivalries among the Indians for the control of fur-supplying areas, turning tribes from agriculture and hunting to commercial trapping and commercial warfare. This warfare became more lethal and destructive since the Indians now armed themselves with guns and muskets, often accepting the direction of white allies who fought to kill and destroy. The rivalry for furs led to new alliances and groupings among the Indians. The most famous of these, the Iroquois Confederacy, formed about 1570, became extraordinarily aggressive in the seventeenth century, ranging widely from the St. Lawrence to the Ohio, as they sought to control and benefit from the European fur trade, conquering and vassalizing other Indian tribes, some of whom were driven far into the west. Since the time of French explorer Samuel de Champlain, the Iroquois had been enemies of the French, whose alliance with the Huron Indians of the upper St. Lawrence valley gave them a position in the fur trade coveted by the Iroquois. Before 1660 the French turned from attacks on the Iroquois to attempts to ally with them and finally back to an aggressive policy. The Dutch and the English sought their friendship and remained on good terms with them. However, from the 1690s to the 1750s, the Iroquois did not launch any general attack on the French, and this neutrality helped balance French and English power in the interior of North America.

The Iroquois Confederacy consisted of five "nations"— Seneca, Cayuga, Oneida, Onondaga, and Mohawk—joined by a sixth, the Tuscarora, driven from the Carolinas by white forces in 1722. The federative aspect of the league involved a Council of Sachems, hereditary leaders who discussed external relations but had no power over the internal affairs of each nation. Within each tribe matriarchy prevailed; not only did the women own all the property and exercise police powers but only males belonging to a certain matrilineage could be chosen as sachems by the women. Iroquois society was based on villages, protected by log palisades, outside of which maize and vegetable fields provided staple foodstuffs.

Far to the south, another confederacy evolved during the seventeenth century, a union of Muskogean-speaking tribes, led by the Muskogee Indians. This Creek "nation" or confederacy arose from the interaction of Spanish and English influences. Courted by Carolina traders from Charleston and Spanish missionaries from Santa Cruz, the Creeks at first sided with the English, furnishing troops and in 1705 allying formally with Carolina. Doubledealing and fraudulent practices by English traders, however, pushed the Creeks into enmity, and they enlisted the support of the Yamasee Indians of South Carolina. The Carolinians, using Cherokee allies, prevailed. The Creeks then made peace with the English but began a long war with the Cherokees. Their policy toward the Europeans became one of neutrality, and they traded with French, Spanish, and English. The other important Indians of the South consisted of Cherokees, Choctaws, and Chickasaws, the first Iroquois and the others Muskogean. Of these, the Choctaws came under Louisiana-French influence while the Cherokees and Chickasaws were courted by the British. All the southern tribes lived in "towns," growing corn and vegetables and hunting for subsistence. Before the coming of the whites, warfare was mild, and such "Indian practices" as scalping did not exist. But trade between different villages and tribes did, carried on by Indian merchants over forest paths. This pre-existing trade prepared the Indians for the coming of white traders. White demands for deer pelts and Indian slaves then revolutionized the culture of the southern Indians while French and English rivalries made them seek alliances and influence over those tribes who, unlike the Creeks, did not remain neutral in the struggle.

CHANGES AND CONFLICTS

From the Gulf of Mexico north to the Great Lakes and in the western parts of the colonies, European rivalries had then profoundly affected Indian society. Not only did new types of warfare and new alliances and groupings of Indians become prevalent, but traditional crafts and social patterns changed. Guns, knives, axes, hoes, blankets, pots and pans, salt, paint and alcohol, at first novelties, became necessities. Yet here the whites on the whole maintained Indians as useful allies, as customers and suppliers and did not covet their lands. The case in areas of concentrated or advancing colonial settlement was different. There, the native Americans, faced with superior European armaments and tactics, lost the battle for survival. Some became peaceful, detribalized, generally poverty-stricken inhabitants of the white colonies; others moved out of their tribal areas to escape white overlordship; still others died in resisting it. In Virginia Indian numbers had dropped by 1670 to about 2,000–3,000, perhaps some 8 percent of those living there in 1608. In New England, where perhaps 25,000 Indians lived in 1600, European diseases had reduced their numbers, probably by half, twenty years later. As in Virginia, initial and wary friendship was replaced by violence as white land-hunger grew. Nor did Puritan views of the Indians as savages and, in periods of warfare, as Satan's agents lead to harmony. Few Puritan ministers were active missionaries and those who were sought to persuade the Indians to accept white authority as well as white religion. The powerful Pequot tribe of southern New England was decimated in 1636–1637 by an alliance of settlers and Narragansett Indians. In 1675–1676, Metamoc, or King Philip, a Wampanoag Indian, led his people in a major uprising joined by other tribes, devastating first much of Plymouth colony, then the upper Connecticut Valley, and threatening the coastal towns. Several thousand colonists were killed. The Indian attacks faltered, Professor Gary B. Nash has argued, less because of English victories than from lack of food, disease, and shortages of guns and ammunition. This failure brought the end of Indian resistance throughout Puritan New England, leaving only the northern Indians, the Penobscot and Abenaki in Maine, who sporadically and often with French encouragement harassed the tiny settlements of the English in that region. In the middle colonies, the Leni Lenape or Delaware Indians, a smaller and less well-organized grouping, faced not only the advancing settlers but felt the weight of pressure from the aggressive Iroquois warriors of upper New York. Under their orders, they moved first to western Pennsylvania to form a buffer between the whites and the Iroquois, then to the Ohio. Further south, the Carolinians also broke Indian resistance. The Iroquoian-speaking Tuscaroras, about 5,000 strong and living on the Roanoke and southwards in North Carolina, were forced out by white settlers in the wars of 1711–1713. They moved north to join their fellow Iroquois in the interior of New York. In South Carolina the Yamasees, a Muskogean-speaking tribe, were routed in 1715–1716 and their survivors absorbed into the Creek nation. Where white settlers prevailed, surviving Indians either continued to live as scattered and dispirited remnants or moved away in search of security elsewhere.

King Philip's War

Eric B. Schultz and Michael J. Tougias

King Philip's War began in June 1675 when a small band of Wampanoag Indians, feeling pressured by the loss of their land to the colonists, raided several farms on the border of the Plymouth colony. The settlers reciprocated with a counterattack, leading to further retaliation by the Indians. From these initial skirmishes, the conflict quickly escalated into one of the bloodiest wars ever fought in American history. For more than a year, no corner of New England was free of carnage and destruction; both sides suffered horrific casualties. In the following excerpt from their book *King Philip's War: The History and Legacy of America's Forgotten Conflict*, authors Eric B. Schultz and Michael J. Tougias describe how this catastrophic event profoundly affected both the colonists and the indigenous peoples.

A mong the handful of seminal events that shaped the American mind and continent, King Philip's War is perhaps the least studied and most forgotten. In essence, the war cleared southern New England's native population from the land, and with it a way of life that had evolved over a millennium. The Wampanoag, Narragansett, Nipmuc, and other native peoples were slaughtered, sold into slavery, or placed in widely scattered communities throughout New England after the war. In its aftermath, the English established themselves as the dominant peoples—and in many New England towns, the only peoples—allowing for the uninterrupted growth of England's northern colonies right up to the American Revolution. As important, King Philip's War became the brutal model for how the United States would come to deal with its native population. Later names like Tippecanoe, Black Hawk's War, the

Trail of Tears, the Salt Creek Massacre, the Red River War, and Wounded Knee all took place under the long, violent shadow of King Philip's War.

King Philip, also called Metacom, was the son of Massasoit, sachem [chief] of the Wampanoag and the man most closely associated with the natives' goodwill toward the struggling Plymouth colony. It seems particularly ironic, then, that Massasoit is seated prominently in our romanticized view of the First Thanksgiving, while the most graphic image of Philip (for those who still study the war) is his severed head skewered on the end of a pike and placed along a major Plymouth thoroughfare for most of a generation. The real tragedy is how we came to embrace one image and lose the other. In removing King Philip's War from our history books, we became, according to the rubric, destined to repeat it. That we did, with a vengeance. . . .

OUTBREAK OF HOSTILITIES

The war erupted on June 20, 1675, along the southern border of Plymouth Colony, and it is startling to see how quickly two peoples, having lived side by side for a half century, could become consumed so quickly and completely with an intense hatred for one another. A small band of Pokanoket (a people of the Wampanoag) warriors left their camp in present-day Warren, Rhode Island, crossed the Kickamuir River, and raided several farms in the English settlement at Swansea. A messenger was immediately dispatched to Governor Josiah Winslow at Marshfield, who on June 22 sent orders to Bridgewater and Taunton to raise a force of two hundred men for the defense of Plymouth Colony's frontier.

Three days after the raid, twenty-year-old John Salisbury of Swansea shot and mortally wounded a marauding Pokanoket. Within a day Pokanoket warriors had ambushed and killed seven English, leaving the entire Swansea settlement of about forty families huddled in three or four secure garrisons. Plymouth and Massachusetts Bay troops attempted to quell the violence by cornering Philip, son of Massasoit and sachem of the Pokanoket, on the Pokanoket peninsula (Warren and Bristol, Rhode Island). However, as the poorly prepared English troops stumbled around Pokanoket territory, Philip slipped across Mount Hope Bay into present-day Tiverton and Fall River, where he drew additional strength from his Pocasset allies. A short time later he would elude the English again when he abandoned his camp in the Pocasset Swamp, crossed the Taunton River, and streaked toward central Massachusetts and the security of his Nipmuc allies.

A year after the incident at Swansea, Plymouth and Massachusetts Bay Colonies lay in shambles. Mendon, Brookfield, Lancaster, Deerfield, Northfield, Wrentham, Worcester, Groton, Rehoboth, Middleboro, and Dartmouth had all been reduced to ashes and abandoned. Swansea itself was left with six structures standing. Marlboro had been destroyed except for a few buildings maintained throughout the war by the military. Other locations such as Hatfield, Springfield, Medfield, Weymouth, Scituate, Sudbury, and Chelmsford faced enormous loss of life and property. Even towns such as Hadley, Northampton, and Taunton, which successfully countered Indian assaults, were scarred by a war that led family and friends to their deaths in faraway towns, kept residents in a constant state of fear and uncertainty, and created a standing army that gobbled up food stores and required an endless stream of tax payments for its support.

Rhode Island found itself the victim of a war it had neither instigated nor declared and suffered as much as its Massachusetts Bay and Plymouth neighbors. Providence lost seventy-two homes and was deserted by most of its inhabitants. Warwick was burned to the ground except for one stone house, while places like Wickford and the ancient settlement of Pawtuxet were utterly destroyed. By March 1676, the area south of the Pawtuxet River had been largely deserted by the English, and by the war's end only the village of Portsmouth and the town of Newport had been spared the ravages of King Philip's War. Connecticut's military played a crucial role in the war, and the colony escaped assault with the exception of Simsbury, which was abandoned and burned to the ground. In that part of the Massachusetts Bay Colony that became present-day Maine, however, King Philip's War led to the destruction and abandonment of all English settlements except Kittery, York, and Wells. In all, more than half of New England's ninety towns were assaulted by native warriors. For a time in the spring of 1676, it appeared to the colonists that the entire English population of Massachusetts and Rhode Island might be driven back into a handful of fortified seacoast cities. One historian noted, "No period of the revolutionary war was, to the interior of any part of the United States, so disastrous."

A STAGGERING DEATH RATE

Between six hundred and eight hundred English died in battle during King Philip's War. Measured against a European population in New England of perhaps fifty-two thousand, this death rate was nearly twice that of the Civil War and more than seven times that of World War II. The English Crown sent Edmund Randolph to assess damages shortly after the war and he reported that twelve hundred homes were burned, eight thousand head of cattle lost, and vast stores of foodstuffs destroyed. Thousands of survivors became wards of the state, prompting churches in England and Ireland to send relief ships to New England's aid.

For all their suffering, the English fared well compared to New England's Native American peoples. During the war, the English attacked and massacred Narragansett and Wampanoag at the Great Swamp in South Kingstown, Rhode Island, along the Connecticut River in present-day Turner's Falls, Massachusetts, and in locations as separate as the Housatonic River in western Massachusetts and the Pawtucket River north of Providence. Some of the most grisly executions were of native women and children trying desperately to flee the war or surrender. One account estimated that three thousand Native Americans were killed in battle. In a total population of about twenty thousand, this number is staggering.

Many of the surviving natives were sold into slavery in the West Indies as part of a scheme designed to replenish colonial coffers depleted by the war. Others migrated west to New York or north to Canada to seek refuge with neighboring tribes. Those allowed to remain, despite having supported the English war effort, often lost their property rights and individual liberties. Never again would the English and the southern New England Indians live side by side as they had prior to King Philip's War.

THE PUEBLO REVOLT OF 1680

TED MORGAN

In 1598, the Spanish soldier Juan de Oñate conquered the region now known as New Mexico. The Hopi and other Pueblo Indians were placed under Spanish rule and reduced to serfdom. One of Spain's primary goals was to convert the Indians to Christianity; to this end, Franciscan friars established missions and attempted to change many aspects of traditional Pueblo culture, such as the practice of polygamous marriage. During the mid-1600s, the Spanish leaders of New Mexico launched a no-holds-barred attack on native religious practices, destroying sacred objects and severely punishing shamans. This act of religious repression spurred the Indians to rise up against their Spanish oppressors. In the following excerpt from *Wilderness at Dawn: The Settling of the North American Continent*, acclaimed author Ted Morgan recounts the events that provoked the only successful Indian revolt against a colonial power.

I n the thinly settled Spanish colonies, Indian labor was the key to survival. A bewildering set of regulations governed labor relations, but, whatever name they went by, they boiled down in practice to the exploitation of a ready-made nation of peons. When the crown said that the Indians were freemen, the translation from the Don Quixote–style Spanish double-talk was that they were free to work for nothing, just as the *hidalgo* [soldier] was free to bear arms and the friars were free to convert. . . .

In New Mexico, there was a stagnation worse than that in

Florida. Pedro de Peralta, who replaced Juan de Oñate as governor in 1610, reported to the viceroy: "No one comes to America to plant and sow, but only to eat and loaf." And how else could they eat and loaf except by exploiting the Indians?

THE MISSIONARIES

Peralta had arrived with nine Franciscans, and by 1616 there were twice that number, fanning out among the Pueblo villages. They used Indian labor to build their churches and houses, and then used them again as sacristans, bell ringers, organists, cooks, and gardeners. The mission influence was twofold. The Spanish took from the Indians their labor and their corn, but they also gave by introducing wheat, cattle, plows, irrigation, lime mortar, roof beams, masonry, and other practical improvements. They taught the Indians trades like carpentry and smithing, and used surplus grain to feed poor Indians outside the missions, which helped them meet their conversion quotas.

Interfering in the Pueblo way of life, they tried to ban polygamy and ceremonial dances. They treated the Pueblos like irresponsible children, as can be seen from the instructions that Friar Ruiz left for his successor in Jemez, thirty miles west of Santa Fe: Don't let the Indian women work in the fields, because all they want to do is "join the older youths in wanton and wicked dalliance." Don't let them sit together in church, because all they do is gossip. Don't let the children at catechism cover the lower parts of their faces with their serapes, "for then they eat grains of toasted maize and chew nasty stuff they are addicted to."

In 1622, Alonso de Benavides arrived in Santa Fe as chief prelate for the New Mexico missions, and also as the representative of the Inquisition, which made him the equal of the governor. After eight years of driving his missionaries to break their conversion records, he wrote a self-promoting *Memorial* for the king in which he claimed that there were now twenty-five missions, each with its own church; over ninety villages; and more than sixty thousand Pueblo Indian converts. According to Benavides, there were more converts than there were Indians in New Mexico.

Under Benavides, the missions spread to Hopi villages in northeastern Arizona. Isolated by the natural buffers of their mesas, the Hopis were astonished to see, in August 1629, three enterprising Franciscans arrive in the village of Awatovi, atop

Antelope Mesa, about sixty miles north of today's Flagstaff, Arizona.

The leader of the three, Francisco Porras, was a remarkably able man, who introduced Spanish plants and animals to promote economic self-sufficiency, organized work details, taught Hopi children to read and write, and built a fine adobe church with a steeple, a copper bell, a choir loft, and an altar stone. He was so capable, in fact, that in 1633 the local shamans, whose authority he was undermining, had him killed by poisoning his food.

THE QUARREL BETWEEN THE FRIARS AND THE GOVERNORS

The mission continued to prosper under his successors, although in the 1650s it was tainted with scandal. Alonso de Posada, one of the Franciscans at Awatovi in 1654, took an Indian mistress and ordered two of the soldiers at the mission to kill her Indian lover. The scandal fueled the quarrel between the friars and the governors, who were constantly trading charges and investigating one another. The crux of the matter was labor management: the governors needed Indians for their private projects, such as tanning hides, weaving, and gathering piñon nuts; but the missionaries wanted the Indians for their own work projects.

One of the friars' weapons against the crown-appointed officials was the Inquisition, which Benavides had brought to New Mexico in 1622. The friars would bring Inquisition charges against a corrupt governor for some religious lapse, as in the case of the governor who came to Sunday mass in Santa Fe and made soldiers who were kneeling in prayer stand up and salute him.

The governors retaliated by investigating the missionaries for brutal treatment of the Indians, charging that the friars made them wear hair shirts and carry heavy crosses in penance. Government policy toward the Indians and the friars changed with the personality of each governor. Governor Lopez, for instance, undermined the friars by giving the village of Tesuque permission to go ahead with their kachina dances. He said they were only "Indian foolishness" and there was no harm in them.

The Franciscans responded by prohibiting the dances throughout New Mexico, and in 1661 they raided a number of villages and destroyed sixteen hundred kachina masks, covering over the kivas (ceremonial rooms).

In 1675, Governor Juan de Treviño decided to cooperate with the friars in stamping out native religious practices, which were now seen as subversive. Forty-seven shamans were arrested. Three were hanged, one hanged himself, and the other forty-three were whipped. At this point, seventy Tewa warriors stormed into Santa Fe to demand the release of the prisoners. The governor complied, contributing to the making of a native leader.

One of the shamans who had been whipped and released was a Tewa Indian named Popé. He fled north to Taos, known for its rebellious spirit, his head filled with plans of vengeance.

For the next five years, he shaped those plans. It was said that a god from the underworld had appeared to him and given him a mission. It was said that three devils had appeared, shooting flames of fire from their extremities, and told him to rid the land of all Spaniards.

LAYING PLANS FOR THE ATTACK

Popé developed a network of emissaries in the villages, who spread the word that the Spanish god had brought drought and hard winters. The Spanish had so burdened them with tasks that they had no time to till their own fields. Not only could they no longer produce the surpluses they needed for trade, they could not even feed themselves. They must bring back their own gods, who would give them more corn than the Spanish god, by wiping out the mission system. They must regain control of their villages by driving the Spaniards out of New Mexico.

Popé's plan required the united action of all the pueblos. On a given day, there would be a simultaneous attack of the thirty-three missions left in the declining system. Santa Fe would be surrounded and cut off, its trails being guarded against messengers. The attack would be timed to begin just before the arrival of the annual provision train from Mexico in September. They would catch the Spaniards at a vulnerable moment.

In 1680, there were about twenty-five thousand Indians left in New Mexico, including six thousand warriors. They outnumbered the 2,350 Spaniards almost three to one. (The Spanish were undermanned for the area they held. Santa Fe, with a population of one thousand, had the biggest garrison—250 men.)

Popé was a charismatic leader with popular support and a remarkable strategic sense. His emissaries in the pueblos offered various incentives, saying that every Indian who killed a

Spaniard would be rewarded with an Indian woman. If he killed four, he would get four; if he killed ten or more, he would have a like number of women. This wasn't a rebellion in the name of freedom. It was a conservative uprising to restore traditional ways, and religious practices that predated the Spaniards.

The revolt was set for August 13, 1680. To alert the pueblos, Popé tied as many knots as there were days until the revolt into ropes of maguey fiber, and sent riders carrying the ropes among the tribes. If the villages agreed, they were to send out smoke signals.

MASSACRE AT THE MISSIONS

In Santa Fe, Christian Indians leaked word of the attack to Governor Antonio de Otermín. In response, Popé advanced the date of the ambush to August 11. That day, a Sunday, Otermín was about to go to mass when Pedro Hidalgo, one of the soldiers from the nearby Tesuque mission, arrived with terrible news. A party of painted warriors had been seen in a ravine outside Tesuque. Father Pio, one of the best-liked missionaries, had gone out to meet them, and saw that they were on the warpath. "What is this, my children, are you mad?" he asked. Those were his last words. After killing Father Pio, the Indians had taken all the mission's cattle and horses and gone into the sierra.

At once Otermín tried to notify his *estancias* (ranches). But the trails were guarded, and his messengers couldn't get through. Those few places that got wind of the rebellion didn't believe the news. The trouble with the territory, Otermín reflected, was that the *estancias* were too far apart.

The scene at Tesuque was repeated at all the missions, and twenty-one out of thirty-three Franciscans were killed. The astonishing thing, a Spanish report noted, was "that all of them rebelled on one day and at one hour." This was unprecedented in New Mexico, where the Indians had been obedient vassals for so many years.

The Indians, it could be said, were only repaying the Spanish, who had hanged their shamans and destroyed the kivas and kachina masks. At Jemez, the friar in charge was taken to the cemetery, stripped naked, and told to get down on his hands and knees. The Indians took turns riding him and whipping him, and finally killed him with war clubs.

At the pueblo of Sandia, south of Santa Fe, the floor of the church and the foot of the communion rail were covered with human excrement. Two chalices and a crucifix were found in a basket of manure, and a full-length statue of St. Francis had its arms hacked off.

In every mission and village, Spanish bodies were piled up in front of altars or in the street. In Santa Fe, Governor Otermín, realizing that the Indians were armed with the weapons of slain soldiers, collected about a thousand Spaniards in the governor's palace and its outbuildings and waited for the attack. The siege began on August 15. Five hundred Indians surrounded the city. Among them was Popé, who wore around his waist a sash of red taffeta taken from the convent at Galisteo.

Otermín fought off the first attack, but a couple of days later the Indian reserves arrived, twenty-five hundred strong. They cut off the water, and by nightfall had set fire to half the city. The whole town, Otermín wrote, "was a torch and everywhere were war chants. . . . What grieved us the most were the dreadful flames from the church and the scoffing and ridicule which the wretched Indians made of the sacred things . . . intoning the *al-abado* [a hymn to the sacraments] and other prayers with jeers."

Otermín was trapped. Outside were three thousand frenzied Indians, bent on massacre. Inside were one thousand Spaniards who had nothing to drink except what they had collected in jars and pitchers. Outside the cries of the warriors, inside the weeping of the women and children. Otermín either had to engage the enemy or die. His men heard mass at dawn on August 20, and the horsemen galloped out, followed by men on foot. Certain of victory, the Indians had spent the night in celebration, singing that the Spanish god was dead. Otermín and his desperate men surprised them, and within a few hours the Indians were in flight, leaving behind three hundred dead. Otermín suffered an arrow wound in the face and a gunshot wound in the chest.

He quickly decided to abandon Santa Fe and headed south with his people toward the Rio Grande. As they marched, they passed the debris of war, burned-out houses, and the rotting carcasses of horses lying in the road. South of Isleta, they joined up with another troop of refugees, led by Lieutenant Governor Alonso García. In mid-September, they reached the Rio Grande, and Otermín took a muster. There were 1,946 persons. The Spanish death toll was 380 soldiers and civilians and twenty-one priests.

REVIVING THE OLD WAYS

It was a triumph for Popé. His two major objectives, to eliminate the mission system and to drive out the Spaniards, had been achieved. For the first and last time in North America, the native people had defeated and thrown out the colonizer, and the land was returned to its original settlers.

Popé at once emphasized the true nature of his rebellion. Every vestige of the conquest had to be expunged. The Indians were told to bathe in the rivers and scrub themselves with soapweed to wash away all traces of baptism. They were told to drop their Christian names and void their Christian marriages. They were told, "Don't speak Spanish, and plant only the crops of your ancestors, maize and beans."

Wearing a bull's-horn headdress, Popé toured the villages, proclaiming the new order. "We are quit with the Spaniards now," he said, "and shall live as we like and settle wherever we see fit." At Santa Ana, south of what would one day be Albuquerque, he presided over a feast at which he cursed the Spaniards and Christianity while drinking from a chalice, and addressed the other Indian leaders as "holy father."

Once again the Pueblo Indians prayed at their kivas. They donned masks and danced the kachina. But soon it became apparent that they could not go back to the old ways, having been Hispanicized beyond return. The invaders had been there since 1600, under fourteen different governors. Only octogenarians remembered pre-Spanish times. Were they supposed to stop planting wheat, uproot their orchards, throw their horses and cattle into the Rio Grande, destroy their guns? Many villagers did not. Some continued to speak Spanish. Some kept their Christian wives. Some hid church vessels. New Mexico's tribal societies had become irretrievably hybrid.

THE SPANIARDS RETURN

Otermín, in the meantime, had settled in El Paso del Norte, today's Ciudad Juárez, Mexico. He and his people were told to stay put until the reconquest of New Mexico could be achieved. But it was twelve years before Diego de Vargas undertook the campaign at his own expense. By that time, Pueblo unity had broken down. Popé turned out to be as repressive as the Spaniards, exacting tribute from the villages. The tribes once again were split into warring factions.

In 1692, de Vargas reconnoitered in New Mexico for four

months, meeting no resistance, and decided that the time was ripe for reconquest. On October 4, 1693, he headed north again, with one hundred soldiers, eighteen Franciscans, some Indian auxiliaries, and seventy-three families of settlers. In Santa Fe, some Tanos Indians had turned the governor's palace into a housing complex, and weren't about to give it up. De Vargas stormed the place, killing between seventy and eighty of the defenders.

The Spaniards were back in New Mexico, but they couldn't repeat their old methods. De Vargas went on a good-will tour of the villages, taking the olive branch to the mesa top. He stood as godfather at the baptism of Indian children. Spanish officials no longer came around every May and October to collect tribute. Indian forms of worship were tolerated, and the beat of drums was heard in the land.

The Pueblos were given a measure of autonomy, while the more distant Hopis were now outside the Spanish sphere of influence. In any case, the eighteenth-century strategic context was different, for New Mexico was now more of a defensive bastion than a mission outpost. An example of the change was that in 1791 a petition arrived in Santa Fe from the Pueblos in Isleta, asking for the removal of a priest because he wouldn't let them perform their corn dance or go out on their traditional rabbit hunt. The priest was removed.

A HOPI ACCOUNT OF THE PUEBLO REVOLT

RETOLD BY EDMUND NEQUATEWA

The following selection reveals the Hopi perspective on the Spanish colonizers, the actions of the Catholic missionaries, and the Pueblo Revolt of 1680. This account was passed down among the Hopis for many generations through oral tradition. The following version was translated into English by Edmund Nequatewa, a member of the powerful One Horned Fraternity, the only society allowed to tell the stories of all the Hopi clans. In his 1936 book *Truth of a Hopi*, Nequatewa permanently recorded this and many other traditionally oral tales so that they would not be lost to posterity.

I t may have taken quite a long time for these villages to be established. Anyway, every place was pretty well settled down when the Spanish came. The Spanish were first heard of at Zuni and then at Awatovi. They came on to Shung-opovi, passing Walpi. At First Mesa, Siky-atki was the largest village then, and they were called Sikyatki, not Walpi. The Walpi people were living below the present village on the west side. When the Spaniards came, the Hopi thought that they were the ones they were looking for—their white brother, the Bahana, their savior.

The Spaniards visited Shung-opovi several times before the missions were established. The people of Mishongovi welcomed them so the priest who was with the white men built the first Hopi mission at Mishongovi. The people of Shung-opovi were at first afraid of the priests but later they decided he was

Edmund Nequatewa, *Truth of a Hopi: Stories Relating to the Origin, Myths, and Clan Histories of the Hopi*, Flagstaff, AZ: Northland Publishing, 1967. Copyright © 1936 by the Northern Arizona Society of Science and Art. Reproduced by permission.

really the Bahana, the savior, and let him build a mission at Shung-opovi.

THE SPANIARDS GAIN CONTROL

Well, about this time the Strap Clan were ruling at Shung-opovi and they were the ones that gave permission to establish the mission. The Spaniards, whom they called Castilla, told the people that they had much more power than all their chiefs and a whole lot more power than the witches. The people were very much afraid of them, particularly if they had much more power than the witches. They were so scared that they could do nothing but allow themselves to be made slaves. Whatever they wanted done must be done. Any man in power that was in this position the Hopi called *Tota-achi*, which means a grouchy person that will not do anything himself, like a child. They couldn't refuse, or they would be slashed to death or punished in some way. There were two *Tota-achi*.

The missionary did not like the ceremonies. He did not like the Kachinas and he destroyed the altars and the customs. He called it idol worship and burned up all the ceremonial things in the plaza.

When the Priests started to build the mission, the men were sent away over near the San Francisco peaks to get the pine or spruce beams. These beams were cut and put into shape roughly and were then left till the next year when they had dried out. Beams of that size were hard to carry and the first few times they tried to carry these beams on their backs, twenty to thirty men walking side by side under the beam. But this was rather hard in rough places and one end had to swing around. So finally they figured out a way of carrying the beam in between them. They lined up two by two with the beam between the lines. In doing this, some of the Hopis were given authority by the missionary to look after these men and to see if they all did their duty. If any man gave out on the way he was simply left to die. There was great suffering. Some died for lack of food and water, while others developed scabs and sores on their bodies.

It took a good many years for them to get enough beams to Shung-opovi to build the mission. When this mission was finally built, all the people in the village had to come there to worship, and those that did not come were punished severely. In that way their own religion was altogether wiped out, because they were not allowed to worship in their own way. All this trouble was a heavy burden on them and they thought it was on account of this that they were having a heavy drought at this time. They thought their gods had given them up because they weren't worshiping the way they should.

Now during this time the men would go out pretending they were going on a hunting trip and they would go to some hiding place, to make their prayer offerings. So to-day, a good many of these places are still to be found where they left their little stone bowls in which they ground their copper ore to paint the prayer sticks. These places are called *Puwa-kiki*, cave places. If these men were caught they were severely punished.

THE MISBEHAVING PRIEST

Now this man, Tota-achi (the Priest) was going from bad to worse. He was not doing the people any good and he was always figuring what he could do to harm them. So he thought out how the water from different springs or rivers would taste and he was always sending some man to these springs to get water for him to drink, but it was noticed that he always chose the men who had pretty wives. He tried to send them far away so that they would be gone two or three days, so it was not very long until they began to see what he was doing. The men were even sent to the Little Colorado River to get water for him, or to Moencopi. Finally, when a man was sent out he'd go out into the rocks and hide, and when the night came he would come home. Then, the priest, thinking the man was away, would come to visit his wife, but instead the man would be there when he came. Many men were punished for this.

All this time the priest, who had great power, wanted all the young girls to be brought to him when they were about thirteen or fourteen years old. They had to live with the priest. He told the people they would become better women if they lived with him for about three years. Now one of these girls told what the Tota-achi were doing and a brother of the girl heard of this and he asked his sister about it, and he was very angry. This brother went to the mission and wanted to kill the priest that very day, but the priest scared him and he did nothing. So the Shung-opovi people sent this boy, who was a good runner, to Awatovi to see if they were doing the same thing over there, which they were. So that was how they got all the evidence against the priest.

Then the chief at Awatovi sent word by this boy that all the priests would be killed on the fourth day after the full moon. They had no calendar and that was the best way they had of setting the date. In order to make sure that everyone would rise up and do this thing on the fourth day the boy was given a cotton string with knots in it and each day he was to untie one of these knots until they were all out and that would be the day for the attack.

KILLING THE ENEMY

Things were getting worse and worse so the chief of Shung-opovi went over to Mishongnovi and the two chiefs discussed their troubles. "He is not the savior and it is your duty to kill him," said the chief of Shung-opovi. The chief of Mishongnovi replied, "If I end his life, my own life is ended."

Now the priest would not let the people manufacture prayer offerings, so they had to make them among the rocks in the cliffs out of sight, so again one day the chief of Shung-opovi went to Mishongnovi with tobacco and materials to make prayer offerings. He was joined by the chief of Mishongnovi and the two went a mile north to a cave. For four days they lived there heartbroken in the cave, making *pahos*. Then the chief of Mishongnovi took the prayer offerings and climbed to the top of the Corn Rock and deposited them in the shrine, for according to the ancient agreement with the Mishongnovi people it was their duty to do away with the enemy.

He then, with some of his best men, went to Shung-opovi, but he carried no weapons. He placed his men at every door of the priest's house. Then he knocked on the door and walked in. He asked the priest to come out but the priest was suspicious and would not come out. The chief asked the priest four times and each time the priest refused. Finally, the priest said, "I think you are up to something."

The chief said, "I have come to kill you." "You can't kill me," cried the priest, "you have no power to kill me. If you do, I will come to life and wipe out your whole tribe."

The chief returned, "If you have this power, then blow me out into the air; my gods have more power than you have. My gods have put a heart into me to enter your home. I have no weapons. You have your weapons handy, hanging on the wall. My gods have prevented you from getting your weapons."

The old priest made a rush and grabbed his sword from the

wall. The chief of Mishongnovi yelled and the doors were broken open. The priest cut down the chief and fought right and left but was soon overpowered, and his sword taken from him.

They tied his hands behind his back. Out of the big beams outside they made a tripod. They hung him on the beams, kindled a fire and burned him.

The Colonies
Come of Age

—| CHAPTER 6 |—

The Anglo-French Wars for Colonial Dominance

William R. Nester

The best-known conflict in the American colonies prior to the Revolution is the French and Indian War of 1754 to 1763, in which the French and English colonial powers and their respective Indian allies squared off against each other. However, as William R. Nester points out in the following selection, during the 1600s and early 1700s, France and England engaged in several smaller wars over their colonial holdings. Each of these colonial wars was part of a larger European conflict, he notes; the battles that took place in the colonies typically were mild compared to the carnage on the European continent. Yet the early Anglo-French wars also had profound effects on the psyche of the American colonists, the author maintains.

Nester is a professor of government and politics at St. John's University in Jamaica, New York. His books include *"Haughty Conquerors": Amherst and the Great Indian Uprising of 1763* and *The First Global War: Britain, France, and the Fate of North America, 1756–1775.*

For over a century and a half, the French and English struggled to carve ever larger empires from the North American wilderness between the Atlantic Ocean, Rocky Mountains, Gulf of Mexico, and Hudson Bay. At first they faced not only each other but also the Spanish, Dutch and, briefly, the

William R. Nester, *The Great Frontier War: Britain, France, and the Imperial Struggle for North America, 1607–1755*, Westport, CT: Praeger, 2000. Copyright © 2000 by William R. Nester. Reproduced by permission.

Swedes. Bloodshed was nearly incessant as these European powers battled among themselves and, more decisively, each fought a series of wars against various Indian tribes to establish and expand their footholds on the continent. In three mid-17th-century wars, the English defeated the Dutch (who had earlier absorbed the few Swedish settlements) and took over their North American holdings. Separately, the French and English stymied Spanish ambitions and contained them west of the Mississippi and in pockets along the Gulf Coast and northern Florida. By the late 17th century, only the French and English remained to fight over North America's eastern half. French settlements in the St. Lawrence valley were now firmly established; Quebec dispatched trading and exploring parties into the Great Lakes and Mississippi valleys that garnered an ever richer horde of furs. Along the Atlantic Coast, the English colonies developed flourishing, diversified economies and spread their hamlets as far west as the Appalachian foothills.

TWO DIFFERENT "EMPIRES"

The character of the French and British North American "empires" differed greatly. Although the French did war against the Iroquois, Natchez, Fox, and other tribes, they did not "conquer" New France; they merely paid very high tolls to the Indians for the privilege of exploiting it. Beyond their narrow ribbon of settlement between Quebec and Montreal, or ports like New Orleans and Mobile, the New France "empire" largely consisted of several scores of ramshackle trading posts, often isolated from one another by hundreds of wilderness miles and resentful Indian tribes. None of those tribes thought themselves French subjects and would have been incensed had it been suggested that they were. Nor did they think of the annual goods dispensed by the French traders as "gifts." Of the goods received from the French, some were exchanged for "rent" and others for furs. The several hundred voyageurs, marines, and missionaries scattered across that wilderness understood clearly that their survival depended on nurturing Indian hospitality and greed, and they became quite adept at doing so by immersing themselves in Indian tongues, customs, marriage, and ambitions.

In contrast, the British had brutally conquered their empire between the Atlantic and the Appalachians with endless streams of settlers armed with muskets, diseases, and ploughs. By 1750, Britain's 1.25 million American subjects had elbowed aside or eliminated the local tribes and towered over New France's 80,000 white inhabitants. The British advantage went beyond raw numbers of settlers. British goods were better made, more abundant, and cheaper than those dispensed by the French. With such overwhelming power, the British could afford to be more assertive and less sensitive toward Indians. In doing so, they fired the hatred of most tribes against them, and even the smoldering emnity of erstwhile allies like the Iroquois and Cherokee.

Throughout the 17th century, the conflict between the French and English was waged primarily through competition for the alliances and trade of various Indian tribes. But as New France and the various English colonies expanded in territory and population, their merchants, soldiers, and privateers increasingly skirmished with each other on forest trails and the high seas. The French and English fought five wars for North America— Huguenot (1627–1629), League of Augsburg or King William's (1689–1697), Spanish Succession or Queen Anne's (1702–1713), Austrian Succession or King George's (1745–1748), and Seven Years' or French and Indian (1754–1763). It was the final war, of course, that proved to be decisive. The last French and Indian War cannot be understood apart from the century and a half of imperialism that preceded it. . . .

THE HUGUENOT WAR

War between England and France broke out in 1628. That year the English privateer Gervase Kirke sailed up the St. Lawrence and demanded Quebec's surrender. Samuel de Champlain, Quebec's founder and leader, rejected the demand. Sailing back down the St. Lawrence, Kirke's force captured that year's supply fleet from France of 400 settlers and provisions crammed aboard five ships, along with nineteen nearby fishing boats; he carried away his loot and vessels to England. Kirke returned the next year with 300 men and three ships. With his ammunition and food supplies exhausted, Champlain could only surrender Quebec and its 100 inhabitants. The English also captured Port Royal in 1629, thus completing New France's conquest. These victories occurred after France and England had signed the Treaty of St. Germain-en-Laye in April 1629, which required, among other things, that New France be returned to France. If the English had held New France, they could have avoided another 130 years of warfare and rivalry with France in North America. . . .

By 1685, over 800 French and several hundred English traders had spread across the Great Lakes, the Ohio and Mississippi valleys, and Hudson Bay. Blood was increasingly shed on lonely trails as rival French and English traders met. In 1685, the governor of New France, Jacque-Rene de Brisay de Denonville, sent Chevalier de Troyes and 90 troops to capture the three English trading posts on lower Hudson Bay, and thereby divert 50,000 furs from English to French markets. In 1686, a trading expedition dispatched by New York governor Thomas Dongan reached the Michilimackinac region to entice those tribes away from the French. Thus did French and English skirmish in the New World four years before they formally went to war in the Old.

KING WILLIAM'S WAR

In 1689, King William's War (War of the Augsburg Succession) broke out between England and France, and soon engulfed much of Europe. William III declared war on France when Louis XIV tried to conquer the English king's native Holland and supported a Catholic Stuart claimant to the English throne. In North America, the warfare quickly assumed the characteristics that would continue through four successive wars. With their armies bogged down in Europe, neither France nor England could commit significant forces to North America. London dispatched a mere four infantry companies to New York and another to Newfoundland. Versailles sent only warships to convoy its annual supply fleet to Quebec. With each war, France and England would boost the number of troops they committed to the New World. But the colonists were mostly forced to decide North America's fate on their own.

Colonial troops and their Indian allies waged war through raids and occasional major campaigns. Over the next few years, the French led war parties of Abenaki against New Hampshire and attacks composed of various tribes to the Hudson and Mohawk valleys. These raids burned Fort Casco, Fort Loyal, Salmon Falls, Schenectady, and York. In response, the English helped finance Iroquois raids along the St. Lawrence valley. An Iroquois raid in July 1689 burned the town of Lachine, a mere seven miles from Montreal. In 1690, an English raiding party voyaged up the Lake Champlain corridor to destroy La Prairie before escaping a French and Indian pursuit. That same year, William Phips led 736 men to capture Port Royal in Nova Scotia.

It was increasingly clear to colonial leaders that raiding could not win the war. In April 1691, representatives of the New England and mid-Atlantic colonies met in New York to plan and launch their first all-out attempt to conquer New France. Pieter Schuyler's raid up Lake Champlain to Montreal's outskirts caused little damage to the French. Phips, meanwhile, organized a fleet of 32 ships and 2,300 troops to sail against Quebec. His fleet anchored before Quebec on October 16 but failed to take the city by storm or destroy it with bombardment. Gales battered the fleet during its ignominious retreat, wrecking several ships and drowning 1,000 men. The expedition had been a disaster.

While life and death struggles would flare along the New England and New France frontiers, the war would be decided elsewhere. At the 1692 Battle of La Hoque, a combined English and Dutch fleet defeated the French navy. Although the war would continue to burn across Europe and the American frontier, the French were hard-pressed to supply New France in the face of British naval supremacy. Raids bloodied the frontier for another half dozen years. The governors of New France and some New England colonies offered bounties for scalps. The Iroquois suffered a humiliating defeat in 1696 when Governor Louis de Baude de Frontenac led 2,000 French and Indians to the Onondaga heartland, whose villages and crops he destroyed.

The Treaty of Ryswick abruptly ended King William's War in 1697. The French agreed to recognize William III as England's legitimate king, along with English claims to Newfoundland and Hudson Bay. Peace in Europe, however, did not extend to North America. The Abenaki continued to war against New England while the Iroquois ravaged the St. Lawrence valley. Several French expeditions along with separate Ottawa and Objibwa war parties attacked the Five Nations. Half of the Iroquois' warriors died in these wars. In 1701, the Iroquois could do nothing to prevent the French from building Fort Detroit to solidify their control over the upper Great Lakes' fur trade. Instead, that same year they meekly accepted a summons by Governor Frontenac to join representatives of 30 tribes at a Montreal council which agreed to a "Great Peace" among them all. That same year, the Iroquois signed a peace treaty with the English at Albany. In both treaties, the Iroquois promised to remain neutral in any war between France and England.

Ironically, while peace finally settled along the northern frontier, war again engulfed Europe, sparked by the death of the childless Spanish king Carlos II. Louis XIV tried to impose his grandson on the Spanish throne and thus extend French control over Spain's Italian and Flemish territory. Other great powers supported other claimants. In 1702, England officially entered what became known as Queen Anne's War or the War of the Spanish Succession. Queen Anne and her government hoped not just to contain Louis XIV's latest aggression but to use the war to seize Spain's Caribbean sugar islands and annual treasure fleet.

During the war, the periodic raids that had all along terrorized the northeast frontier increased in number and ferocity. Abenaki attacked the cities of Casco, Wells, Winter Harbor, York, and Deerfield, slaughtering hundreds of settlers and dragging hundreds of others into captivity. Caughnawaga Iroquois raided Schenectady. Iroquois raids burned and looted along the St. Lawrence valley. Western Indians attacked the Iroquois. Bounties were once again offered for enemy scalps and prisoners. Privateers captured hundreds of enemy merchant ships.

All the raiding aside, no significant campaigns occurred until 1708 when Colonel Benjamin Church launched an unsuccessful attack on Port Royal. Another attack failed the following year. Then, in 1710, an English fleet finally captured not only Port Royal but all the small French settlements dotting the Bay of Fundy. These campaigns were overshadowed in 1711 when Sir Hovenden Walker sailed toward Quebec with a fleet of 14 warships, 31 transports, and 11,000 troops, of which 4,300 were composed of seven regular regiments and 6,500 provincial troops. Walker's campaign was the first time that England had sent substantial numbers of troops to aid its American colonies. Given the expedition's fate, the regulars would have been better off not leaving England. Shortly after entering the St. Lawrence, much of the fleet ran aground in a thick fog. In all, nine ships broke up and over 900 men drowned. Walker ignominiously ordered the remnants of his command back to Boston. As historian Ian Steel points out, "New France's survival in 1711, as in 1690, was due to incompetence and misfortune."

While King William's War had flared along Britain's northern American frontier, Queen Anne's War spread to the south. As in the northeast, victory in the southeast depended on forging Indian alliances against one's enemies. The southeast's most powerful Indian group was the Creek confederation, which included seven tribes of 15,000 people in 60 villages. Enemies surrounded the Creek, including the Choctaw and Chickasaw to the west, the Guale and Apalachee allied with Spain to the southeast, and the Cherokee to the north. Hoping to get iron and guns, the Creek had invited Spanish missionaries and merchants to their realm in 1681. The Spanish faith and goods, however, spawned greeds and jealousies that threatened the fragile confederacy. By 1685, the Creek had expelled the Spaniards and invited South Carolina merchants, who left their religion at home. English-armed Creeks began raiding Spanish missions in northern Florida along with their enemies to the west. As elsewhere, the influx of European diseases offset any material advantages. Smallpox ravaged the Creek during the 1690s. The French complicated the southeast's complex power distribution when they founded the colony of Louisiana with posts at Biloxi in 1699 and Mobile in 1701.

When news of the War of the Spanish Succession reached South Carolina, Governor James Moore organized and dispatched an expedition to take St. Augustine. While the defenders withstood the siege, a Spanish fleet arrived, forcing the English to abandon their own ships and artillery and retreat overland to South Carolina. Unable to take Florida with provincial troops, Moore then tried to exterminate it by supplying Creek war parties. The frontier war sputtered on for years, with all tribes suffering hundreds of deaths and dozens of burned villages. The French entered the fray, allying with the Choctaw against the Creek and sending privateers to seize English merchant ships. Carolinian volunteers accompanied a large Creek army that devastated the Choctaw lands in 1711. The following year, the Creek and the French signed a neutrality treaty that held until 1763.

Meanwhile, war had broken out between the three southern colonies and the Tuscarora in 1711. Over the next two years, the English launched several ever larger campaigns of Creek, Catawba, Cherokee, and provincial troops against Tuscarora villages. In 1713, Tuscarora remnants fled north all the way to New York to seek shelter among the Iroquois, who adopted them as a sixth member of their confederacy. With the Franco-Creek neutrality and Tuscarora's disappearance, the southeast escaped the large-scale fighting that engulfed the northeast during the next two Anglo-French wars.

Under the 1713 Treaty of Utrecht ending Queen Anne's War, Versailles ceded English claims to Newfoundland, Hudson Bay,

Acadia except for Isle Royale (Cape Breton), and Isle Saint-Jean (Prince Edward Island); recognized English sovereignty over the Iroquois; and permitted the English to trade in French territory. France's ally, Spain, lost nothing in North America, but did have to grant England the strongholds of Gibraltar and Minorca in the Mediterranean. England reaped huge benefits from the war, along with greater defense commitments.

The Utrecht Treaty is a classic example of a peace accord that sowed the seeds of future conflicts. The failure to delineate these territorial trades and fulfill other tenets unleashed a half century of conflicting claims that only war could resolve. Most controversial of all was Article 15, which seemed to allow for free trade among all the tribes and asserted British sovereignty over the Iroquois. Did free trade permit Englishmen to peddle their goods at the gates of French trading posts? If not, just where were the territories of the Iroquois and other tribes drawn? The English and French proclaimed the Iroquois as British subjects; the Iroquois rejected that distinction.

These ambiguities aside, by European standards, Utrecht inaugurated a relatively strong peace between England and France that lasted until 1744. Both sides used those 27 years to expand their respective North American empires. The French founded settlements in the Great Lakes, Mississippi valley, and Louisiana territories. In Louisiana, the French established Fort Rosalie in 1716, Fort Toulouse in 1717, and New Orleans in 1719. In the upper Mississippi valley, they established Fort de Chartres in 1720 and Fort St. Philippe in 1726. On Isle Royale in 1717, the French began building fortress Louisbourg. In 1720, the French rebuilt a trading post at the Niagara River mouth and fortified it in 1726. In 1731, Fort Frederic arose at Lake Champlain's southern narrows. In addition to these forts, the French traded at several score smaller posts scattered at cross-trails throughout the eastern woodlands, western prairies, and even high plains as far as the Assiniboine and Missouri rivers. Thus did the French construct a chain of forts and settlements in a vast crescent from the Gulf Coast, up the Mississippi valley, over to the Great Lakes, and down the St. Lawrence valley. Although the links in this chain were far apart, they served effectively as magnets for regional trade and barriers to contain the English east of the Appalachian mountains.

These French advances only spurred the English to consider ways to sever that chain. A 1735 Board of Trade report maintained that although the Appalachian Mountains "may serve at present for a very good frontier, we should not propose them for the boundary of your Majesty's Empire in America . . . British Settlements might be extended beyond them, and some small forts erected on the great Lakes . . . whereby the French communications from Quebec to the River Mississippi might be interrupted."

TRADE RIVALRIES

The perennial efforts of the English to divert furs from the Great Lakes to Albany began to bear considerable fruit in the 1720s. Trade missions to the village of Irondequoit on Lake Ontario garnered furs bound for Montreal. The amount of furs reaching Albany increased tenfold between 1716 and 1724. Then, in 1725, the English established a trading post at Oswego on Lake Ontario, and fortified it in 1727. Supplies were conveyed along the 217-mile route from Albany to Oswego almost entirely by water, up the Mohawk River, over the half-dozen-mile portage of the Great Carrying Place, down Wood Creek to Lake Oneida, and then down the Onondaga River to Oswego. From there, the English canoed to the upper Great Lakes to solicit trade.

The English post on Lake Ontario was a painful thorn in the side of French Canada. As Cadwallader Colden noted, the "remote Indians . . . formerly used to go down to the French at Montreal, and there buy our English goods at second Hand, at above twice the Price they now pay for them at Oswego." Father Francois Piquet worried that Fort Oswego "not only spoils our trade, but puts the English into communication with a vast number of our Indians, far and near. It is true that they like our brandy better than English rum; but they prefer English goods to ours, and can buy for two beaver-skins at Oswego a better silver bracelet than we sell at Niagara for ten."

The French responded by threatening to erect a rival post at Oswego, but they lacked the low-priced, high-quality goods that would have enabled them to compete. According to historian Colin G. Calloway, the rival trading posts at Oswego and Niagara made "the Six Nations' economic dependence on European trade . . . complete, and the profits flowed almost entirely in one direction." This was, of course, the same pattern of dependence and exploitation that had been and would be repeated across North America. That dependence caused the Iroquois to insist that those two forts remain free from attack should another war break out between France and England. . . .

During this time, England and France not only remained at peace, but actually allied against Spain in an inconclusive war between 1718 and 1721. The French captured Pensacola but restored it with a peace treaty. Spain and England fought during 1728 and 1729 without a decisive victory for either side. Surprisingly, Georgia's establishment in 1733 did not immediately provoke another war. Having bolstered its northern frontiers, the Crown tried to cement its empire's southern end by issuing a charter to James Oglethorpe to found Georgia. Oglethorpe led a party of settlers to lay out Savannah in 1733 and in subsequent years established a series of forts and settlements along the coast down to the St. John's River. Despite Spanish protests against what it claimed were infringements on its territory, fighting did not break out between the two kingdoms until 1739, when Madrid's violations of its peace treaty with England led to the undeclared War of Jenkins' Ear. In 1739, an English fleet sacked Portobello, Panama. That early success, however, was eclipsed in 1740 when an expedition against St. Augustine once again failed to capture that Spanish stronghold. The English suffered an even worse disaster in 1741 when disease killed half their troops besieging Cartegena, a Spanish fort on the South American coast. Although Georgian troops did repell a Spanish invasion in 1742, a 1743 attack on St. Augustine once again failed miserably. Colonials provided the bulk of English troops in these campaigns. The heavy losses soured the Americans' enthusiasm for fighting far from their own homes.

KING GEORGE'S WAR

In 1740, the Emperor Charles VI died without a male heir. Over the next few years, most of Europe's powers joined this War for the Austrian Succession. In October 1743, the Bourbon kings of Spain and France signed the Treaty of Fontainbleau, reviving their old Family Compact. The British and French fought on the continent and oceans for at least a year before Versailles formally issued a war declaration in March 1744.

In North America the struggle was known as King George's War. Once again Indian raids burned and killed along the northern frontier. Much of the fighting took place in Nova Scotia and Cape Breton. The French got in the first blow by an attack on Canso in May 1744, but failed to capture Annapolis Royal two months later. In 1745, Governor William Shirley organized an expedition of 3,000 New England troops, led by William Pepperell aboard 52 ships commanded by Admiral Peter Warren, which successfully besieged and took Louisbourg. All of the 4,460 French soldiers and civilians were transported back to France. It was a crippling blow to French power in the region. To this, the French could only respond with more raids against New England. In 1746, Rigaud de Vaudreuil led 400 Canadians and 300 Indians down the Connecticut River to capture and burn Fort Massachusetts. In June 1747, Chevalier Boucher de Niverville led a raid on New Hampshire and destroyed five forts and 100 houses. On the night of February 11–12, 1747, Captain Nicolas-Antoine Coulon de Villiers led 250 Canadians and Micmac against Grand Pre's 500 defenders commanded by Lieutenant Colonel Arthur Noble. Achieving a complete surprise, Villiers' men killed Noble and 70 of his men and captured the rest. Elsewhere, the Choctaw fought against the French from 1746 to 1749, while many Ohio valley tribes conspired but did not openly war against the French during that same period. From the Great Lakes to the Gulf, Indians looked to the English to supply their trade-goods needs. . . .

The war cost France much of its naval and merchant fleet. British warships and privateers reigned supreme, capturing 2,457 prizes from 1745 through 1748 alone. What ships the British did not destroy, the French often lost through mismanagement and bad luck. In spring 1746, for example, a 76-ship French fleet set sail to retake the British conquests in North America. Storms and disease killed 3,000 as the fleet reached Nova Scotia and then returned to France. The English fleet blockaded St. Lawrence Bay, provoking near starvation among the Canadians and the dwindling of Indian allies as the supply ships bringing their gifts were seized.

As in previous wars, the events in North America were but sideshows to the bloodbath drenching Europe. While the British succeeded on the high seas and at Louisbourg, they barely held on in Europe. The worst threat to England occurred in 1745 when the Jacobite Stuart Prince Charles landed in Scotland and tried to spark a Scottish revolt. The threat died when the Duke of Cumberland annihilated Charles' army at Culloden in 1746 and then torched the homes of suspected Jacobite supporters.

By 1748, the European powers had exhausted their treasuries and manpower with no decisive winner. Diplomats negotiated a cease-fire in April and in October 1748 signed the Treaty of

Aix-la-Chapelle. The treaty secured most of Britain's objectives including breaking up the Bourbon alliance, preserving the European power balance, and forcing France to both repudiate the Jacobite pretender to England's throne and withdraw from the Netherlands. The treaty, however, brought no change to North America; all captured territory was returned to the previous owner. Nor did the treaty clarify the imperial boundaries blurred by the 1713 Utrecht Treaty.

The decade of war against Spain and then France burned two lasting images into many Americans' memories. One was the debacle before Cartegena, where English incompetence and arrogance contributed to the deaths of thousands of colonists. The other was Louisbourg, where American initiative and courage conquered France's most powerful fortress in the western hemisphere. The Crown then shattered this colonial triumph when it restored Louisbourg with the Treaty of Aix-la-Chapelle. The war deepened a budding sense of American nationalism.

GEORGIA: THE LAST OF THE THIRTEEN COLONIES

JOHN C. MILLER

Founded in 1732, Georgia was the last of the original thirteen British colonies to be established in North America. John C. Miller describes Georgia's unique early history in the following passage from his book *This New Man, the American: The Beginnings of the American People.* He explains that Georgia's chief founder, English politician James Oglethorpe, carefully planned the colony as a philanthropic endeavor. Under Oglethorpe's design, English prisoners—primarily debtors and other minor criminals—would be transported to Georgia and given a chance to rebuild their lives. However, the author writes, this idealistic plan was ultimately doomed to fail. Miller taught for many years at Stanford University in Palo Alto, California, where he held the position of Robinson Professor of U.S. History. His books include *The First Frontier: Life in Colonial America* and *The Colonial Image: Origins of American Culture.*

During the reigns of Elizabeth I and James I, Spain had stood as the great obstacle to England's territorial aspirations in North America. Although by 1730 Spain's military and naval power was hardly more than a shadow of what it had been in the seventeenth century when the Iberian kingdom had dominated Europe as well as the New World, Spain still remained in possession of Saint Augustine. (In 1821, when Florida was annexed by the United States, St. Augustine became the oldest city in the republic.) From this base, the Spaniards incited the Indians to attack the frontier of South Carolina; the exposed settlements suffered heavy losses, particularly during the Tuscarora War of 1711–1713. Although the Tuscarora Indians were ultimately defeated and forced to take refuge with their blood brothers, the Iroquois (after 1713, in consequence, the Five Nations became known as the Six Nations), so much havoc was wreaked on the frontier that in 1729, at the request of the settlers, South Carolina was converted into a royal colony. Nevertheless, the British government failed to give the settlers the protection they demanded. It was left to private enterprise, aided, it is true, by a parliamentary subsidy, to act in support of the strategic interests of the empire.

Still, considerations other than the protection of the frontier against Spaniards and Indians were involved in the decision to establish a buffer colony to the south of South Carolina. From the days of Queen Elizabeth, overseas expansion had been regarded as a means of solving England's social and economic problems. The colonies were expected to absorb England's surplus population, including the unemployed, sturdy beggars, jailbirds, street women, and destitute orphans. The dregs of society were deemed good enough to be colonists.

OGLETHORPE'S DESIGN FOR GEORGIA

By the early part of the eighteenth century, when England no longer seemed overpopulated and workers were required at home, the English government became less inclined to make the colonies a dumping ground for the destitute, although criminals continued to be exported in ever-increasing numbers. In the meantime, however, humanitarianism—an integral part of the eighteenth-century Enlightenment—began to animate some highly placed Englishmen. Among them was General James Oglethorpe, a Tory member of Parliament who, as a result of serving on a parliamentary committee to investigate English prisons, became convinced that something had to be done for debtors. At this time, a man could be imprisoned by his creditor for a debt as small as a shilling, and conditions in the prisons to which debtors were consigned resembled those of the stygian pit.

Besides being a humanitarian and a Tory, Oglethorpe was also an imperialist. . . . As an imperialist, Oglethorpe was distinguished by his hatred of Spain and his eagerness to see En-

gland appropriate Spanish territory in the New World. Oglethorpe's imperialism was also economic: he recognized that
powerful and rich as the British Empire was, it had not realized
the dream of the early empire builders by providing the mother
country with a source of spices, silk, tea, coffee, cocoa, dye-
wood, cochineal, and other tropical products upon which the
greatness of empires was believed to depend.

Although Oglethorpe's territorial and economic objectives
lay in the Caribbean, his attention was drawn irresistibly to the
plight of South Carolina. Exposed on the south to the Spaniards
in Saint Augustine, the South Carolinians were forced to withstand the attack of Indians, particularly the Choctaw and Yamasee tribes, who were armed and supplied by Spain for the
express purpose of laying waste the farms and plantations of
those colonists. South Carolina sorely needed support and protection in its wars with the Spaniards and their savage protégés.
Oglethorpe was determined to defend South Carolina by erecting an English buffer colony on its southern flank. This colony
was named Georgia in honor of George II, the King of England.
In 1732, Parliament gave Oglethorpe and his associates a patent
to the territory running from the southern boundary of South
Carolina to Spanish Florida.

A COLONY WITH A DIFFERENCE

Georgia was a unique colony; it was a proprietary colony under the jurisdiction of 21 trustees whose tenure was limited to
a period of 21 years. The arrangement more closely resembled
a mandate under the League of Nations than the organization
of a conventional proprietary colony. Moreover, Georgia was
the only colony from which the original sponsors did not expect
to make money: the trustees held the land "in trust" for the
state. And in marked contrast to other charters, the Georgia
charter did not oblige the trustees to establish representative institutions in the area of their grant.

But the paramount difference between Georgia and other
colonies was that Georgia owed its existence to a financial
grant by the British government. Parliament contributed about
90 percent of the financial support received by Georgia: private
benefactions accounted for the remainder. Part of the reason for
Parliament's heavy outlay for Georgia was the fact that most
of the trustees, including Oglethorpe himself, were members
of Parliament.

Quite as much as Puritan New England, Georgia was a planned society. But unlike the Puritan colonies, it was not intended to be a sanctuary for oppressed religious groups; instead, for the first time, a colony was founded at least in part for the purpose of rehabilitating the victims of social and economic injustice.

Since this was to be a semimilitary colony—the Spaniards could be counted upon to react sharply to a British intrusion upon territory claimed by His Catholic Majesty—Oglethorpe insisted that the colonists be sober, industrious, God-fearing Protestants. Roman Catholics were barred because it was feared that they might side with the Roman Catholic Spaniards. From his observation of English prisons, Oglethorpe was convinced that they contained large numbers of worthy poor—the victims of unduly severe laws, particularly those applying to debtors. But he had no thought of emptying the prisons indiscriminately: habitual criminals were to remain where they were, safely behind bars. Oglethorpe's idea was to select from the inmates of the prisons only those victims of misfortune who possessed the qualities required of pioneers—especially pioneers who were probably going to have to fight for their lives. He did make one exception to this rule: in 1743 he bought an entire cargo of Irish convicts at 5 pounds a head. He simply could not resist this bargain.

PROHIBITING SLAVERY AND ALCOHOL

As South Carolina had shown, nothing was more calculated to weaken a colony militarily than black slavery. Obliged to hold down a large slave population at home, white South Carolinians could not give their undivided attention to defending themselves against the Spaniards and Indians. Primarily for this reason, Oglethorpe and the trustees prohibited slavery in Georgia. It is significant that slavery was not excluded from the colony by the charter of 1732 but by a law enacted in 1735 "for rendering the Colony of Georgia more Defencible." All Negroes, not merely slaves, were excluded from the colony.

Certainly Oglethorpe was not an abolitionist. Oglethorpe himself was a director and later deputy governor of the Royal African Company. He and several of the trustees profited from the slave trade: by prohibiting slavery in Georgia they were acting against their own financial self-interest. Nevertheless, Oglethorpe did not put his opposition to slavery, and to blacks in general, in Georgia wholly upon military grounds. Although he profited from the slave trade, he thought it a dirty business: slavery, he said, was "against the gospel, as well as the fundamental law of England. We refused, as trustees, to make a law permitting such a horrid crime." He was resolved that Georgia, the scene of a unique experiment in philanthropy, should not be infected by an institution so contrary to the principle of goodwill toward men.

Because he was dealing with prison inmates and destitute people, some of whom had gotten into trouble because of their weakness for strong drink, and because Georgia was primarily a military colony, Oglethorpe prohibited the importation of hard liquor (beer and wine were permitted). Also for reasons of military defense, the settlers were compelled to live in compact towns and villages. The economic interests of the empire were served by the requirement that the colonists plant the kind of crops decreed by Oglethorpe and the trustees.

By this means, Oglethorpe hoped to achieve the age-old dream of mercantilists: to make England and its colonies independent of outside sources of supply. Each landowner was required to plant at least 1,000 mulberry trees for every hundred acres owned. The prospectus of the colony held out hope that Georgia would produce wine, silk, oil, dyes, etc. Even the Indians were promised benefits: "the example of a whole colony who shall behave in a just, moral, and religious manner," Oglethorpe observed, "will contribute greatly towards the conversion of the Indians, and taking off the prejudices received from the profligate lives of such who have scarce anything of Christianity but the name."

To prevent the development of the plantation system, which, as South Carolina had demonstrated, weakened the war-making potential of a colony, Oglethorpe and the trustees restricted to 500 acres the amount of land any single individual could own. On the other hand, every adult male was assured of possessing at least 50 acres of land. Since land was held on a feudal and semimilitary tenure, it could not be sold or exchanged without the trustees' consent, and restrictions were imposed upon the devising of land by testament.

Thus the occupations, morals, and freedom of choice of the early Georgians were even more closely regulated than in the Puritan colonies. After all, a New Englander could plant what he pleased, hold slaves, and nip a drink or two. But the poor

Georgians could do none of these: they sowed and reaped as they were told, drank nothing stronger than wine (which they could not afford), and had no black slaves to do the work a white man was unwilling to do.

THE PRICE OF PATERNALISM

In 1732, Oglethorpe personally led a party of 112 settlers, most of them charity cases, ashore at Savannah. But the so-called "Great Migration" occurred in 1736, when several thousand colonists arrived in Georgia. Not all the settlers were English debtors and worthy poor. At Oglethorpe's invitation, Moravians, Salzburgers, Palatines, English, Irish, Scots, and several "Italian silk men" settled in Georgia. Next to Pennsylvania, Georgia was the most cosmopolitan of the English colonies.

The founders of Georgia drew upon over a century and a half of experience in the establishment of overseas settlements. In consequence, they avoided many of the pitfalls into which prior promoters of colonies had fallen. They recognized that it was necessary to pay the passage of settlers, sustain whem while they were engaged in clearing lands and building houses, and supply them with clothing and tools.

In Georgia, for the first time in the history of an English settlement overseas, the colonists were given so much charitable aid that they were encouraged to let the government take care of them. As late as 1738, some settlers were still being supplied from the public commissaries. Even the Indians who were also maintained at the government's expense began to depend upon handouts rather than upon hunting and fishing. When the trustees closed the public commissary in 1739, many of the settlers left the colony in disgust, and the red men reluctantly again took up their bows and arrows.

The price of this kind of paternalism was the denial of individual liberty. Having no representative institutions, the colonists worked, lived, and drank according to directives laid down by the trustees. Many protested vehemently against this denial of the rights of Englishmen: they were, they said, "exposed to as an arbitrary a government as Turkey or Muscovy ever felt." Criticism of the trustees or of the local officials in charge was met with threats of hanging. More whites were whipped and imprisoned in Georgia, it was alleged, than in all the rest of British America. If the Georgians could be believed, they were being reduced to slavery at the same time that they were denied black slaves.

Not the least of the Georgians' grievances was the prohibition upon the importation of rum. Not only did this act of the trustees deprive the settlers of the consolation of strong drink— all the more necessary, it was said, in a hot climate. It also prevented trade with the West Indies, where Georgians were eager to sell lumber, staves, barrels, and agricultural products in exchange for rum and sugar.

In the hope that religion, that other great consoler of mankind, would atone for the loss of strong drink, the trustees distributed thousands of pious tracts among the settlers. John and Charles Wesley, the founders of Methodism, came to Georgia to inspire the colonists with Christian zeal. John Wesley prescribed for Georgians more fasting, cold water, and acts of penance: he said he wished to see Georgia not a rich but a religious colony. But the settlers continued to complain that they suffered from "fevers, wasting and tormenting Fluxes, most excruciating Cholicks, and Dry-Belly Aches; Tremors, Vertigoes, Palsies, and a long Train of painful and lingering nervous Distempers; which brought on to many a cessation from Work and Life; especially as Water without any Qualification was the chief Drink."

Georgians did not really experience the horrors, as they pictured them, of prohibition: in the absence of any effective enforcement machinery, large quantities of rum and other spirituous liquor were imported. But rum had to be paid for in cash, and this drained the colony of specie. One Georgian reported that the interdiction placed upon rum actually promoted its use. "As it is the nature of mankind in general, and of the common sort in particular," he observed, "more eagerly to desire and more immoderately to use those things which are most restrained from them."

THE TRIUMPH OF THE PLANTATION SYSTEM

The exclusion of black slaves from Georgia occasioned one of the first debates in America over slavery. Significantly, far less concern was expressed over the effect of slavery upon the blacks than upon the whites. The proponents of slavery made the point that by being deprived of the opportunity to own slaves, they were denied one of the important rights of Englishmen. Liberty-loving Englishmen demanded the right to hold slaves also on the time-honored ground that only blacks could do the heavy work of clearing land and planting crops in the hot sun. (In the white man's mythology, blacks never felt the heat.)

It was primarily the English settlers who clamored for slaves: the Scotch settlers at Darien, Georgia, and the Salzburg Germans who colonized Ebenezer, Georgia, declared their abhorrence of slavery. "As freedom to them must be as dear as to us, what a scene of horror it must bring!" the Scotch exclaimed.

Although the trustees resisted the demand of the English settlers for black slaves, many were imported under the designation "servants." Finally, in 1750, in response to pressure from the Georgians themselves, Parliament legalized rum and black slavery in the province—with the stipulation, however, that slaves be instructed in Christianity and protected from inhumane treatment. Under the terms laid down by Parliament, slaves could not be made to work more than 16 hours a day. In the hope of preventing the complete triumph of black slave labor, the law required that slaveholders maintain one white worker for every four Negroes.

As Oglethorpe and the trustees had foreseen, the introduction of black slavery meant the triumph of the plantation system. As a result, the small, independent farmer was pushed off the best soil, and thousands of black-slaves were imported to work the large estates. Georgia, in short, became very much like any other Southern colony. In 1752, when Georgia became a royal colony, the resemblance was complete.

Thus, largely as a result of the actions of Georgians themselves, Oglethorpe's vision of an egalitarian society from which black slavery and the plantation system were forever barred was snuffed out. The kind of paternalistic control and the limitations imposed upon the acquisitive instinct were antithetical to the American Dream. What the majority of the settlers wanted was an open society in which every man had a chance to acquire an unlimited amount of land, hold as many slaves as he could buy, drink what he pleased, and plant the crops that brought in the largest and quickest returns.

The Surge of European Immigration

Bradley Chapin

From the mid-1600s on, the population of colonial America grew at an astounding rate, Bradley Chapin explains in the following passage from his book *Early America*. He states that the main factor behind this rapid population growth was immigration from Europe. While the vast majority of immigrants hailed from the British Isles, he writes, sizable groups also arrived from the European continent. They left in order to escape the religious intolerance, violent wars, and economic hardships that plagued much of Europe, drawn by the promise of religious freedom, land, and work in the colonies. A professor of history for many years at Ohio State University in Columbus, Chapin is the author of *Criminal Justice in Colonial America, 1606–1660* and the editor of *Provincial America, 1600–1763*.

The estimated population at the end of the colonial era, 2,780,369 persons excluding Indians, was 80 percent white and 20 percent black. Not surprisingly, the people who had come or whose ancestors had come from the British islands made up the large majority, 78 percent, with the English accounting for about 60 percent, the Scots over 8 percent, the Scots-Irish 6 percent and the Irish almost 4 percent. The largest group from the European continent was German, almost 9 percent of the total. Though neither the Dutch nor the French were emigrating people, they accounted for about 1 and 2 percent of the total. The growth of population from immigration and natural increase had been amazingly rapid. In the century after 1660, the white population grew at a rate of 13 percent each year.

The forces of European push and American pull caused the emigration. American pulling power continued to be the promise of land, jobs, and religious freedom. In varying combinations, intolerance, war, and economic distress created the European push. For example, during the reign of Louis XIV (1643–1715) the French king's policies inadvertently contributed to the strengthening of his English enemy. In 1685 he began an active persecution of the French Protestant minority, the Huguenots. Fleeing from France in all directions, many came to America and settled along the coast from New England to South Carolina. Louis made the Rhine Valley the scene of his wars and at least four times between 1674 and 1707 his armies ravaged the Rhenish Palatinate, creating urgent causes for Germans to leave.

England's domestic and foreign wars also contributed to the movement of people. In 1715 and again in 1745, Scotland rose in arms for the Stuart pretenders to the British throne. Overwhelmed in battle, the highlanders swelled the stream of Scots who had been leaving steadily in search of economic opportunity. By the Treaty of Utrecht (1713), Britain obtained French Acadia (Nova Scotia). Subsequently fearing the native French as security risks, the board of trade ordered them deported and caused the Acadians to be scattered thinly among the mainland colonies. The wars sent many British soldiers and sailors to America, where some deserted and others chose to stay after serving their time.

Policies of religious uniformity in France, the Germanies, and Great Britain made conditions intolerable for religious minorities. In the Germanies, the Peace of Westphalia (1648) recognized three major religions—Catholic, Lutheran, and Calvinist—and then established the rule that the people of each principality must follow the religion of the prince. The rule produced a kaleidoscope of persecution. A person adhering to any one of the recognized faiths might find himself the object of persecution if his prince was of a different religion. In addition there were substantial numbers of Germans who rejected the standard religions. These were the Pietists: United Brethren and Moravians, Amish, Dunkards, Mennonites, and Schwenckfelders. In England, Stuart policy pushed nonconformists out of the realm. It also squeezed the Catholics of southern Ireland and the Scots-Irish Presbyterians of Ulster (northern Ireland). In both areas, Parliament denied all political rights to those who would not support the Anglican Church.

Economic distress caused many farmers to look to America for a new start. A century of war had created great instability in the Rhine Valley. To all of the hazards of agriculture, war added the recurring possibility that invading armies would consume or destroy crops. Times were particularly hard in Ireland and Ulster. English kings made large land grants there and English landlords gouged their tenants. In Ulster they doubled and trebled the rents when old leases expired. English economic interests would not tolerate Irish competition. Responding to pressure, Parliament barred Irish meat and dairy products from the English market and virtually destroyed growing textile industries in Ireland and Ulster with the Woolens Act of 1699.

ENTICING EUROPEANS TO THE COLONIES

The promoters of colonies fished in these pools of misery with success. The understanding came early that the wealth of America could be realized only by putting large numbers of people on the land. From the first efforts of the London Company of Virginia through the settling of Georgia in the mid-eighteenth century, corporations and proprietors sold America by vigorous promotional campaigns. . . . William Penn excelled as a promoter. As a Quaker missionary in the 1670's he twice visited the Rhine Valley. The Rhenish sectaries responded to his pamphlets and from its founding Philadelphia became the great port of entry for German and other immigrants.

Through most of the colonial period, England had no overall policy for the control of movement within the empire or for immigration into it from foreign countries. In 1740, Parliament required seven years residence before an alien in the colonies could be naturalized. Policy, varying from colony to colony and from time to time in a single colony, was pragmatic and based on self appraisal of local needs. Yet certain broad regional trends are discernible. The New England colonies pursued conservative immigration policies. The large increase of people there was self-generated, so that New England remained more purely English than other sections. To the south, the attitude toward immigration related directly to the need for labor. In the late seventeenth and early eighteenth centuries, the middle and southern colonies encouraged immigration. The southern colonies especially used the headright system extensively. The system paid the cost of transporting immigrants by granting land to the person who paid for the passage. Later the system of redemptioneers largely replaced the headrights. The redemptioneer was a person whom an agent obtained by fair means or foul and transported to America. The agent then sold the redemptioneer's labor for a term of years. To satisfy the demand for labor, agents resorted to kidnapping and a large number of persons began their life in America as "kids." British courts added to the outgoing stream by exporting vagabonds and condemned criminals.

THE BIRTH OF "THE MELTING POT"

In the earliest days of Virginia settlement, a ballad writer, encouraging people to go out, emphasized the overriding purpose. "We hope to plant a nation, wherein none before hath stood." In the older, racial sense of the word "nation" the purpose had been realized by the mid-eighteenth century. Regardless of the diversity of the people—in language, law and sentiment—the new nation was English. This created the dilemma for the non-English immigrant. To what degree should they and could they maintain their own language, religion, and customs?

The agencies that could keep ethnic cultures alive were family, church, and school. Most immigrant groups brought family and church with them, but some surrendered their identities quickly while others maintained major elements of their culture almost indefinitely. Language obviously made a difference. Those who spoke English in whatever local form—the Irish, Scots-Irish, and Scots—soon became a species of Englishmen. Of the people who did not speak English, the Swedes and French were soon assimilated, but the Dutch and Germans kept major features of their culture through the colonial period and beyond. Though a distinct language was significant, it did not guarantee ethnic survival. The number and concentration of a people seems to have been the critical factor. Though Irish, Scots, and Scots-Irish came in large numbers, they tended to scatter. The Scots-Irish went or were shoved along to the frontier, where by definition people were spread thinly. Many Irish went to Virginia and North Carolina, where most began their American lives as indentured servants on individual plantations. The Scots went wherever opportunity took them. The Swedish settlements on the Delaware were relatively compact and contiguous. Though the Swedes had been in the area for a dozen years before the English arrived, they were so few in number that they were absorbed easily. The French were neither numerous nor concentrated.

CULTURAL SEPARATISM

Only the Dutch and the Germans combined most of the factors that favored cultural survival. The Germans came in large numbers and concentrated themselves in eastern Pennsylvania. The Dutch, though less numerous, had established a definite jurisdiction in the naturally cohesive Hudson Valley. . . . The churches of the Dutch and German homelands maintained contact and interest in their American extensions. Both the Germans and the Dutch maintained schools. The most obvious evidence of cultural survival was the regular, daily use of the parent language. The Dutch maintained theirs in family, school, and church. On the eve of the American Revolution judges complained that they could not get twelve English speaking men to make up a jury in Albany. The Germans resisted the use of English in their core institutions. Children went to school and all went to church and heard lessons and services in German. A flourishing German language press provided books, pamphlets, almanacs, and, by the time of the Revolution, over three dozen newspapers in Pennsylvania. This cultural persistence still shows in a created sub-language, Pennsylvania Dutch (Deutsch, or German) and in the survival of some of the pietistic communities. As recently as 1972, the Amish won recognition of the value of their different way of life in a United States Supreme Court case.

One area in which ethnic separation failed absolutely was government. Early in the Pennsylvania experience, Germans established a distinct community at Germantown, a suburb of Philadelphia. Under the direction of Francis David Pastorius, Germantown became a staging area through which many Germans passed on their way to permanent homes. From 1691 to 1707, a separate court sat there. Germantown Germans tried their cases in a German court. On one occasion the court cleared a man who was under indictment at the Philadelphia quarter sessions for a serious crime. As a result of the jurisdictional collision, the Pennsylvania government shut down the Germantown court and its record concludes plaintively "from thence no more Courts were kept at Germantown." Law would be made, enforced and judgment rendered in English institutions.

Africans in America: Enslavement and Resistance

Jon Butler

Jon Butler is the William Robertson Coe Professor of American Studies and History at Yale University in New Haven, Connecticut. He also serves as the chair of the history department and as codirector of the Yale Center for the Advanced Study of Religion. His publications include *Religion in Colonial America, The Huguenots in America: A Refugee People in New World Society,* and *Awash in a Sea of Faith: Christianizing the American People.*

In the following selection, taken from his book *Becoming America: The Revolution Before 1776,* Butler examines the solidification of race-based slavery in colonial America. According to the author, Africans did not become a significant part of the American labor force until the 1680s, when the importation of African slaves drastically increased. The enslaved Africans endured incredible hardships, Butler maintains, but they also actively resisted their lot in a variety of ways, ranging from work slowdowns to violent revolts against their white masters.

T he history of Africans in America differs dramatically from the history of Europeans in America. Where the African experience in America centered on themes of capture, enslavement, and coercion, the history of Europeans in

Jon Butler, *Becoming America: The Revolution Before 1776,* Cambridge, MA: Harvard University Press, 2000. Copyright © 2000 by the President and Fellows of Harvard College. Reproduced by permission.

America centered on themes of choice, profit, and considerable freedom. The African and European experiences never duplicated and seldom paralleled each other. Yet Africans and their experience in America powerfully intersected the decline of the Indian population and the outpouring of non-English immigrants to America to recast the seventeenth-century colonies and become the American future.

THE SUDDEN TURN TO SLAVEHOLDING

In 1680 slavery was uncommon, strange, and even exotic in the British mainland colonies. British colonists certainly knew what it was. They knew it meant ownership of other human beings. They knew it gave owners untrammeled power to buy, sell, and compel labor from the enslaved and to own their offspring. As the eighteenth century progressed, they tightened slaveholding and treated bonded men and women with ever greater severity. They consistently corralled Africans' behavior and wrung from them every conceivable advantage of labor and creativity, often through unimaginable mental and physical cruelty. The principal impetus for this action was simple: profit. Slaveholding attracted European colonists intent on realizing the dreams that brought them to America even when it subjected others to horrific suffering.

As late as 1680 the English mainland colonies knew few Africans and little slavery. In the Chesapeake colonies of Maryland and Virginia, Africans accounted for only 5 percent of the population in 1680, and English indentured servants comprised more than 90 percent of the hired labor force. Between 1650 and 1680 the minor slavery that existed in the Chesapeake remained loose and relatively informal. Its legal articulation was sparse, and its social leakage substantial. The Maryland and Virginia legislatures passed few laws enunciating a comprehensive slave "code" before 1690, and from the 1650s into the 1680s, surprising numbers of Africans lived as free residents, completing labor terms more akin to those of indentured servants, after which they were freed by their owners. Some free Africans farmed land they owned, and a few, like Anthony Johnson of Accomack County, Virginia, owned African slaves themselves. Yet by 1700 the free Africans had disappeared—fled or been reenslaved, no one knows—probably because the English settlers' sudden turn to extensive slaveholding after 1680 made them a threat, a preview of the ways that increased slaveholding would transform seventeenth-century colonial society almost beyond recognition.

Why the rush to slaveholding after 1680? Complex causes created the change. First, the supply of British and continental European indentured servants declined as the colonial demand for labor continued and accelerated, especially after 1680. English officials complained less about overcrowding at home, and rumors of mistreatment of indentured servants in America abounded. As a result, the immigration of servants from England to America declined in the last quarter of the seventeenth century and failed to satisfy the rising labor demands of colonial farmers, especially in the Chesapeake and the Carolinas. The immigration statistics for the first decade of the eighteenth century reflect the result: between 1700 and 1709, only 1,500 indentured English, Scottish, and continental European indentured servants arrived in America, while imported Africans numbered 9,000. By the first decade of the eighteenth century, then, captured Africans outstripped indentured servants by a ratio of at least 6–1 and established a pattern of colonial labor consumption not broken until the American Revolution.

Second, captive Africans consistently became easier to obtain. The Royal African Company, which had been granted a monopoly for the British slave trade in 1672, eagerly exploited the growing market in the still small British mainland colonies. By the 1690s the company's success produced demands to open the market to competitors, and when the Crown ended the monopoly in 1698 new entrepreneurs plunged into the trade. London, Liverpool, and especially Bristol slave traders soon accounted for the great bulk of eighteenth-century mainland colony slave imports, but colonists also entered the trade. Between 1680 and the 1740s colonial merchants and ship owners began to specialize in slave trading—John Guerard, Richard Hill, Benjamin Savage, and Joseph Wragg in Charleston and Godfrey Malbone, Abraham Redwood, the Wanton family, and Samuel Vernon in Newport, Rhode Island, among others. In addition, the increasing reach of international commerce into all the colonies meant that enslaved Africans were also more easily available from Spanish, French, and especially Dutch traders. By 1710, then, the increasing numbers of colonists who wanted Africans enjoyed considerable choice in both Africans and merchants.

But why slaves? Why not some form of indentured servitude, especially since the English treated at least some Africans as indentured servants before 1650 and since both the English Civil War (1645–1649) and the Glorious Revolution (1688–1689) raised the English commitment to personal freedom? The reasons lodged in slaveholding's attraction. Slavery furnished laborers that European immigration could not stock. Slavery ameliorated the uncertainties that indentured servitude engendered. Slavery imposed a formal legal silence upon laborers denied the rights that indentured servants claimed for shelter, clothing, and even education. And slavery offered lifetime service while indentured servants completed their labor in three or four years. Even if masters breached indenture contracts without fearing lawsuits and even if few servants actually pursued complaints, the comparative point was obvious: slaves offered more attractive, longer-term investments even as they also conveyed new kinds of status to their owners.

THE FOCUS ON AFRICAN SLAVERY

But why not Indians rather than Africans? Indian slavery existed in the American colonies from the mid-seventeenth century past the American Revolution. But Indian slavery never prospered. Too many Indians remained free, too many resisted slavery, and too many escaped too easily into a countryside they knew intimately, in striking contrast to captured Africans, who found the countryside even more unfamiliar than did the Europeans in America. Indian slavery existed in colonial America, but it remained an oddity.

The focus on Africans had two causes. Again, one involved convenience. In the sixteenth and seventeenth centuries Europeans discovered in Africa a ready and rapidly expanding supply of slaves. Europeans could purchase captives in African wars that they could then sell as laborers in the New World colonies. A fateful Benin agreement with a Portuguese trader in 1472 to allow the trade of precious metals and "slaves" began a trade that devastated Old World Africa. A rapidly accelerating New World demand for slaves escalated wars among African nations. Previously incidental captives became prime booty to be sold to multiplying numbers of European traders hurrying back to Africa to acquire fresh captives for eager New World markets.

Second, Western perceptions of African culture induced Europeans to ask few, if any, questions about the legal and moral basis of their own behavior. Europeans had long labeled Africans as foreign, heathen, and differently colored, regardless

African captives were crammed into a slave ship's hold, where they endured horrific conditions during the voyage to America.

of African national and cultural differences and without help from pseudo-scientific nineteenth-century concepts of "race." African "government" seemed chaotic and incapable. Africans were "savage" and libidinous. And they were not white, or not what passed for "white" in a Europe actually overflowing with considerable varieties of skin color among its peoples. In short, Africans might be human, but Europeans also perceived them as different, disagreeable, and dispensable, ideal candidates for an enslavement that very quickly became indelibly American.

In turning to slavery so widely after 1680, English and other European colonists in America joined a slave trade that became the largest forced human migration in history. Anomalies typified this transformation. Even at its height slave imports to Britain's mainland colonies remained a minor part of the much larger New World slave trade. Ninety-five percent of the captured Africans brought to the New World between 1700 and 1760 went to places other than the British mainland colonies: 400,000 arrived in the Dutch Caribbean, 400,000 in Spanish America, 1,000,000 in the British Caribbean, 1,000,000 in the French Caribbean, and 1,300,000 in Portuguese Brazil. By contrast, only about 250,000 captured Africans came to the British mainland colonies.

The dramatic rise in slave imports after 1680 nonetheless

held immense implications for the development of Britain's eighteenth-century mainland colonies. Before 1680 English immigrants constituted the single largest group arriving in the mainland colonies and made up nearly 90 percent of all foreign arrivals in the colonies. But after 1700 and down to the American Revolution, Africans constituted the largest group of arrivals in the colonies and outstripped all European immigrants combined. Africans failed to outnumber European immigrants only between 1750 and 1759 and between 1770 and 1775, although even in those years they still outnumbered any single group of European immigrants. The number of imported Africans climbed from 9,000 between 1700 and 1709 to 40,000 in the 1730s, then doubling to 80,000 in the 1760s, with a dip to 50,000 in the 1750s. Between 1700 and 1775, African imports dropped to less than 20,000, largely because prerevolutionary political tension reduced the demand for slaves among anxious farmers and planters.

SLAVERY IN THE VARIOUS COLONIES

Slaveholding became especially prominent in the southern colonies but also prospered in the north. Through the 1670s indentured servants outnumbered slaves in Maryland estate inventories almost four to one. But by the 1690s slaves outnumbered indentured servants four to one. Africans constituted 13 percent of the Maryland population by 1704 and 30 percent of it by 1764. Africans constituted 6 percent of Virginia's population in 1680, 20 percent by 1720, and almost 40 percent by 1760. In South Carolina, this rate grew both higher and faster. The West Indies planters who settled the colony in the 1680s overwhelmingly rejected indentured servitude and turned to slaveholding for imported agricultural labor, just as they had done in the West Indies. Enslaved Africans outnumbered Europeans there by 1710 and constituted two-thirds of the colony's population by 1720.

Population changes in the middle and northern colonies were impressive but not so dramatic. By 1770 Pennsylvania contained more than 4,000 slaves, although the proportion of slaves seldom exceeded 3 percent between 1690 and 1770. As early as 1698 New York contained about 2,000 slaves, or about 12 percent of the population, a legacy, in part, of long-standing Dutch slave trading. But Africans climbed to about 15 percent of the colony's population at mid-century, and in 1771 the colony still contained 20,000 Africans amid 150,000 Europeans.

Even New England knew slavery. Rhode Island always contained the largest percentage of slaves in the region, a by-product of the extensive slave trading pursued by its merchants and shippers. Perhaps reflecting this fact, Rhode Island's enslaved population also fluctuated considerably, 6 percent in 1708, almost 12 percent in 1755, then back to 6 percent in 1771. In Connecticut, enslaved Africans never topped 3.2 percent of the population (in 1762), although this low ratio still placed more than 4,500 slaves in the colony. In Massachusetts, the most "English" of all the colonies, enslaved Africans made up only 2.1 percent of the population in 1764. Yet by the Revolution, more than 5,000 Africans lived in this northern colony where captured Africans had been present since the 1630s and where their antiquity in the land was scarcely younger than the settlement of their Puritan owners.

CHARACTERISTICS OF THE AFRICANS' ORDEAL

Death, agony, and bittersweet resilience characterized the African experience in the mainland colonies. Death not only came unusually early, at least by comparison to the experience of European colonists, but in circumstances Europeans never knew. The experience of slavery for Africans began with the deaths of compatriots and kin in local wars. Then more of it came in the infamous "middle passage" from Africa to America, where 10 percent of slaves packed aboard a vessel died regularly and where entrapment on a ship fraught with disease or commanded by an incompetent captain sometimes brought the death rate higher. Then death stalked Africans in America. Typically, they survived less than five years. Sometimes they did not make it through even one year in America: eight of the thirty-two slaves John Mercer bought in Virginia between 1733 and 1742 died in their first year of service, for example. The causes were not difficult to locate: lack of resistance to European and American diseases, unfamiliar foods, poor housing, and depression and anomie [alienation], which produced sufficient suicides to prompt owners to complain about the problem. Unlike inanimate property, Africans could and did destroy themselves, a prospect owners feared and resented.

The agony centered on slaveholding itself, and after 1680 European colonists in the mainland settlements constructed a slaveholding of intense control and manipulativeness, a distinctly modern institution that laid the foundation for the even more powerful slaveholding of the postrevolutionary antebellum era. Everywhere in the eighteenth-century mainland colonies, European slaveholders produced an increasingly authoritarian institution ever more concerned with owners' power, slave discipline, and what they regarded as African "misbehavior." Seventeenth-century legislation was often brief in the extreme. But after 1680 assemblies from the Carolinas to New England continuously expanded "slave law" to tighten owners' control and better control slave behavior. Sometimes this happened fitfully, as after "incidents" like the 1712 New York City slave revolt, the 1739 Stono Rebellion in South Carolina, and the rumor of a slave revolt in New York City in 1741. Legislators felt that the rapidly growing enslaved population needed taming, as did those who employed slaves. Thus when New York revised its slave code in 1731 it prohibited Africans from owning or possessing guns and also fined owners for letting slaves wander alone at night.

The eighteenth-century colonial slave laws were not uniform. South Carolina's slave laws were more brutal than those of Virginia and Maryland, though all were harsh enough. South Carolina more readily subjected Africans to death and specified cutting ankle cords, slitting noses, and "gelding" or castration than did Virginia, although everyone sanctioned the whip for almost all offenses. Yet from South Carolina to New York and Rhode Island, legislation everywhere tightened slaveholding. In the process American colonists made modern American slavery primarily between 1680 and 1770. They did not inherit it. Seventeenth-century mainland colony slavery established crucial principles about the ability of one person to own another. Eighteenth-century mainland colony slavery created the modern system of human and legal interrelationships that left a devastating and indelible imprint on America, its society and its conscience. . . .

FORMS OF RESISTANCE

The two principal rebellions of the colonial era, the 1712 New York City revolt and South Carolina's 1739 Stono Rebellion, never freed captured Africans as their planners hoped. The New York City rebellion lasted only one evening and the Stono Rebellion several days and both cost many African lives. But the two rebellions, plus rumors of revolts in Annapolis, Maryland, in 1740 and in New York City again in 1741, terrorized Europeans. They gave ominous meaning to signs of African-

American community and resolve: sustained, persistent labor resistance that ranged from tool breakage, slack work, and running away to assault against Europeans and even homicide.

Running away and work resistance, not revolution, became the most common form of African resistance to slavery and also helped to create community and strengthen individual resolve. Few captured Africans were lucky enough to manage permanent escapes. The wilderness was as strange to them as to Europeans, and slave owners possessed overwhelming powers of chase, detection, and capture. Despite these difficulties, Africans continually resisted owners by running away, even if only for short periods of time, and by resisting work. Runaways produced a peculiar newspaper culture in which runaway advertisements in the *Virginia Gazette* and the *South Carolina Gazette* became a small literary genre. Owners tried to raise alarm among slaveholders almost inured to such departures while attempting to describe the uniqueness of the missing African in ways that would engineer his or her return.

Work resistance could be more subtle. In South Carolina, slaves resisted the arduous labor of pounding rice by hand. Owners recognized the hardship and the cost: one observer described rice pounding as "the severest work the negroes undergo and costs every planter the lives of several slaves annually." Africans sometimes complained about particular jobs, occasionally winning an owner's understanding but most often suffering punishment and a return to work. Some resistance verged on rebellion. Africans sabotaged tools, ruined processed crops, and burned barns. They murdered owners with a wide range of techniques from assault to poisoning. After the 1739 Stono Rebellion, planters in South Carolina and elsewhere feared that such episodes were bringing them closer to an even larger confrontation.

Resistance, flight, and murder reinforced community among Africans. Initiating resistance required cooperation from friends, who made identification of individual culprits difficult, and from relatives, who hid runaway Africans who bolted. Resistance took root in the growing reality of kinship among Africans originally from highly diverse cultures, in a growing sense of place, and in a knowledge that Africans were the backbone of a burgeoning economy and culture whose achievement they guaranteed but whose reward they were denied. Even in the face of retributive Europeans, captured Africans had created community under conditions experienced by no other immigrants to America.

CULTURAL PROGRESS IN THE COLONIES

LOUIS GOTTSCHALK AND DONALD LACH

A professor of history for over thirty years at the University of Chicago, Louis Gottschalk published a number of books about the Marquis de Lafayette's life, including his role in the creation of the United States. Donald Lach held the position of Bernadotte E. Schmitt Professor of Modern History at the University of Chicago and wrote extensively concerning the influence of Asia on Europe during the early modern era. Together they coauthored *Europe and the Modern World* and *Toward the French Revolution: Europe and America in the Eighteenth-Century World*, from which the following selection is excerpted. Gottschalk and Lach describe the cultural flowering of colonial America in such areas as science, philosophy, literature, higher education, the establishment of libraries, and the birth of the free press.

I n the Anglo-American colonies the growth of trade and commerce during the eighteenth century increased, in turn, the interchange of ideas and quickened the intellectual life and untraditional tendencies of the colonists. As long as the colonial settlements had remained widely scattered and isolated, ideas had tended to remain static, unaffected by outside impacts, and unable to congeal into a common consciousness and public opinion. But the wandering merchant and sailor, the itinerant peddler and shoemaker, and other tradesmen circulated both their wares and the current views from community to community; and, as roads and transportation facilities improved, the communication of ideas improved with them.

In the early days it had often been virtually impossible to find one's way through the forest even when traveling between the largest colonial centers. The few scattered inns had been unspeakably dirty and unsafe, and it was not uncommon for the landlord to assign a single room to several travelers regardless of congeniality or sex. By the middle of the eighteenth century, however, roads and inns had improved greatly on the main routes. Travel had increased sufficiently by 1732 to warrant the publication in Boston of the first American guidebook, *The Vade Mecum [Handbook] for America, or a Companion for Traders and Travelers.* This book set forth the roads and distances between important points from Boston to Jamestown and included information about local fairs and other attractions. The greater number of coastwise vessels and their increased tonnage and better accommodations also encouraged travel among the colonists, and the seaboard location of the settlements was an inducement to maritime transportation.

Still another factor in the stimulation of colonial thought was the growth in population and importance of the towns. Cities, large and small, tend to be centers of new ideas, new inventions, new associations of people, new styles of dress, new tastes in food, new schemes of politics and economics, new ventures in trade, and new contacts in culture. True enough, during the entire colonial period and for a century to come, the great majority of Americans lived a rural existence. Nevertheless, centers like Boston, New York, and Philadelphia became increasingly important focal points, and in their midst were fashioned the articulate forces of intellectual and political ferment. All were seaports and had access to contemporary European thought.

INTELLECTUAL CLUBS

In this cosmopolitan atmosphere of the cities there sprang up a host of clubs, founded for various purposes and with varying degrees of seriousness, but nearly all intent upon things of the spirit—in every sense of the word. Some of these clubs' names are intriguing. For example, New York could boast of the Hungarian and the Hum Drum clubs. Newport possessed the Philosophical Club (but this might have been a misnomer, for a contemporary tells us that, though the members drank punch and smoked, he "was surprised to find that no matters of philosophy were brought upon the carpet" and "they talked of privateering and the building of vessels"). Philadelphia had among its organizations a Beefsteak Club and a literary-scientific society called "the Junto."

The latter club, founded in 1727 by Benjamin Franklin, was a debating society where young literati read and discussed papers. As an outgrowth of the Junto, Franklin and others founded the American Philosophical Society in 1743. Its secularist purpose was shown by its encouragement of "all philosophical experiments that let light into the nature of things, tend to increase the power of man over matter, and multiply the conveniences and pleasures of life." Included in its membership were some of the outstanding minds in the colonies, together with such eminent European scientists as French chemist Antoine-Laurent Lavoisier, Swedish botanist Carolus Linnaeus, and French naturalist Georges-Louis Leclerc de Buffon and such *philosophes* [philosophers] as Marquis de Condorcet and Marquis de Chastellux (not to mention Marquis de Lafayette). In connection with the Junto, Franklin was instrumental in building up a subscription library that contained scientific works, and that he did not fill its shelves with theological books—as the libraries of the colonial colleges did—was indicative of the new rationalism he did so much to promulgate.

THE COLONIAL PRESS

The growth of towns likewise encouraged the rise of a periodical press. The first regular newspaper, the *Boston News-Letter*, appeared in 1704, a small, dull periodical that managed to keep itself alive by printing only innocuous items that would give no offense to the political authorities. Fifteen years later two more papers entered the field, and in 1721 James Franklin, Benjamin's brother, founded the *New England Courant*, resisting the dissuasions of his friends, who assured him that America did not need another newspaper. By 1765 the colonists were reading about forty-three newspapers, three of them in German.

Many of these journals had short lives, and few had real literary merit. They freely copied interesting news items from each other, often weeks or months old, since, in the absence of other means of communication, stale news was still news. They seldom were as large as modern tabloids. They nearly always carried little advertisements or "notices" on every page, and the front page was generally devoted almost entirely to such notices. Benjamin Franklin's paper, the *Pennsylvania Gazette*, was entertaining and influential, while two southern journals, the

South Carolina Gazette and the *Virginia Gazette*, had literary standards surpassing those of any New England papers.

Despite some censorship the colonial press exerted a considerable influence on its readers, who turned to it for information about events overseas and in neighboring colonies. A victory for American intellectual and legal independence occurred in 1735 when John Peter Zenger, editor of the *New York Weekly Journal*, was acquitted of charges brought by New York's governor in a case involving the reinterpretation of the English law of libel and hence the principle of freedom of the press. The jury's verdict was later termed by Gouverneur Morris, himself a leader in the American Revolution to come, "the morning star of liberty which subsequently revolutionized America."

COLLEGES AND UNIVERSITIES

The first universities established in the New World were founded in Mexico City and Lima in 1551, under the auspices of the Catholic Church. Likewise, the first universities founded in the Anglo-American colonies were launched under religious control—in these instances, Protestant. The oldest is Harvard, authorized in 1636 by a vote of the Massachusetts General Court and endowed by John Harvard, a Charlestown minister, so that young men might in turn become ministers. The second-oldest college is William and Mary, established in 1693 during the reign of the royal pair after whom it was named. The third college to be established was Yale, founded in 1701 as a Puritan institution intended to educate young men "for publick employment both in Church and Civil State." Its endowment came from Elihu Yale, who had amassed a fortune from the East Indian trade. In the middle of the eighteenth century came the great religious outburst known as "the Great Awakening," and it led to the founding of four new colleges—Princeton (1746), which was Presbyterian; Brown (1764), which was Baptist; Rutgers (1766), which was Dutch Reformed; and Dartmouth (1770), which was Congregational. King's College, an Anglican institution, was founded in 1754 and was presently to change its name to "Columbia," in keeping with political innovations.

These institutions were sectarian, and their curricula were traditionally Classical. In America as in Europe, Latin had still been the language of scholarly writing in the seventeenth century, and a knowledge of Greek, though not so essential to learning, had been regarded as desirable. But the eighteenth-century Franklin was self-educated, and his early education had included no Latin, Greek, formal philosophy, or pure science. He conceived of an educational institution whose curriculum would include such utilitarian studies as surveying, navigation, accounting, mechanics, agriculture, physics, chemistry, history, civics, government, trade, commerce, international law, and modern languages as well as the Classics. This was the Academy, and later the College, of Philadelphia. Franklin thereby became the founder of the first institution of higher learning in the Western world to afford training in vocations and trades as well as in the learned professions, in contemporary problems as well as in Classical and theological lore, and in the practical and applied sciences as well as scientific theory. His college became a model for many subsequent American colleges—whether for better or for worse is still a highly debated point. In 1765 a medical school was established in Philadelphia, the earliest of its kind in North America.

ALMANACS, BOOKS, AND LIBRARIES

In general, colonial institutions of higher learning were marked by rigidity and conservatism of thought and by mediocrity of scholarship. In the general impetus, however, to the advancement of learning that marked the middle decades of the eighteenth century, colonial scholarship seems to have improved appreciably. The intellectual tastes of the colonists were reflected in the books that they read. A farmhouse would probably contain—if the household were literate—a Bible, of course, and a hymn book, and an almanac. Almost every printing house in the colony produced its almanac. The almanac was a small annual magazine, with encyclopedic information—recipes, sermon texts, lists of pills, short stories and poems, interest tables, weather prognostications, distances between taverns, aphorisms, jokes, essays, and astronomical information of sorts. The almanac's accuracy was open to grave doubts, but the average colonist probably seldom entertained them. The best-known was Franklin's *Poor Richard's Almanac*, but it had to compete with a host of rivals.

The townspeople were more catholic than the farmers in their reading, and colonial importers and printers managed to provide an ever-growing number of readers with the latest literature from England and the Continent. Political philosophers John Locke and Charles-Louis de Montesquieu were among the especially popular writers, articulating as they did the colonists' own thoughts on natural law and right. Of course, the Classics also found ready buyers. Franklin, as printer, was able to place before his customers works by Seneca, Ovid, Francis Bacon, John Dryden, Locke, John Milton, and Jonathan Swift. Such books soon found their way into private libraries, several of which were worthy of respect.

Meanwhile, those who could not afford to amass book collections of their own had their intellectual appetites at least partly satisfied by the founding of small libraries in the larger cities. Since 1621, when the earliest known library in the Anglo-American colonies was established for Indians, the number of libraries had grown. Here again Franklin's resourcefulness showed itself to advantage, when he instituted the first subscription library in America in connection with the Junto. Together with a small number of mechanics and tradesmen, he started a library by the practical expedient of pooling modest savings. In Franklin's words: "The institution soon manifested its utility, was imitated by other towns, and in other provinces. The libraries were augmented by donations; reading became fashionable; and our people, having no public amusement to divert their attention from study, became better acquainted with books; and in a few years were observed by strangers to be better instructed and more intelligent than people of the same rank generally are in other countries." Franklin was to maintain afterward that the new libraries "perhaps have contributed in some degree to the stand generally made throughout the colonies in defense of their privileges."

COLONIAL LITERATURE

Except for Franklin, no great literary figure appeared in the colonies, North or South, before 1776. Few outstanding works of art or belles lettres were produced on the frontier. As the towns grew, literary productivity grew with them. But writings were generally political and historical tracts rather than novels or poetry or drama. John Woolman, a New Jersey Quaker, tailor, traveler, and reformer, produced a series of pamphlets in the period around the Treaty of 1763 carrying such titles as *Some Considerations on the Keeping of Negroes* and *A Word of Remembrance and Caution to the Rich*. John Wise, Massachusetts pastor, defended the Congregational theory of politics in *The Churches' Quarrel Espoused* (1710) and *A Vindication of the Government of the*

New-England Churches (1717), and other pastors in pamphlets and sermons dealt with the problems of popular government. Samuel Sewall's diary and Mary Rowlandson's story of her captivity among the Indians were works of interesting personal record but of little literary merit. The writing of history was seriously cultivated on the frontier. Cotton Mather's *Magnalia Christi Americana [A History of Christ's Wonderful Works in America]* (1702), Cadwallader Colden's *History of the Five Nations of Indians* (Iroquois) (volume I published in 1727), and Thomas Hutchinson's *History of the Province of Massachusetts Bay* (three volumes, of which the first appeared in 1764) were the most lasting eighteenth-century efforts. In these American historical accounts, the Indian appeared as a significant figure, even sometimes coloring the author's prose with a touch of the formal metaphorical style of the Indian oration and treaty.

Much of the better colonial literature was in the form of sermons. Despite the fact that the importation of Europe's growing rationalism was pushing America's educated classes into a secular and deistic trend on religious questions, the clergy continued to be the intellectual guides of at least the less educated. Many clerics were anti-Anglican. A revivalist wave, sometimes called the "Great Awakening," spread through America, beginning in the 1730's, in much the same way that Quietism, Pietism, Jansenism, and Wesleyanism had spread through Europe. Jonathan Edwards, a native-born, controversial, unrelenting, strict Calvinist theologian, George Whitefield, visiting from England, and other ministers of various denominations preached through the country a "new light," a new emotional rapport with God, which found expression in the rapid growth of evangelistic sects like the Baptists and the founding of new colleges like Princeton, Brown, Rutgers, and Dartmouth. Their sermons were frequently printed and widely read.

In other fields of cultural development America also showed the effects of its youth. The great luminary of American science—as of other lines of American cultural achievements—during the colonial period was Franklin. His *Experiments and Observations on Electricity* (1751) set forth, among other things, the daring experiment with a kite that decisively confirmed the identity of lightning and electricity. Other scientists—like David Rittenhouse in astronomy and Benjamin Rush in medicine—were worthy but less outstanding.

Though colonial America had its poets—particularly Philip

Freneau and the Hartford group known as the "Connecticut Wits"—and its artists—particularly John Singleton Copley— these men were imitative and of little genius and were to produce most of their best works only in the period following the Declaration of Independence. One eighteenth-century poet, however, deserves special mention. Edward Taylor (1645–1729) privately gave expression to his apparently devout and meditative soul in poems, published only in 1937, that critics now regard as of superior distinction.

Although the New World had as yet produced few great artists, writers, and scientists, the important thing was that, however few, they were beginning to think of themselves as Americans and of their culture as native, no matter how dependent upon European origins and influences. Even in cultural matters America was learning to stand more or less alone.

ADVICE TO A YOUNG TRADESMAN

BENJAMIN FRANKLIN

Benjamin Franklin was perhaps the most prominent cultural figure of eighteenth-century colonial America. Self-educated and self-made, he was a true renaissance man, excelling in such diverse fields as business, politics, scientific research, practical invention, philosophy, and comedic literature. *Poor Richard's Almanac,* his annual publication of weather forecasts sprinkled with wise and witty sayings, was intensely popular and made him a fortune. Franklin invested much of his money in his community, funding fire departments, libraries, schools, and other civic improvements. His writings often stressed the colonial ideals of hard work, thriftiness, and upright character, as demonstrated in the following essay from July 1748.

To my Friend A.B.
 As you have desired it of me, I write the following Hints, which have been of Service to me, and may, if observed, be so to you.

Remember that TIME is Money. He that can earn Ten Shillings a Day by his Labour, and goes abroad, or sits idle one half of that Day, tho' he spends but Sixpence during his Diversion or Idleness, ought not to reckon That the only Expence; he has really spent or rather thrown away Five Shillings besides.

Remember that CREDIT is Money. If a Man lets his Money lie in my Hands after it is due, he gives me the Interest, or so much as I can make of it during that Time. This amounts to a consid-

Benjamin Franklin, "Advice to a Young Tradesman, Written by an Old One," *The American Instructor: or Young Man's Best Companion*, by George Fisher, Philadelphia: B. Franklin and D. Hall, 1748.

erable Sum where a Man has good and large Credit, and makes good Use of it.

Remember that Money is of a prolific generating Nature. Money can beget Money, and its Offspring can beget more, and so on. Five Shillings turn'd, is *Six:* Turn'd again, 'tis Seven and Three Pence; and so on 'til it becomes an Hundred Pound. The more there is of it, the more it produces every Turning, so that the Profits rise quicker and quicker. He that kills a breeding Sow, destroys all her Offspring to the thousandth Generation. He that murders a Crown, destroys all it might have produc'd, even Scores of Pounds.

Remember that Six Pounds a Year is but a Groat a Day. For this little Sum (which may be daily wasted either in Time or Expence unperceiv'd) a Man of Credit may on his own Security have the constant Possession and Use of an Hundred Pounds. So much in Stock briskly turn'd by an industrious Man, produces great Advantage.

ESTABLISHING GOOD CREDIT

Remember this Saying, *That the good Paymaster is Lord of another Man's Purse*. He that is known to pay punctually and exactly to the Time he promises, may at any Time, and on any Occasion, raise all the Money his Friends can spare. This is sometimes of great Use: Therefore never keep borrow'd Money an Hour beyond the Time you promis'd, lest a Disappointment shuts up your Friends Purse forever.

The most trifling Actions that affect a Man's Credit, are to be regarded. The Sound of your Hammer at Five in the Morning or Nine at Night, heard by a Creditor, makes him easy Six Months longer. But if he sees you at a Billiard Table, or hears your Voice in a Tavern, when you should be at Work, he sends for his Money the next Day. Finer Cloaths than he or his Wife wears, or greater Expence in any particular than he affords himself, shocks his Pride, and he duns you to humble you. Creditors are a kind of People, that have the sharpest Eyes and Ears, as well as the best Memories of any in the World.

Good-natur'd Creditors (and such one would always chuse to deal with if one could) feel Pain when they are oblig'd to ask for Money. Spare 'em that Pain, and they will love you. When you receive a Sum of Money, divide it among 'em in Proportion to your Debts. Don't be asham'd of paying a small Sum because you owe a greater. Money, more or less, is always welcome; and your Creditor had rather be at the Trouble of receiving Ten Pounds voluntarily brought him, tho' at ten different Times or Payments, than be oblig'd to go ten Times to demand it before he can receive it in a Lump. It shews, besides, that you are mindful of what you owe; it makes you appear a careful as well as an honest Man; and that still encreases your Credit.

Beware of thinking all your own that you possess, and of living accordingly. 'Tis a Mistake that many People who have Credit fall into. To prevent this, keep an exact Account for some Time of both your Expences and your Incomes. If you take the Pains at first to mention Particulars, it will have this good Effect; you will discover how wonderfully small trifling Expences mount up to large Sums, and will discern what might have been, and may for the future be saved, without occasioning any great Inconvenience.

Waste Not, Want Not

In short, the Way to Wealth, if you desire it, is as plain as the Way to Market. It depends chiefly on two Words, INDUSTRY and FRUGALITY; i.e. Waste neither Time nor Money, but make the best Use of both. He that gets all he can honestly, and saves all he gets (necessary Expences excepted) will certainly become RICH; If that Being who governs the World, to whom all should look for a Blessing on their honest Endeavours, doth not in his wise Providence otherwise determine.

1603

Elizabeth I, queen of England, dies and is succeeded by her cousin James I, the first of England's Stuart monarchs. He quickly alienates the Puritans by insisting on the divine right of royalty to govern with absolute authority.

1606

William Brewster and other Puritan Separatists establish a congregation in Scrooby, England. James I charters the Virginia Companies of London and Plymouth. The London Company launches three ships of settlers in December.

1607

The London Company's ships reach Chesapeake Bay in April. The settlers found the colony of Jamestown, Virginia, the first permanent English settlement in North America. Powhatan, chief of the local Indians, saves the colonists from starvation in the autumn by providing them with food. In December, Captain John Smith is captured by the Indians and undergoes what is most likely a mock execution ceremony, which ends when Powhatan's daughter, Pocahontas, pleads for his life.

1608

The Virginia colonists almost abandon Jamestown in January but decide to stay after a supply ship arrives from England. The first women colonists arrive in October. John Smith is made head of the settlement in the autumn; he demands that the settlers "work or starve." He also attempts to intimidate the Indians into submission, but Powhatan responds by refusing to trade with the settlers and withholding food supplies. Samuel de Champlain establishes the first permanent French settlement in North America at Quebec in Canada. Some of the Separatists from Scrooby leave England to seek refuge from religious persecution in Holland.

1609

Hostilities increase between Powhatan and Jamestown. Seven ships carrying four hundred settlers arrive from England. The winter of 1609–1610 is termed the "starving time" by the Jamestown colonists; by the spring of 1610, only sixty of five hundred settlers remain alive. Henry Hudson explores the upper coast of North America for the Dutch. In November, New Mexico is officially made a royal colony of Spain.

1610

In May, Sir Thomas Gates arrives in Virginia and loads the surviving Jamestown colonists onto his ship, intending to return to England. However, they encounter a relief fleet headed by Governor De La Warr and turn back to the colony. The Spanish found Santa Fe in New Mexico.

1612

John Rolfe begins cultivating tobacco; within a few years, the tobacco trade becomes Virginia's main source of income.

1613

The Jamestown colonists kidnap Pocahontas, holding her for ransom. French Jesuits establish a mission in present-day Maine; within weeks, a military expedition from Jamestown destroys it on the grounds that the territory is part of Virginia's grant.

1614

In April, John Rolfe marries Pocahontas, and a truce is made with Powhatan. Rolfe ships his first tobacco to England in June. Dutch trader Adriaen Block explores the Hudson Bay region; the Dutch set up fur-trading posts on Manhattan Island and at Fort Orange (Albany).

1617

From this year until 1619, an outbreak of European diseases greatly reduces the Indian populations of Virginia and New England.

1619

The earliest representative colonial assembly, the House of Burgesses, convenes in Jamestown during the summer. In August, twenty blacks arrive in Jamestown aboard a Dutch ship; their exact legal status remains unclear, but they probably were indentured servants. The Virginia Company gives a land grant to William Brewster and his group of Separatists in the Netherlands (the Pilgrims).

1620

The Virginia Company of Plymouth is reorganized as the Council for New England. On September 16, the Pilgrims set sail for America from Plymouth, England, on board the *Mayflower*. They arrive at Cape Cod in November and establish the colony of Plymouth in present-day Massachusetts. Nearly half the colonists die during the winter.

1621

In the spring, Massasoit, leader of the Wampanoags, sends two English-speaking Indians, Samoset and Squanto, to negotiate a treaty with the Pilgrims. Squanto teaches the colonists agricultural and survival skills. The Pilgrims hold the first Thanksgiving celebration in the fall. The Dutch West India Company is formed to colonize New Netherland.

1622

In March, Opechancanough (Powhatan's successor) leads a devastating attack on the Virginia colonists. News of the massacre creates general hysteria in Plymouth, straining the Pilgrims' relations with the Wampanoags.

1624

The London Company's charter is revoked, and Virginia is made a royal colony. The Dutch West India Company dispatches its first colonizing expedition to New Netherland.

1625

Charles I becomes king of England; he will increase the persecution of Puritans. Dutch colonists establish the town of New Amsterdam on Manhattan Island.

1626

The Dutch buy Manhattan Island from the Indians. Eleven African slaves are brought to New Amsterdam.

1627

Thomas Morton angers the Pilgrims by celebrating May Day at Merry Mount.

1628

Myles Standish attacks Merry Mount and sends Thomas Morton back to England. A settlement is founded at Salem, Massachusetts.

1629

Charles I dissolves Parliament. The Massachusetts Bay Company receives a royal charter.

1630

Under the auspices of the Massachusetts Bay Company, a large group of Puritans arrives in New England. They establish the Massachusetts Bay Colony, including the town of Boston.

1631

Roger Williams immigrates to Massachusetts and begins preaching, first in Salem and then in Plymouth.

1632

The Calvert family receives a charter from Charles I to establish the colony of Maryland as a haven for Catholics.

1633

The first secondary school, Boston Latin School, begins instruction.

1634

The first colonists arrive in Maryland. A small English settlement takes root in Wethersfield, Connecticut. Anne Hutchinson immigrates to Boston, where she begins holding religious meetings in her home.

1635

Roger Williams is banished from Massachusetts Bay for his religious and political beliefs.

1636

Roger Williams founds the colony of Providence in present-day Rhode Island. Hartford, Connecticut, is settled by Puritans from Massachusetts. The first American college, Harvard, is established at Cambridge, Massachusetts. War breaks out between the Pequot tribe and the New England colonists. The Antinomian controversy sharply divides the Massachusetts Bay Colony.

1637

The Pequot War ends during the summer with the virtual extermination of the tribe. In November, Anne Hutchinson is tried before the Massachusetts General Court and sentenced to banishment. Hutchinson and a number of her followers relocate to Portsmouth, Rhode Island; other Antinomians move to New Hampshire. Puritans from Massachusetts found the colony of New Haven in present-day Connecticut.

1638

In March, Swedish colonists arrive in the Delaware River valley, where they build Fort Christina.

1639

The first printing press in the English colonies is set up at Cambridge, Massachusetts.

1640

Charles I finally recalls Parliament to raise new taxes to support his military goals; however, the body is dominated by Puritans who oppose the king.

1641

Massachusetts becomes the first American colony to officially recognize slavery in its legal code. The Massachusetts Bay Colony extends its jurisdiction over the four English settlements in New Hampshire.

1642

Civil war erupts in England between the Cavaliers (supporters of the king) and the Roundheads (supporters of Parliament, mostly Puritans).

1643

On May 19, the Puritan colonies of Massachusetts Bay, Plymouth, Connecticut, and New Haven form the New England Confederation for mutual aid and defense. War breaks out between New Netherland and the Algonquian Indians; the conflict rages until 1645.

1649

The English Civil War ends with the defeat of the Cavaliers. With Puritans firmly in control of Parliament, England is declared a commonwealth. Charles I is beheaded; Virginia declares its loyalty to his exiled son, Charles II. Many prominent Cavaliers immigrate to Virginia. The Maryland Assembly passes the Toleration Act, the first law in the colonies that protects freedom of worship.

1650

Anne Bradstreet's *The Tenth Muse*, the first book of poetry by an American colonist, is published in London.

1652

Parliament sends a fleet and commissioners to Virginia and Maryland to establish Puritan-controlled governments in those colonies. Massachusetts annexes the English settlements in Maine.

1653

Puritan leader Oliver Cromwell becomes Lord Protector of England.

1654

New Sweden takes Fort Casimir from the Dutch. The Protestant-dominated Maryland Assembly repudiates the colony's policy of religious toleration and forbids Catholics to worship openly. Jewish colonists arrive in New Netherland, the first such group to migrate to North America.

1655

Dutch troops conquer New Sweden and annex the territory to New Netherland.

1656

The first Quakers arrive in the Massachusetts Bay Colony, where they are quickly arrested and banished for religious nonconformity.

1657

Oliver Cromwell returns Maryland to the Calvert family proprietors; religious toleration is restored.

1658

Cromwell dies and is succeeded by his son, who proves unable to continue the Protectorate.

1659–1660

Puritan persecution of Quakers reaches its height; four Quakers are executed in New England during these years.

1660

The Stuart monarchy is restored to England with the crowning of Charles II.

1661

Virginia passes the first colonial law that recognizes permanent chattel slavery for blacks.

1662

Connecticut receives a royal charter allowing it to absorb the colony of New Haven.

1663

Rhode Island obtains a royal charter that specifically recognizes freedom of conscience. Charles II grants a charter for the Carolina territory to a group of eight proprietors.

1664

In March, Charles II grants his brother James, the duke of York, a large tract in North America that includes New Netherland. In August, the English capture New Netherland without firing a shot; they rename it New York. English settlement of New Jersey begins.

1670

English settlers found Charleston in modern South Carolina.

1672

Virginia sets a bounty on the head of maroons—runaway slaves who form secret communities in forests or swamps.

1673

War breaks out between England and the Netherlands; the Dutch recapture New York on July 30. French-Canadian explorer Louis Jolliet and Jesuit missionary Jacques Marquette become the first Europeans to travel down the Mississippi River; they reach the Arkansas River before turning back.

1674

The English regain control of New York on November 10. In December, Marquette founds a mission at present-day Chicago, Illinois.

1675

King Philip's War begins in the Plymouth colony in June and quickly escalates into the most devastating conflict of the colonial era. In New Mexico, the governor arrests forty-seven Pueblo shamans in an attempt to stamp out native religious practices.

1676

King Philip's War ends in August; many of the defeated Native Americans are sold into slavery in the West Indies. In Virginia, Bacon's Rebellion begins when Nathaniel Bacon leads an unauthorized military campaign against local Indians. His actions place him at odds with the royal governor, who moves to stop him. On September 19, Bacon's forces capture and burn Jamestown. In October, Bacon unexpectedly dies of disease, and the rebellion disintegrates rapidly. New Jersey is divided into East Jersey and West Jersey.

1677

An English investigator reports to the Crown that Massachusetts has become overly independent and intransigent; he recommends that the colony be placed under direct royal control.

1679

New Hampshire is made a royal colony separate from Massachusetts.

1680

In August, the Pueblo Revolt takes place when the Pueblo Indians, led by Popé, drive the Spaniards out of New Mexico.

1681

Charles II grants William Penn a charter for Pennsylvania, which is to serve as a refuge for Quakers.

1682

On April 9, French explorer Sieur de La Salle reaches the mouth of the Mississippi River; he claims the vast river basin for

France, naming it Louisiana. In October, William Penn arrives in Philadelphia, Pennsylvania.

1684

Massachusetts's charter is revoked, and it becomes a royal colony.

1685

Charles II dies; his Catholic brother, the duke of York, succeeds him as James II. Sieur de La Salle leads an expedition with the intent of founding a settlement at the mouth of the Mississippi, but he mistakenly makes landfall on the coast of Spanish Texas and establishes a base at Matagorda Bay.

1686

James II establishes the Dominion of New England, which merges Massachusetts, Plymouth, Connecticut, Rhode Island, New Hampshire, and Maine. (New York and the Jerseys are added in 1688.) He eliminates the existing colonial assemblies and places the Dominion under a single royal governor, Edmund Andros.

1687

Sieur de La Salle is murdered by his own men; the French colonizing effort in Texas disintegrates.

1688

In February, Quakers in Pennsylvania issue the first written protest against slavery in the English colonies. The Glorious Revolution begins in England when parliamentary leaders, frustrated by the pro-Catholic and anti-Parliament actions of James II, invite his Protestant daughter, Mary, and her Dutch husband, William of Orange, to assume the English throne as joint sovereigns. William and Mary arrive in England in November; shortly thereafter, James II flees to France.

1689

William III and Mary are crowned king and queen of England. When news of the Glorious Revolution reaches Boston in April, New Englanders overthrow Governor Andros and dismantle the Dominion of New England. In May, a similar rebellion takes place in New York when colonist Jacob Leisler and his followers seize control of the government.

In July, Coode's Rebellion occurs when Protestant supporters of William and Mary take over the capital of Maryland. The War of the League of Augsburg (King William's War) begins between the French and the English.

1690

French and Indian forces attack Fort Casco and Fort Loyal in Maine, Salmon Falls in New Hampshire, and Schenectady in New York. Troops from New England capture Port Royal, Canada, in May. America's first newspaper, *Publick Occurrences*, starts publication in Boston but is soon suppressed for criticizing the government.

1691

Massachusetts is granted a new charter, which provides for a royal governor and a representative assembly. Plymouth and Maine are consolidated with Massachusetts. A royal governor arrives in New York, and Jacob Leisler is executed for treason. Maryland officially becomes a royal colony; religious toleration is greatly reduced. The French retake Port Royal.

1692

Witchcraft trials in Salem, Massachusetts, result in the execution of nineteen people. William Penn's charter is revoked, making Pennsylvania a royal colony.

1693

Virginia receives a royal charter to establish the College of William and Mary, the second college in the English colonies. Spanish forces reconquer the Pueblo Indians and restore Santa Fe as the capital of New Mexico.

1694

William Penn's proprietary rights to the colony of Pennsylvania are restored. Queen Mary dies without children.

1697

The Treaty of Ryswick ends King William's War.

1698

The Royal African Company's monopoly in the English slave trade is broken, allowing American competition; after this date, the large-scale importation of black slaves will rapidly increase in the colonies. The Spanish found Pensacola, Florida.

1699

The French found Biloxi within the colony of Louisiana (in present-day Mississippi).

1700

The non-Indian population of the English colonies in America surpasses 250,000, approximately 30,000 of whom are black slaves.

1701

The Iroquois Confederacy signs peace treaties with France and England, vowing to remain neutral in any future conflict between the European colonies. The French establish Mobile in present-day Alabama and Detroit in present-day Michigan. Yale, the third colonial college, is founded in Connecticut. Delaware is given the right to its own legislative assembly, separate from Pennsylvania, although it continues to have the same governor.

1702

Following the death of William III, Mary's sister Anne ascends the English throne. In May, England officially enters the War of the Spanish Succession (Queen Anne's War). An expedition from South Carolina attacks St. Augustine but fails to capture the Spanish fort. East and West Jersey are united as the royal colony of New Jersey.

1704

On February 29, the French and Indians massacre colonists at Deerfield, Massachusetts. The *Boston News-Letter*, the first continuously published newspaper in America, is founded.

1706

In August, French and Spanish forces launch an unsuccessful attack on Charleston, South Carolina. Albuquerque is established in New Mexico.

1710

After two unsuccessful attempts in the two previous years, the English capture Port Royal, Canada.

1711

An English attempt to conquer Quebec ends in disaster when the war fleet is shipwrecked. The Tuscarora War begins in the Carolinas.

1712

In April, a rebellion of about two dozen slaves occurs in New York City, in which fourteen whites are killed. In the aftermath, approximately seventy blacks are jailed; twenty-seven are condemned to death. On May 9, North and South Carolina are officially separated.

1713

Queen Anne's War ends with the Treaty of Utrecht; France cedes Acadia (renamed Nova Scotia), Newfoundland, and Hudson's Bay to England. Forced out of the Carolina region by white settlers, the Tuscarora Indians flee to the north, where they join the Iroquois Confederacy.

1714

Queen Anne dies without an heir; George of the House of Hanover, a German prince descended from James I, becomes George I, king of England.

1715

The Yamasee War starts in South Carolina; by 1716, the Yamasee tribe will be routed by white settlers. George I restores Maryland to the fourth Lord Baltimore, a Protestant.

1719

The French establish New Orleans, Louisiana.

1727

George II succeeds his father, George I, as king of England. Benjamin Franklin founds the Junto, a debating society, in Philadelphia.

1728

A Russian expedition led by Danish explorer Vitus Bering discovers Alaska and the Bering Strait.

1730

The religious revival known as the Great Awakening begins in the colonies.

1731

Benjamin Franklin and other leading citizens of Philadelphia establish the first circulating library in colonial America.

1732

Georgia, the last of the original thirteen colonies, is founded. Benjamin Franklin publishes the first issue of *Poor Richard's Almanac* in Philadelphia.

1735

In the first victory for freedom of the press in America, John Peter Zenger, editor of the *New York Weekly Journal*, is acquitted of libel charges brought by New York's governor. After this decision, colonial newspapers become increasingly vocal on political issues.

1736

Benjamin Franklin founds the volunteer Union Fire Company in Philadelphia.

1739

Evangelist George Whitefield arrives in Philadelphia and commences his first tour of the American colonies. French explorers Pierre and Paul Mallet reach present-day Colorado, becoming the first Europeans to see the Rocky Mountains from the Great Plains. On September 9, the Stono Rebellion (the first major slave uprising in America) begins in South Carolina; approximately one hundred slaves burn seven plantations and kill twenty white colonists before the revolt is crushed.

1740

An English expedition, largely made up of colonial troops from Georgia, besieges St. Augustine without success. A slave conspiracy is discovered in Annapolis, Maryland.

1741

Rumors of an impending slave revolt in New York City lead to public hysteria; thirty-five suspected conspirators (including four whites) are executed.

1742

Colonists in Georgia repulse a Spanish invasion.

1743

Benjamin Franklin and other prominent Philadelphians found the American Philosophical Society for the promotion of scientific knowledge.

1744

King George's War, the American front of the War of the Austrian Succession, begins.

1745

New England troops capture the French fortress of Louisbourg on Cape Breton Island, near Nova Scotia.

1746

Princeton College is founded in New Jersey.

1748

In October, King George's War ends with the Treaty of Aix-la-Chapelle, which returns all captured North American territories to their prewar owners.

1750

The non-Indian population of the thirteen English colonies reaches 1.25 million. Blacks, almost all of whom are enslaved, make up approximately 20 percent of the population.

FOR FURTHER RESEARCH

GENERAL HISTORIES OF THE COLONIAL PERIOD

W.W. Abbot, *The Colonial Origins of the United States: 1607–1763*. New York: Wiley, 1975.

Charles M. Andrews, *The Colonial Period of American History*, 4 vols. New Haven, CT: Yale University Press, 1964.

Herbert Aptheker, *The Colonial Era*. New York: International Publishers, 1959.

Oscar Theodore Barck Jr. and Hugh Talmage Lefler, *Colonial America*. New York: Macmillan, 1968.

W.J. Eccles, *The French in North America, 1500–1783*. East Lansing: Michigan State University Press, 1998.

John E. Pomfret, *Founding the American Colonies, 1583–1660*. New York: Harper & Row, 1970.

Thomas L. Purvis, *Colonial America to 1763*. New York: Facts On File, 1999.

Arthur Quinn, *A New World: An Epic of Colonial America from the Founding of Jamestown to the Fall of Quebec*. Boston: Faber and Faber, 1994.

John A. Schutz, *The Dawning of America: 1492–1789*. St. Louis, MO: Forum Press, 1981.

John Anthony Scott, *Settlers on the Eastern Shore, 1607–1750*. New York: Knopf, 1967.

Tee Loftin Snell, *The Wild Shores: America's Beginnings*. Washington, DC: National Geographic Society, 1974.

Marion L. Starkey, *Land Where Our Fathers Died: The Settling of the Eastern Shores: 1607–1735*. Garden City, NY: Doubleday, 1962.

Harry M. Ward, *"Unite or Die": Intercolony Relations, 1690–1763*. Port Washington, NY: Kennikat Press, 1971.

David J. Weber, *The Spanish Frontier in North America*. New Haven, CT: Yale University Press, 1992.

Henri and Barbara van der Zee, *A Sweet and Alien Land: The Story of Dutch New York*. New York: Viking, 1978.

ANTHOLOGIES OF PRIMARY DOCUMENTS

Susan Castillo and Ivy Schweitzer, eds., *The Literatures of Colonial America: An Anthology*. Malden, MA: Blackwell, 2001.

Bradley Chapin, *Provincial America, 1600–1763*. New York: Free Press, 1966.

David A. Copeland, *Debating the Issues in Colonial Newspapers: Primary Documents on Events of the Period*. Westport, CT: Greenwood Press, 2000.

John Demos, *Remarkable Providences: Readings on Early American History*. Boston: Northeastern University Press, 1991.

Jack P. Greene, ed., *Settlements to Society: 1584–1763*. New York: McGraw-Hill, 1966.

David Hawke, ed., *U.S. Colonial History: Readings and Documents*. Indianapolis: Bobbs-Merrill, 1966.

Faith Jaycox, *The Colonial Era: An Eyewitness History*. New York: Facts On File, 2002.

Myra Jehlen and Michael Warner, eds., *The English Literatures of America, 1500–1800*. New York: Routledge, 1997.

John C. Miller, ed., *The Colonial Image: Origins of American Culture*. New York: George Braziller, 1962.

Carla Mulford, ed., *Early American Writings*. New York: Oxford University Press, 2002.

T.J. Stiles, ed., *The Colonizers*. New York: Perigee Books, 1998.

BIOGRAPHIES OF IMPORTANT INDIVIDUALS

H.W. Brands, *The First American: The Life and Times of Benjamin Franklin*. New York: Doubleday, 2000.

Cyclone Covey, *The Gentle Radical: A Biography of Roger Williams*. New York: Macmillan, 1966.

Richard S. Dunn, *Puritans and Yankees: The Winthrop Dynasty of New England, 1630–1717*. Princeton, NJ: Princeton University Press, 1962.

Mary K. Geiter, *William Penn*. New York: Longman, 2000.

Michael G. Hall, *The Last American Puritan: The Life of Increase Mather, 1639–1723*. Middletown, CT: Wesleyan University Press, 1988.

Lauran Paine, *Captain John Smith and the Jamestown Story*. New York: Hippocrene Books, 1973.

Josephine K. Piercy, *Anne Bradstreet*. New York: Twayne, 1965.

Norman K. Risjord, *Representative Americans: The Colonists*. Lanham, MD: Rowman & Littlefield, 2001.

Kenneth Silverman, *The Life and Times of Cotton Mather*. New York: Harper & Row, 1984.

Arthur Bernon Tourtellot, *Benjamin Franklin: The Shaping of Genius: The Boston Years*. Garden City, NY: Doubleday, 1977.

Carole Chandler Waldrup, *Colonial Women: 23 Europeans Who Helped Build a Nation*. Jefferson, NC: McFarland, 1999.

Selma R. Williams, *Divine Rebel: The Life of Anne Marbury Hutchinson*. New York: Holt, Rinehart, and Winston, 1981.

Grace Steele Woodward, *Pocahontas*. Norman: University of Oklahoma Press, 1969.

THE PILGRIMS AND THE PURITANS

Kate Caffrey, *The Mayflower*. New York: Stein and Day, 1974.

Allen Carden, *Puritan Christianity in America: Religion and Life in Seventeenth-Century Massachusetts*. Grand Rapids, MI: Baker Book House, 1990.

John Demos, *A Little Commonwealth: Family Life in Plymouth Colony*. New York: Oxford University Press, 2000.

Francis Dillon, *The Pilgrims*. Garden City, NY: Doubleday, 1975.

Everett Emerson, *Puritanism in America, 1620–1750*. Boston: Twayne, 1977.

Thomas J. Fleming, *One Small Candle: The Pilgrims' First Year in America*. New York: W.W. Norton, 1964.

Crispin Gill, *Mayflower Remembered: A History of the Plymouth Pilgrims*, New York: Taplinger, 1970.

Cyril Leek Marshall, *The Mayflower Destiny*. Harrisburg, PA: Stackpole Books, 1975.

Perry Miller and Thomas H. Johnson, *The Puritans*, 2 vols. New York: Harper & Row, 1963.

Samuel Eliot Morison, *Builders of the Bay Colony*. Boston: Houghton Mifflin, 1964.

Alden T. Vaughan, ed., *The Puritan Tradition in America, 1620–1730*. Columbia: University of South Carolina Press, 1972.

George M. Waller, ed., *Puritanism in Early America*. Lexington, MA: D.C. Heath, 1973.

George F. Willison, *Saints and Strangers*. New York: Ballantine, 1965.

WITCHCRAFT TRIALS IN NEW ENGLAND

Paul Boyer and Stephen Nissenbaum, *Salem Possessed: The Social Origins of Witchcraft*. Cambridge, MA: Harvard University Press, 1974.

Laurie Winn Carlson, *A Fever in Salem: A New Interpretation of the New England Witch Trials*. Chicago: Ivan R. Dee, 1999.

John Putnam Demos, *Entertaining Satan: Witchcraft and the Culture of Early New England*. New York: Oxford University Press, 1982.

Sanford J. Fox, *Science and Justice: The Massachusetts Witchcraft Trials*. Baltimore, MD: Johns Hopkins Press, 1968.

Richard Godbeer, *The Devil's Dominion: Magic and Religion in Early New England*. New York: Cambridge University Press, 1992.

Larry Gragg, *The Salem Witch Crisis*. New York: Praeger, 1992.

David D. Hall, ed., *Witch-Hunting in Seventeenth-Century New England: A Documentary History, 1638–1692*. Boston: Northeastern University Press, 1991.

Chadwick Hansen, *Witchcraft at Salem*. New York: George Braziller, 1969.

Frances Hill, *A Delusion of Satan: The Full Story of the Salem Witch Trials*. New York: Doubleday, 1995.

Frances Hill, ed., *The Salem Witch Trials Reader*. Cambridge, MA: Da Capo Press, 2000.

Peter Charles Hoffer, *The Devil's Disciples: Makers of the Salem Witchcraft Trials*. Baltimore, MD: Johns Hopkins University Press, 1996.

Carol F. Karlsen, *The Devil in the Shape of a Woman: Witchcraft in Colonial New England*. New York: W.W. Norton, 1987.

Mary Beth Norton, *In the Devil's Snare: The Salem Witchcraft Crisis of 1692*. New York: Knopf, 2002.

Enders A. Robinson, *The Devil Discovered: Salem Witchcraft, 1692*. New York: Hippocrene Books, 1991.

THE GREAT AWAKENING

J.M. Bumsted and John E. Van de Wetering, *What Must I Do to Be Saved? The Great Awakening in Colonial America*. Hinsdale, IL: Dryden Press, 1976.

Edwin Scott Gaustad, *The Great Awakening in New England*. Gloucester, MA: Peter Smith, 1965.

Alan Heimert and Perry Miller, eds., *The Great Awakening: Documents Illustrating the Crisis and Its Consequences*. Indianapolis: Bobbs-Merrill, 1967.

David S. Lovejoy, *Religious Enthusiasm and the Great Awakening*. Englewood Cliffs, NJ: Prentice-Hall, 1969.

Darrett B. Rutman, ed., *The Great Awakening: Event and Exegesis*. New York: Wiley, 1970.

AFRICAN AMERICANS, SLAVERY, AND INDENTURED SERVANTS

Allan Kulikoff, *Tobacco and Slaves: The Development of Southern Cultures in the Chesapeake, 1680–1800*. Chapel Hill: University of North Carolina Press, 1986.

Edmund S. Morgan, *American Slavery, American Freedom: The Ordeal of Colonial Virginia*. New York: W.W. Norton, 1975.

Kenneth Morgan, *Slavery and Servitude in Colonial North America: A Short History*. New York: New York University Press, 2001.

William D. Piersen, *From Africa to America: African American History from the Colonial Era to the Early Republic, 1526–1790*. New York: Twayne, 1996.

Abbot Emerson Smith, *Colonists in Bondage: White Servitude and Convict Labor in America, 1607–1776*. Chapel Hill: University of North Carolina Press, 1947.

Lawrence William Towner, *A Good Master Well Served: Masters and Servants in Colonial Massachusetts, 1620–1750*. New York: Garland, 1998.

Betty Wood, *The Origins of American Slavery: Freedom and Bondage in the English Colonies*. New York: Hill and Wang, 1997.

Donald R. Wright, *African Americans in the Colonial Era: From African Origins Through the American Revolution*. Arlington Heights, IL: Harlan Davidson, 1990.

John van der Zee, *Bound Over: Indentured Servitude and American Conscience*. New York: Simon and Schuster, 1985.

COLONIAL REBELLIONS AND SLAVE REVOLTS

Sally Smith Booth, *Seeds of Anger: Revolts in America, 1607–1771*. New York: Hastings House, 1977.

John B. Frantz, ed., *Bacon's Rebellion: Prologue to the Revolution?* Lexington, MA: D.C. Heath, 1969.

Douglas Edward Leach, *Roots of Conflict: British Armed Forces and Colonial Americans, 1677–1763*. Chapel Hill: University of North Carolina Press, 1986.

Jerome R. Reich, *Leisler's Rebellion: A Study of Democracy in New York, 1664–1720*. Chicago: University of Chicago Press, 1953.

Wilcomb E. Washburn, *The Governor and the Rebel: A History of Bacon's Rebellion in Virginia*. Chapel Hill: University of North Carolina Press, 1957.

Stephen Saunders Webb, *1676: The End of American Independence*. New York: Knopf, 1984.

Thomas Jefferson Wertenbaker, *Torchbearer of the Revolution: The Story of Bacon's Rebellion and Its Leader*. Princeton, NJ: Princeton University Press, 1940.

THE COLONIAL WARS

Russell Bourne, *The Red King's Rebellion: Racial Politics in New England, 1675–1678*. New York: Atheneum, 1990.

Alfred A. Cave, *The Pequot War*. Amherst: University of Massachusetts Press, 1996.

James D. Drake, *King Philip's War: Civil War in New England, 1675–1676*. Amherst: University of Massachusetts Press, 1999.

John Ferling, *Struggle for a Continent: The Wars of Early America*. Arlington Heights, IL: Harlan Davidson, 1993.

David Horowitz, *The First Frontier: The Indian Wars and America's Origins, 1607–1776*. New York: Simon and Schuster, 1978.

Francis Jennings, *The Invasion of America: Indians, Colonialism, and the Cant of Conquest*. Chapel Hill: University of North Carolina Press, 1975.

Douglas Edward Leach, *Flintlock and Tomahawk: New England in King Philip's War*. New York: Macmillan, 1958.

Robert Leckie, *"A Few Acres of Snow": The Saga of the French and Indian Wars*. New York: Wiley, 1999.

Jill Lepore, *The Name of War: King Philip's War and the Origins of American Identity*. New York: Knopf, 1998.

Howard H. Peckham, *The Colonial Wars, 1689–1762*. Chicago: University of Chicago Press, 1964.

Michael J. Puglisi, *Puritans Besieged: The Legacies of King Philip's War in the Massachusetts Bay Colony*. Lanham, MD: University Press of America, 1991.

Joseph Lister Rutledge, *Century of Conflict: The Struggle Between the French and British in Colonial America*. Garden City, NY: Doubleday, 1956.

Ian K. Steele, *Warpaths: Invasions of North America*. New York: Oxford University Press, 1994.

Alden T. Vaughan and Edward W. Clark, eds., *Puritans Among the Indians: Accounts of Captivity and Redemption, 1676–1724*. Cambridge, MA: Harvard University Press, 1981.

NATIVE AMERICANS

James Axtell, *The Invasion Within: The Contest of Cultures in Colonial North America*. New York: Oxford University Press, 1985.

———, *Natives and Newcomers: The Cultural Origins of North America*. New York: Oxford University Press, 2001.

Colin G. Calloway, ed., *The World Turned Upside Down: Indian Voices from Early America*. Boston: St. Martin's Press, 1994.

William Cronon, *Changes in the Land: Indians, Colonists, and the Ecology of New England*. New York: Hill and Wang, 1983.

Karen H. Dacey, *In the Shadow of the Great Blue Hill*. Lanham, MD: University Press of America, 1995.

Matthew Dennis, *Cultivating a Landscape of Peace: Iroquois-European Encounters in Seventeenth-Century America*. Ithaca, NY: Cornell University Press, 1993.

Francis Jennings, *The Ambiguous Iroquois Empire: The Covenant Chain Confederation of Indian Tribes with English Colonies from Its Beginnings to the Lancaster Treaty of 1744*. New York: W.W. Norton, 1984.

Karen Ordahl Kupperman, *Indians and English: Facing Off in Early America*. Ithaca, NY: Cornell University Press, 2000.

———, *Settling with the Indians: The Meeting of English and Indian Cultures in America, 1580–1640*. Totowa, NJ: Rowman & Littlefield, 1980.

Ann Marie Plane, *Colonial Intimacies: Indian Marriage in Early New England*. Ithaca, NY: Cornell University Press, 2000.

Daniel K. Richter, *Facing East from Indian Country: A Native History of Early America*. Cambridge, MA: Harvard University Press, 2001.

Charles M. Segal and David C. Stineback, *Puritans, Indians, and Manifest Destiny*. New York: Putnam, 1977.

Alden T. Vaughan, *New England Frontier: Puritans and Indians, 1620–1675*. New York: W.W. Norton, 1979.

COLONIAL LIFE AND SOCIETY

Herbert Applebaum, *Colonial Americans at Work*. Lanham, MD: University Press of America, 1996.

Carol Berkin, *First Generations: Women in Colonial America*. New York: Hill and Wang, 1996.

Patricia U. Bonomi, *Under the Cope of Heaven: Religion, Society, and Politics in Colonial America*. New York: Oxford University Press, 1986.

Carl Bridenbaugh, *Cities in the Wilderness: The First Century of Urban Life in America, 1625–1742*. New York: Knopf, 1955.

David D. Hall, *Worlds of Wonder, Days of Judgment: Popular Religious Belief in Early New England*. New York: Knopf, 1989.

David Freeman Hawke, *Everyday Life in Early America*. New York: Harper & Row, 1988.

Jane Kamensky, *The Colonial Mosaic: American Women, 1600–1760*. New York: Oxford University Press, 1995.

Gloria L. Main, *Peoples of a Spacious Land: Families and Cultures in Colonial New England*. Cambridge, MA: Harvard University Press, 2001.

Parke Rouse, *Planters and Pioneers: Life in Colonial Virginia*. New York: Hastings House, 1968.

Laurel Thatcher Ulrich, *Good Wives: Image and Reality in the Lives of Women in Northern New England, 1650–1750*. New York: Knopf, 1982.

Helena M. Wall, *Fierce Communion: Family and Community in Early America*. Cambridge, MA: Harvard University Press, 1990.

Stephanie Grauman Wolf, *As Various as Their Land: The Everyday Lives of Eighteenth-Century Americans*. New York: Harper-Collins, 1993.

ART, CULTURE, AND EDUCATION

James Axtell, *The School upon a Hill: Education and Society in Colonial America*. New Haven, CT: Yale University Press, 1974.

Daniel J. Boorstin, *The Americans: The Colonial Experience*. New York: Random House, 1958.

Lawrence A. Cremin, *American Education: The Colonial Experience, 1607–1783*. New York: Harper & Row, 1970.

Everett Emerson, ed., *Major Writers of Early American Literature*. Madison: University of Wisconsin Press, 1972.

Ned C. Landsman, *From Colonials to Provincials: American Thought and Culture, 1680–1760*. New York: Twayne, 1997.

Harrison T. Meserole, ed., *Seventeenth-Century American Poetry*. Garden City, NY: Anchor Books, 1968.

Samuel Eliot Morison, *The Intellectual Life of Colonial New England*. New York: New York University Press, 1956.

Max Savelle, *The Colonial Origins of American Thought*. Princeton, NJ: D. Van Nostrand, 1964.

Thomas J. Wertenbaker, *The Golden Age of Colonial Culture*. New York: New York University Press, 1949.

Louis B. Wright, *The Cultural Life of the American Colonies, 1607–1763*. New York: Harper & Brothers, 1957.

Louis B. Wright et al., *The Arts in America: The Colonial Period*. New York: Scribner, 1966.

INDEX